BUILDING THE
WORKINGMAN'S
PARADISE

THE HAYMARKET SERIES

Editors: Mike Davis and Michael Sprinker

The Haymarket Series offers original studies in politics, history and culture, with a focus on North America. Representing views across the American left on a wide range of subjects, the series will be of interest to socialists both in the USA and throughout the world. A century after the first May Day, the American left remains in the shadow of those martyrs whom the Haymarket Series honors and commemorates. These studies testify to the living legacy of political activism and commitment for which they gave their lives.

Forthcoming titles:

Selling Culture: Magazines, Markets, and Class at the Turn of the Century by Richard Ohmann

Imagineering Atlanta by Charles Rutheiser

Bearing North by Paul Smith

Anything But Mexican: Chicanos in Contemporary Los Angeles by Rudi Acuna

The Invention of the White Race, Volume 2: The Origin of Racial Oppression in Anglo-America by Theodore Allen

Miami by John Beverley and David Houston

The Cultural Front: The Left and American Culture in the Age of the CIO by Michael Denning

Power Misses by David James

Messing with the Machine: Modernism, Postmodernism and African-American Fiction by Wahneema Lubiano

Public Transport by Eric Mann

Black Avant-Garde Film by Ntongela Masilela

Queer Space by Kevin McMahan

Dancing on the Brink: The San Francisco Bay Area at the End of the Twentieth Century by Richard Walker

BUILDING THE WORKINGMAN'S PARADISE

The Design of
American Company Towns

———————◆———————

MARGARET CRAWFORD

VERSO
London • New York

First published by Verso 1995
© Margaret Crawford 1995
All rights reserved

Verso
UK: 6 Meard Street, London W1V 3HR
USA: 180 Varick Street, New York NY 10014–4606

Verso is the imprint of New Left Books

ISBN 0–86091–421–6
ISBN 0–86091–695–2 (pbk)

British Library Cataloguing in Publication Data
A catalogue record for this book is available from the British Library

Library of Congress Cataloging-in-Publication Data
Crawford, Margaret.
    Building the workingman's paradise : the design of American
company towns / Margaret Crawford.
        p.   cm. — (Haymarket series)
    Includes bibliographical references and index.
    ISBN 0–86091–421–6. — ISBN 0–86091–695–2 (pbk.)
    1. Company towns—United States—History.   2. Industries—
United States—History.   3. Industrial relations—United States—
History.
I. Title.
HT123.C688   1995
307.76′7′0973—dc20   95–37264
                                                                  CIP

Typeset by M Rules
Printed and bound in Great Britain by the Bath Press

CONTENTS

ACKNOWLEDGMENTS

As this book proceeded slowly over the years, many individuals and institutions provided invaluable assistance. When the book began as a doctoral dissertation, my committee offered personal support, intellectual guidance, and rigorous criticism. Sandy Jacoby's advice started me off in the right direction, Dolores Hayden's questions and comments consistently challenged me, Thomas Hines and Eric Monkonnen provided much-needed encouragement, and Marty Wachs was a thoughtful and acute reader. Gwendolyn Wright and Francesco Dal Co also offered useful advice and encouragement during the early days of research. Other scholars generously shared their own research with me, including Janet Ball, John Pastier, Claudia Isaac, Kim Wallace, and Connie Gustafson. Earle Draper, who died in 1993, spent many hours going over his company town experiences with me. The Edward A. Dickson History of Art Fellowship from UCLA provided funding for travel and a year of research. The staffs of many libraries made the research possible: the University Research Library at UCLA, the Environmental Design Library at Berkeley, the Avery Library at Columbia University, the Olin Library at Cornell University, the Library of Congress, the Baker and Graduate School of Design Libraries at Harvard University, the Chicago Historical Society, the Department of Labor Library and public libraries in Mt Union, Pennsylvania, Worcester, Massachusetts, Spartanburg, South Carolina, Gainesville, Georgia, and Torrance, California. The Norton Company, Johnson and Johnson, and the Phelps-Dodge Corporation also furnished important information.

More recently, Mike Davis deserves thanks for his patient belief in the book, the History Theory and Design seminar at USC for providing valuable feedback, and Vic Liptak, Steve Callis, and Howard Smith for their help with the illustrations. I am grateful to my husband, Marco Cenzatti, for providing both personal and intellectual support. Our trips together to English industrial sites first generated my interest in company towns and his work on industrial restructuring has been a constant stimulus to my own thinking. Finally, I want to thank my mother, Virginia Crawford, for her significant contributions to this project. In addition to her interest and enthusiasm from the very beginning, she traveled thousands of miles with me visiting company towns around the country. I'm sorry she won't be able to read the finished book.

INTRODUCTION

This book is a study of the design of American company towns. Spanning the 150-year evolution of the company town as a distinctive urban form, it focuses on the transformation of company town planning from a vernacular building activity to a professional design task, undertaken by architects, landscape architects, and city planners. This culminated in the years 1913–25, when the "new" company town flourished. This book is the first history of the "new" company town, but in order to explain fully the shift between these two essentially different eras, it is necessary to retell the earlier history of the company town, reframed within a comprehensive and critical framework. The result is a new interpretation of the American company town. Although focusing specifically on the physical form of the company towns, this book breaks new ground by locating design within the constraints set by social and economic determinants. This portrays the built environment of the company town not as a static physical object, but as the product of a dynamic process, shaped by industrial transformation, class struggle, and reformers' efforts to control and direct these forces.

First, any history of the company town must answer a basic question: What is a company town? The *Encyclopedia of Social Sciences*' definition serves the purposes of this book: "a community inhabited chiefly by the employees of a single company or group of companies which also owns a substantial part of the real estate and houses."[1] This excludes other common uses of the term to describe locales with a dominant "industry," such as Detroit or Washington DC, or a dominant business enterprise. It also eliminates other types of industrial communities that are often confused with company towns – industrial towns like Homestead, Pennsylvania, that depended on a single employer, but were developed by private interests;[2] experimental and communitarian settlements, such as New Harmony, Indiana, Amana, Iowa, and Oneida, New York, that were economically based on industry or agriculture, but were communally owned; and housing projects or suburbs intended for industrial workers but developed separately from industrial facilities.

Historically, company towns, dependent on the nature and viability of the industry that supported them, have appeared in many different forms, locations, and situations. They constituted an early form of urbanization: in 1645, the Braintree Iron Works established the first company town in America. After this, settlements based on mining, timber-cutting and sawmilling, iron manufacturing, and rope and gun production spread across the land. The introduction of mechanized production at the beginning of the nineteenth century spawned even more towns, following industrial frontiers from the textile mills of New England to the coalmines of Pennsylvania, Maryland, and West Virginia, south to Alabama's coalfields and iron mines, west to the copper mines of upper Michigan, the silver and copper mines of the Far West, and, finally, to the cotton mills of the South. By the beginning of the twentieth century, suburban company towns were proliferating on the boundaries of large manufacturing cities and, during World War I, the Federal Government built its own industrial suburbs near shipyards and munitions plants. In 1930 the Bureau of Labor Statistics estimated that more than two million people were living in company towns. But shortly after, the effects of the Depression and changes in labor laws decreased their number, and the company town gradually disappeared from the American landscape.[3]

Underlying the enormous diversity of the American company town is a basic division that is of fundamental importance in interpreting its physical form. On one side is the industrial landscape, shaped by the processes that engendered it; and on the other, the model town, a concrete demonstration of a social or physical ideology.[4] The industrial landscape represents the direct translation of the technical and social necessities of a particular method of industrial production into a settlement form. Based on expediency, the industrial landscape, like most vernacular forms, depended on precedent. As the pragmatic sponsors of new company towns endlessly reproduced successful buildings and plans, so they produced multiple versions of the same settlement or housing types. This process, highly responsive to the demands of industrial processes or regional circumstances, produced generalized company town typologies. In contrast, model towns, usually the product of a single individual's ideology of religion, labor, or design, tended to be specific and unique. Attempts to mitigate the effects of economic logic by imposing social and physical planning, these towns emphasized conceptual order and symbolic form over the demands of industry. Intent on introducing social or physical innovation, their sponsors often ignored local conditions and followed the dictates of larger philosophical, social, or religious movements.

Alexander Hamilton proposed the first model town in 1792, but over the next century economic landscapes were the dominant form of company town. To relieve the harshness of industrial necessity, a minority of company town owners improved living and working conditions. They accompanied their reforms with a "discourse of benevolence," initially grounded in notions of Christian stewardship but increasingly justified by economic rationality. Built in 1883, the town of Pullman, Illinois, George Pullman's answer to the widening rift between capital and labor, represented a new model. A watershed between older styles of paternalism and the professionalized welfare methods of the twentieth century, Pullman influenced a new generation of "model" company towns, based on Progressive concepts of management and labor relations administered by trained professionals. In order to deter unionization and reduce labor turnover, the "new" company town attempted to attract workers by providing significantly better working and living conditions.[5]

By 1910, architects, planners, and landscape architects had taken over the design of the "new" company town. Unlike vernacular expression, professional design explicitly effaced the visual connection between the living environment and its industrial origins. Overlays of social and physical planning rendered the company town's industrial origins almost unrecognizable. This study examines this significant but little known chapter of company town history. Part I describes the gradual transformation of the industrial landscape into the "new" company town. Chapters 1 and 2 cover the evolution of the company town in an era of rapidly increasing industrial productivity, beginning in 1790 when Samuel Slater started spinning yarn with machines propelled by waterpower and culminating just over a century later, when the Pullman strike dramatized the conflicts of a fully capitalist economy and society. Chapter 1 examines the growth and decline of the New England textile industry and Chapter 2 covers the boom period following the Civil War, fueled by the iron and steel industries. The Pullman strike, the product of a period of increasing labor struggles, led industrialists and reformers to rethink the premises of the company town. Their proposals are discussed in Chapters 3, 4, and 5. Beginning with the Progressive era, a succession of different groups undertook the reform of the company town – urban and political reformers, the industrial betterment movement, proponents of Frederick Taylor's scientific management theories, tenement reformers, and finally, architects, landscape designers, and urban planners.

Part II consists of detailed studies of four designers of "new" company towns: Grosvenor Atterbury, Bertram Goodhue, John Nolen, and Earle S. Draper. Representing all three design professions – architecture, landscape architecture, and city planning – they built company towns across America. Building on the Norton Company's extensive welfare program, Atterbury "Americanized" the English garden city as an industrial garden suburb: Indian Hill, Massachusetts, one in a series of idealized New England company towns. Goodhue applied a similar approach to his design for Tyrone, New Mexico, introducing Mexican imagery in keeping with the region and the climate. Tyrone brought urban sophistication to the mining frontier, previously known for its primitive living conditions. Nolen, a city planner, standardized their approaches, creating a generalized method for planning company towns, that he adapted in numerous plans for towns as diverse as Kistler, Pennsylvania, Kingsport, Tennessee, and Union Park Gardens, Wilmington, Delaware. Earle S. Draper, a former employee of Nolen's, settled in the South and specialized in planning textile mill towns. In towns like Chicopee, Georgia, Draper redesigned the mill town as a rural landscape. Employing a range of social and physical strategies, each of these designers drew very different conclusions from their experiences in company towns.

REREADING THE COMPANY TOWN

Despite the extent and importance of company towns, a general history of American company towns has yet to appear. The subject has attracted the interest of a broad range of disciplines, including economics, geography, political science, sociology, labor and social history, as well as the histories of architecture, landscape architecture, and urban planning. In the absence of general works, there are a number of notable small-scale studies, interdisciplinary works focusing on single industrial communities. These range from studies of New England textile towns to mid-Atlantic iron plantations to Southern mill villages. Their community focus allows an in-depth examination of the multiple dimensions of a company town, emphasizing the interactions between a particular industry, a specific firm, a regional setting, and a group of workers.[6]

These works, however, deal primarily with nineteenth-century towns. By the end of the century an increasingly concentrated economy, specialized industrial structure, and complex corporate organization made it more difficult for historians to present such a coherent picture. Industrial communities began to respond to national rather than to regional economies, corporate decisions affecting towns were based on industry-wide strategies, and professionals applied standardized management and industrial relations policies. Labor began to organize on a national scale and architects' and planners' designs complicated the direct expression of the industrial needs that had characterized vernacular settlements. In response, historical approaches became more specialized, focusing on specific aspects of the company town. Some works dealt only with planning or architecture, while others portrayed company towns as episodes in the larger history of labor, industrial relations, or firms. A particularly wide gap exists between those who look at the company town as a physical environment and those who address its economic, labor, and social aspects.[7]

The aim of this study is to bridge this gap and serve as a corrective to overspecialized studies of company town design. In general, discussions of the physical form of company towns have fallen into four categories, focusing on formal, professional, economic, or social control issues. The first treats the company town as a chapter in the formal evolution of American urban or suburban planning, or as an episode in the career of notable architects and planners.[8] This emphasizes the continuity of design traditions, presented in exclusively aesthetic terms, while ignoring the specific design issues presented by the social and economic conditions of the company town. A second, overlapping category depicts the history of company town design as a demonstration of professional achievement.[9] Histories of landscape architecture and planning treat company town commissions as significant contributions to the development of the professions. Many biographers also present company town commissions as landmarks in individual careers.

The last two categories, responding to the narrow focus of previous scholarship, take more critical positions. Marxist historians make a direct link between the evolution of company town design and broad transformations in the American economy, while others portray the company town as a mechanism to control the unruly masses, and the designer as a physical agent of social control.[10] In spite of their opposing points of view, both approaches suffer from overgeneralization. On the one hand, writers who ignore the social and economic forces portray designers as all-powerful creators, while on the other, writers who do take these issues into consideration depict the designers as powerless, pawns in the hands of capitalist development or individual capitalists. Both schools tend to view the company town as a one-dimensional phenomenon, rarely differentiating between different types of company town or the widely varying regional, industrial, social, and labor contexts in which they developed.

In order to situate the physical form of the company town in a more complete and flexible explanatory framework, I discuss company town design as part of several larger contexts, one element in a complex configuration where economic development, industrial restructuring, geographical shifts, immigration, ethnic divisions, and labor struggles are as significant as reform, aesthetics, and professional advancement. By including both a broad survey and detailed case studies, I hope to address two scales of explanation, presenting the big picture without neglecting the significance of individual company towns. At both scales, I introduce three historical discussions that illuminate the actions and motivations of the three main groups who shaped the "new" company town: capitalists, workers, and reformers, including designers. These focus on industrial restructuring, labor history, and the critical history of progressive reform.

One difficulty scholars of company towns face is accounting for the process that creates, alters, and destroys company towns: the dynamic of capitalist development.[11] To emphasize the importance of change as an inherent aspect of the company town, I have drawn on studies of industrial restructuring, a body of economic literature that attempts to explain large-scale changes in industrial organization, involving the introduction of new technologies, changes in the labor process, and new patterns of geographic location during a particular period. To ensure the continued expansion of industrial growth, which was threatened by recurring economic and political crises, industrial firms and sectors went through periods of extensive restructuring. In each period, the particular form industrial restructuring took was shaped not only by the demands of capital for the reorganization of production, but also by the history of class relations and ongoing changes in social organization.[12]

This study attempts to locate the development of new and different types of company town within this broad dynamic of capitalist development. Michel Aglietta has divided the history of American capitalism into three discrete periods. The first, from 1800 to 1873, was marked by the gradual penetration of the United States by the capitalist organization of production, the second, lasting until World War I, introduced an extensive regime of accumulation based on competitive capitalism, and the third, lasting until the mid-1960s, was an intensive regime known as Fordism, characterized by mass production and mass consumption, regulated by the state. In Aglietta's periodization, shifts from one regime to the next occurred through transitional phases of restructuring.[13] These phases correspond to the appearance of significant new models for company towns: the first, around 1825, coincides with the appearance of Lowell, Massachusetts, the second, with the founding of Pullman in 1883, and the third, in 1914, with the appearance of the "new" company town. This suggests that employers utilized the company town as a regulatory mechanism, a physical setting that aided in accommodating specific groups of workers to new forms of industrial production.

Restructuring took place in space as well as in time. Geographer David Harvey has pointed out the importance of the "spatial fix" for successful industrial restructuring.[14] Changing location or reorganizing space creates new spatial settings that renew possibilities for industrial growth and expansion. The specific characteristics and histories of these different settings made their own demands on industrial development. As it expanded into new regions, each industrial sector continually generated new settlement typologies. Their changing forms and locations reflected both the temporal instability and the "inconstant geography" of capitalism.[15] Company towns were often outposts introducing industrial capitalism into previously unexploited territory and, later, nostalgic ruins of the same industry, abandoned in a continuing cycle of creation and destruction. Over the course of more than a century, a series of shifts in industry and geography generated a succession of company town types: the mill village, the corporate city, the lumber camp, the mining town, the industrial suburb, and the satellite city.

Aglietta's concept of industrial restructuring, which stresses the importance of social organization and class relations in structuring industrial production, suggests that workers played active roles in shaping company towns. However, most studies of early company towns overemphasize the role of technology as the overriding factor in the organization of the town, while scholars of later towns exaggerate the power of the employer, depicting his relationship to his employees, whether benevolent or overbearing, as almost completely unilateral. Adding labor history to the history of the company town points out the inaccuracy of these interpretations. Although company towns created a "diffuse" relationship between employers and workers, blurring the boundaries between working and living spheres, and making employees more than usually vulnerable to their employers' control, workers rarely were passive.[16] In company towns across the country, they actively participated in struggles to define their living and working conditions. Company towns became important sites of labor strife, dramatizing the continuing conflicts between capital and labor, ethnicity and Americanization, and discipline and democracy that marked industrializing America.[17]

Paradoxically, however, the "new" company town was widely publicized as a solution to labor unrest. Although acutely aware of the Pullman strike and other labor upheavals in company towns, many employers also saw company towns as a way of avoiding labor problems. The record of labor organizing, unionization, and strikes during this period reveals labor activity as the specific incentive to many "new" company town commissions. After 1900, there is a startling correlation between strikes and other labor struggles and the subsequent appearance of new company towns. Trying to forestall strikes, prevent unionization, and improve labor relations, employers hoped that "new" company towns would serve as *tabulae rasae* on which they could renegotiate their relationship with their employees. These negotiations usually included significant concessions to workers' interests, such as better living conditions, home ownership, parks, and recreational facilities.

Problematizing the discourse of reform adds another necessary critical dimension to the story of the "new" company town. After 1900, social reformers, scientific management experts, welfare secretaries, and design professionals, each claiming expert knowledge of industrial life, began to introduce changes into the company town. Their presence further complicated the already complex relationship between capital and labor. Their mission of "efficiency and uplift" combined social concern and self-interest in equal parts.[18] Attempting to mediate between capital and labor, they expanded the realm of middle-class professional values into the industrial environment. Critical studies of the Progressive era, looking beyond its often self-serving ideology, have revised our picture of this ethos of reform, bringing their assumptions to the surface and describing the limitations of their reforms.[19] The design professions, sharing a similar commitment to imposing physical order, fostering social efficiency, and extending professional mandates, have rarely been subjected to such critical scrutiny.

This study approaches design with a similar skepticism. Many scholars of company town architecture and town planning have played the role of tourist in company towns, focusing primarily on what is visible. This allows them to make what Eric Monkonnen has called the "architectural fallacy," reading economics, politics, and society through buildings.[20] As a result, they have been unduly impressed by the deceptive attractions of physical appearance. As the Commission that investigated the Pullman strike observed, "aesthetic features are admired by visitors, but have little money value to employees, especially when they lack bread."[21] Thus, rather than using design excellence as the primary framework of analysis and evaluation as many previous scholars have done, this study locates the major determinants of physical design in the external needs that generated them. However, although the designers' role was highly structured by factors beyond their control, it would be a mistake simply to view them as physical agents of the employers' desire to control their workers. Company sponsorship removed many conventional obstacles to town planning, such as individual ownership, the need for profit, and the lack of centralized control, without necessarily imposing any formal or physical definitions on the result. This gave designers the freedom to decide exactly how social and economic components could be translated into aesthetic choices and allowed them to define their own position toward both the client – the capitalist – and the user – the worker.

PART I

THE INDUSTRIAL
LANDSCAPE
TRANSFORMED:
1790–1890

1

TEXTILE LANDSCAPES: 1790–1850

Shortly after the American Revolution, the question of industry entered the American consciousness. Although American cities, thriving with entrepreneurial activity, already amply demonstrated the effects of private commercial enterprise, the few industries that existed – mining, iron working, and lumber milling – were located in remote settlements, far from the scrutiny of most Americans. However, even these isolated industrial activities aroused suspicion. Puritan clergymen and nearby farmers attacked their purely economic motives and destructive technologies, seeing them as violations of the social and religious values necessary to an agricultural economy.[1] Once the introduction of mechanized industry became imminent, local conflicts about the value of industrialization expanded to a national scale. Both sides in this hotly contested debate were convinced that decisions about American industrialization would set an irrevocable course for the new nation.

One reason for the intensity of the discussion was the example set by the English model of industrial development. Although Americans regularly committed industrial espionage in an attempt to acquire England's patented industrial secrets, they worried about the harmful social and physical effects of England's industrial transformation. Concentrated in the North-West, textile manufacturing had produced filthy, crowded, and chaotic cities such as Manchester and Leeds, where a new class of industrial wage-earners lived and worked in wretched conditions. Ways of avoiding these horrors preoccupied advocates and opponents of industrialization alike. Zachariah Allen, a strong supporter of American industry, concluded a horrified account of his tour of the English textile districts by exclaiming, "God forbid . . . that there ever may arise a counterpart of Manchester in the New World."[2]

These debates identified a fundamental contradiction in American capitalism that would be posed again and again over the next century and a half: the conflict between the market rationality of industrial development with profit as its ultimate consideration, and the social rationality that religious, ethical, or democratic principles demanded. The best-known positions in these debates, those of Alexander Hamilton and Thomas Jefferson, simply echoed these polarities. Hamilton's advocacy of "manufactures" was based on his conviction that economic growth should be a national priority. He feared that, without the economic power generated by industrialization, the United States would be unable to defend itself. Jefferson focused on the dangers an industrial proletariat posed to the egalitarian class system he believed was necessary to a democratic order.[3]

While Jefferson and Hamilton argued about the conditions under which industrialization should be undertaken, more practically, associations to promote "manufactures" formed, and venturesome entrepreneurs started to construct textile towns.[4] Speculative representations of the form American industry would take, these early company towns encapsulated in physical form the contradiction between economic and social rationality. On the one hand, the "model" company town attempted to ameliorate purely economic concerns with social and physical planning, and on the other, the "economic landscape" directly translated the technical and social necessities of industrial production into a settlement form.

Whether driven by ideals or built solely for profit, company towns expressed the tensions inherent in their creation, and invariably became sites of struggle. As industrialization proceeded, conflicts between capitalists and workers over the organization of production were exacerbated by conflicts over living conditions. Civil society also imposed its own interests – first, through expressions of public concern; later, by invoking the power of the state to investigate and regulate conditions in company towns. From the beginning, employers used paternalism to resolve the contradictions such controversy exposed, attempting to reconcile their interests with those of their workers to the satisfaction of outsiders. Employers used their control over workers' daily lives to impose various types of structured dependency. Although "paternalism" refers to all varieties of "enforced benevolence" that interfere with a person's liberty of action for that person's good,"[5] employers rarely just practiced paternalism, but linked their actions to a broader justificatory ideology – a "discourse of benevolence" that directly addressed concerns about the negative social effects produced by industrial development and capitalist social relations. Frequently adjusted to fit the changing realities of American capitalism, both paternalistic practices and the discourse of benevolence changed considerably over time. Ironically, however, the intensity of paternalistic relationships often heightened the tensions already present in the hierarchical social order of the company town, and led to further disruption.

THE MODEL TOWN

Even before Americans had fully mastered the techniques of textile manufacturing, the first "model" company towns were under construction. In the absence of practical experience, advocates of both the Hamiltonian and Jeffersonian positions proposed ideal solutions. Two early model towns, Paterson, New Jersey, and Humphreysville, Connecticut, served as concrete demonstrations of these opposing theories of physical and social planning.[6] Both towns claimed to offer comprehensive answers to what their sponsors anticipated would be the important questions posed by industrialization. Although neither accurately forecast the form American industrial development would eventually take, their alternative forms introduced the basic issues that subsequent discussions of company towns would debate. Like later model towns, they were influential partly as the result of the publicity they received. Both the inflated claims of their sponsors and the outraged responses of their critics posed their benefits and dangers in extreme terms, establishing a tradition that would continue into the twentieth century.

In August 1792, Alexander Hamilton, Secretary of the Treasury, and Tench Coxe, his Assistant Secretary, both militant advocates of American industrialization, hired Pierre L'Enfant, recently discharged from his work on the new capital at Washington, to design a grandiose industrial town for a site on the Passaic River in northern New Jersey.[7] The new town, officially sponsored by the Society for Useful Manufactures, was to furnish tangible proof that importing industrial capitalism would not necessarily impose England's "dark satanic" mills onto the virgin landscape of America. In his *Report on Manufactures*, Hamilton proposed establishing large-scale manufacturing units financed by substantial amounts of capital and regulated by the state. In opposition to the *laissez-faire* English approach, Hamilton emphasized careful control and extensive planning. Projected onto a *tabula rasa*, his visionary "national manufactory" would be a highly rationalized settlement.[8]

Hamilton's ambitious plans depended on capitalizing the town at the unprecedented sum of one million dollars, at that time more than the total worth of all corporations operating in the United States. Although cotton textiles, identified as a "critical sector of extraordinary importance in establishing industry," would provide its economic base, the proposed town would produce a full range of manufactured products. Since the Great Falls of the Passaic, 77 feet high, generated enough waterpower for an unlimited number of factories, the Society bought 700 acres and optimistically incorporated a city 6 miles square in anticipation of future growth. Hamilton's enthusiastic prospectus attracted investors from as far away as Amsterdam and convinced the state of New Jersey to charter the corporation, invest 10,000 dollars, and exempt it from taxes for ten years. In return, the town was named after its governor, William Paterson. With more than 250,000 dollars pledged, development began.[9]

L'Enfant's plan matched Hamilton's ambitions. Ignoring existing structures, he projected a visionary scheme, which local newspapers predicted would "far surpass anything yet seen in this country." L'Enfant adapted the diagonal plan of Washington to the site's rugged topography, planning a capital of manufactures organized around a series of broad diagonal avenues, 200 feet wide, radiating from an elevated point in the center of the town: "I have taken advantage of a rising ground to reserve the summit of it for the erection of some public building, carrying the street from thence according as the accidental opening may admit prolonging them at a distance." The industrial area maintained an equally grand scale. A massive stone aqueduct would divert the Passaic's waters 7 miles along a series of multi-leveled classical arches; monumental mills would line the banks along both sides of the power canal, and a broad "airline road," – a straight roadway lined with trees – would carry Paterson's products directly to Newark and New York City.[10]

Translating Hamilton's abstract economic vision into reality inevitably generated arguments about how to achieve his goals. L'Enfant's vision of the new physical forms in which American capitalism could clothe itself clashed with the priorities of the Society's directors. Although both consciously avoided any similarities to Europe's notorious industrial heartlands, the directors refused to reconcile the functional imperatives of industry and investment with the planner's abstract mode of representation. L'Enfant borrowed the most prestigious urban type of the period, the capital city, for Paterson's plan, adapting diagonally radiating streets, monumental avenues, and magnificent arches to exalt industrial purpose into a national imperative. Ignoring such honorific aspirations, the directors of the Society tried instead to create an ideal setting for industrial efficiency. Unimpressed by the grandeur of L'Enfant's symbolic order, the Society organized the town around industrial production, replacing the public building L'Enfant envisioned as Paterson's center with a functional core of factories.[11]

While outlining their plans for housing Paterson's workers, the directors, almost inadvertently, delineated a completely new social and physical order. Subdividing the site into equal quarter-acre lots, they allocated identical cottages to fifty families. Each tiny house was 24 × 19 feet, a story and a half high, with a cellar and a garret. They set aside four larger lots to build more substantial houses for the skilled mechanics who would supervise the operation. Workers could rent, buy houses with twenty-year mortgages at 5 percent, or purchase lots; these flexible arrangements were more concerned with attracting workers than with controlling them.[12] Family housing implied a family labor system, an arrangement that supported Hamilton's argument that industry would not reduce an already limited agricultural labor force, but would employ "those previously unemployed," particularly women and children. Paterson's planning introduced a new spatial order into America. If L'Enfant's grand plan symbolized the future projected for industry, the Society's represented the actual contradictions it would bring. If the uniform grid of identical cottages promised equality and a uniform standard of living, the core of factories imposed the rationalized and repetitious logic of mechanized production.

Frustrated by opposition and lack of progress, L'Enfant angrily quit the project in 1792, leaving nothing built. The Society for Useful Manufactures fared little better; most of its promised capital never appeared, the collapse of the stock market in 1792 bankrupted major stockholders, and projected government support did not materialize. In the absence of any conception of industrial relations, the workers posed unanticipated problems. Skilled English mechanics could not set up the basic machinery for cotton manufacturing, while American workers, dissatisfied with their wages, went out on strike – the first industrial strike in America. Unable to deal with this unprecedented event, the Society retaliated by closing down the factory – the first American lock-out. In 1794, without funds, the enterprise was abandoned and Paterson reverted to its former condition as an agricultural village.[13]

The Society's plans for Paterson provoked enormous controversy. The Society was attacked as a government-supported corporation that would drive small producers out of business and criticized for being a monopoly providing "exclusive privileges" to a wealthy few at the expense of farmers and small manufacturers. In a heated debate with Tench Coxe in the pages of the *American Museum*, George Logan, a farmer and advocate of *laissez-faire* economics, accused the Society of threatening republican principles. Logan feared that the accumulation of wealth and power in Paterson would inevitably lead to the oppression and neglect of the masses.[14] Although Paterson's opponents interpreted the enterprise's industrial failure as a vindication of their criticism, the town in fact was too far ahead of its time to be viable, demanding economic and social conditions that did not yet exist. The first professionally planned company town, Paterson was an ambitious prototype for a settlement type that would not reappear for another century.

THE PATERNALISTIC ORDER

Ten years after Paterson's failure, Colonel David Humphreys founded another industrial settlement to demonstrate a specific ideological program. If Paterson embodied Hamilton's position in the factory controversy, the mill village of Humphreysville exemplified a Jeffersonian approach. Unconcerned about industry's physical representation, Humphreys hoped to alter its social order. A friend and admirer of Jefferson, Humphreys, while Ambassador to Spain, had imported Merino sheep to begin a wool industry in the United States. Already influenced by Jefferson's fears about the negative effects of urban concentration on America's developing democracy and the political dangers of creating a class of industrial workers, Humphreys's own tour of European factories further convinced him of the need for a new system of factory life. Opposed to massive industrial concentrations such as Paterson, he intended to prove that small-scale individual efforts could solve the "factory problem."[15]

In keeping with Jefferson's belief that necessary industries should be kept small and isolated in rural areas, Humphreys built a small wool mill and village along the Naugatuck River in southwest Connecticut. Although Humphreys's mills, tucked away in a picturesque clearing, physically resembled other early textile villages, they operated under a new set of premises. Determined to avoid the "demoralizing" effects of factory labor and maintain what he regarded as adequate moral standards, Humphreys created the first system of industrial labor management in America, an ideology of control based on moral guardianship imposed both in and out of the factory. Instead of following the English example of hiring families, Humphreys imported a completely new workforce – the daughters of local farmers and orphans from almshouses in New York. The young women were paid, but the orphans, called "apprentices," were provided with room and board but no wages.[16]

Humphreys's labor system was literally paternalistic; he assumed parental authority over his apprentices, organized their accommodation, and personally administered a complex daily regime. Housing his young workers in "model" boarding houses in groups of fifteen, he supplied them with comfortable beds and fresh vegetables while imposing a strict routine of early bedtimes and early rising to go to work. After work and on Sundays, he required the workers to attend his school, taught by professional teachers who checked the boys' progress with regular examinations. A carrot and stick regime of rewards and punishments disciplined both work and leisure. Those who excelled in each class were rewarded with prizes of books and money, while monitors enforced the silence and order Humphreys demanded.

The boys' work in the mills, however, formed the heart of Humphreys's ideology of improvement, based on the widely held Calvinist belief that labor was both morally and socially improving. Humphreys's self-congratulatory "Poem on the Industry of the United States of America," written at the time of the founding of Humphreysville, celebrated the advantages of labor:

> From industry the sinews strength acquire
> The limbs expand, the bosom feels new fire.
> Unwearied industry pervades the whole

Nor lends more force to body than to soul.
Hence character is form'd, and hence proceeds
Th' enlivening heat that fires to daring deeds.[17]

To ensure such physical and moral benefits, Humphreys discouraged "negligency and idleness" in the factory, insisting that "the labor at stated hours is easy, but must be performed." He rewarded his workers' diligence and proficiency with a series of prizes given for skill in various manufacturing tasks. Many observers saw Humphreys's efforts as serving a larger social good, since these orphans might not otherwise have had the opportunity to engage in "improving" labor.

As the daughter of his mill superintendent observed, "Col. Humphreys omitted nothing that could arouse the ambition or promote intellectual improvement among the operatives, although he did it after a grand military fashion."[18] He wrote plays that the operatives performed on holidays and organized the boys into his own private militia, putting them through their drills himself. Humphreys's system functioned very efficiently. Healthy living conditions resulted in very low absenteeism in the factory and visitors noted that "rewards and encouragements of various kinds have nearly superseded the necessity of punishment" and "there has not been for some time past a single bad subject on the black list." Humphreys's absolute control allowed him to dismiss on the spot any apprentice he considered immoral.[19]

Humphreys's heavily coercive paternalism represented an extension of authoritarian family relations into the industrial realm. He claimed power over his orphans *in loco parentis*, legitimizing power outside the family by appealing to roles within it. Humphrey's contemporaries accepted this relationship, describing the apprentices as "appear[ing] extremely well-satisfied with their condition, being well fed, clothed and lodged, like the members of a well-regulated and happy family."[20] Richard Sennett has argued, however, that such paternalism inflates and distorts the paternal role by magnifying the element of egoistic benevolence to the exclusion of other parental qualities. Rather than encouraging growth and independence, paternalism demands continual subservience, loyalty, and appreciation.[21]

In the context of the debates of the time, which considered industrial labor to be degrading, many observers considered Humphreys's moral guardianship to be exemplary. Humphreysville was widely praised for definitively answering many of the troubling questions posed by the factory controversy. Timothy Dwight, later President of Yale, wrote that the town established three fundamental points about industry: that manufactures could be carried on with success; that workmen could remain healthy; and that a deterioration of morals was not necessarily inherent in manufacturing activities.[22] Jefferson demonstrated his support by ordering coats made from Humphreys's wool for himself and his cabinet. The state of Connecticut recognized Humphreys's achievement in "converting into an active capital the exertions of persons who would otherwise be idle and, in many instances, a burden to the community," by exempting the village from taxes for ten years and, ironically, exempting his apprentices from military duty.[23]

THE TEXTILE LANDSCAPE

Humphreysville's paternalism, like Paterson's model plan, found few imitators. Instead, expediency rather than ideology prevailed. At the same time as L'Enfant was laying out grand boulevards and Humphreys was drilling his apprentices, a more modest but viable textile town was evolving along the Blackstone River valley in northern Rhode Island. In 1790, Samuel Slater, a recent immigrant from England, finally succeeded in replicating the first Arkwright spinner in America. Using waterpower, he mechanized the spinning of cotton yarn – the first mass-production industry in America. Unaware of Hamilton and Humphreys's sophisticated arguments about industrialization, Slater used an ad hoc approach, based on circumstances and precedent; instead of inventing a specifically American system, he simply adapted English practices to local conditions. As other aspiring industrialists adopted and reproduced his successful practices, they became known as the Slater or Rhode Island system.[24]

Existing conditions shaped the developing industry. In contrast to the large-scale and well-capitalized corporations Hamilton advocated, Slater and other investors, small partnerships of merchants, had limited capital and preferred not to take risks. They scaled mills to existing markets and available waterpower. Since only yarn spinning had been mechanized, making cloth still required skilled handloom weavers, thus limiting the amount that could be produced. Individual mills thus remained small; most operated with fewer than a hundred workers tending no more than a thousand spindles. Northern Rhode Island's topography, broken by networks of small river valleys, reinforced these practices by offering numerous cheap mill sites along waterfalls and rapids in remote areas. A small investment in dams and waterworks would divert enough fast-flowing water into a power canal to drive a wheel to power the mechanical spinning frame.[25]

The area's hilly terrain was difficult to cultivate, and so provided Slater with a labor force – rural families unable to survive by farming its rocky soil. If Slater was unfamiliar with Hamilton's discourse on employing those previously unemployed, facing the same labor shortage, he solved the problem by resorting to a traditional practice – the English family system. He recruited families from rural areas, advertising for "poor families having the

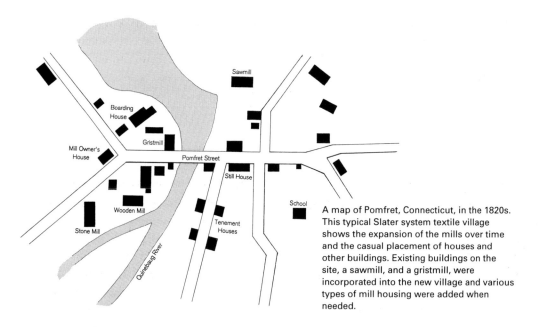

Sawmill

Boarding House

Gristmill

Mill Owner's House

Pomfret Street

Still House

Wooden Mill

Stone Mill

School

Tenement Houses

Quinebaug River

A map of Pomfret, Connecticut, in the 1820s. This typical Slater system textile village shows the expansion of the mills over time and the casual placement of houses and other buildings. Existing buildings on the site, a sawmill, and a gristmill, were incorporated into the new village and various types of mill housing were added when needed.

largest number of children." The entire family operated as an economic unit: unskilled children tended the spinning machines, fathers performed skilled jobs in the mill or worked on nearby farms, and the mother wove at home or in the factory. Their combined pay provided a living wage for families who could not otherwise achieve an adequate standard of living.[26]

The mills' remote locations, the poverty of their workers, and the English precedent of providing housing for workers encouraged mill owners to build their own settlements. By 1815, more than 170 small mills were operating in the area around Pawtucket, creating a landscape of tiny villages which, according to an early visitor, "appear to spring up as if by magic in the bosom of some forest around the waterfall which serves to turn the mill wheel . . . sprinkled among the glens and meadows of solitary watercourses."[27] Picturesque rather than monumental or satanic, these mill villages constituted the first successful industrial landscape in America, a reproducible type of company town, which literally translated the productive demands of the Slater system into a spatial order. This distinctive settlement type was duplicated in hundreds of rural mill villages scattered not only across southeastern New England but up and down the Atlantic coast from Maine to Maryland, wherever fast-flowing streams and local capital were available.[28]

Without conscious planning, the morphology of the mill village revealed a spatial hierarchy that satisfied the needs of textile manufacturing but was still shaped by agrarian

Willimantic, Connecticut in 1824. Even after the advent of the Waltham system, numerous Slater system textile villages continued to thrive along small rivers all over New England. The enlarged mills now dominate the village. Courtesy of Rhode Island Historical Society.

tradition. The primary determinant was the water supply; the availability of waterpower determined the location of the village; its size was determined by the size of the mill, which depended on the amount of waterpower. The village began with the damming of a river's natural flow into narrow power canals that channeled energy to the mill. The most efficient location for a mill was between the canal and the road that brought raw materials in and carried finished yarns and cloth out. The prototypical form of Slater's first mill at Pawtucket, a narrow rectangle topped with a cupola adapted from numerous English precedents, was followed by subsequent mills. The mill's form and structure suggested familiar building types such as meeting houses, but as mills increased in size and number, they soon dominated the village.[29]

The settlement clustered around the mill recreated the traditional linear street design and an open field pattern of the New England village in a new industrial context. Unlike the imposed order of the mill and its waterworks, the surrounding village, an informal mix of buildings, pastures, and garden plots, rarely followed any pattern. The mill owner began by constructing only the necessary structures: housing for the workers and a company store. Cash-poor mill owners preferred to pay wages in kind rather than in cash, so they deducted rent and store purchases from workers' wages. Later, if the mill was successful, churches, schools, or commercial buildings would be added. Housing rarely followed a single prototype; duplexes were the most common type of mill housing, but mill owners also built detached cottages, small tenements, and boarding houses. To save money, they constructed mill houses in groups of duplicated units. This introduced a regularity into the pastoral setting, but this newly repetitive order was limited to small groupings and thus barely disturbed the vernacular order. Overall, variety rather than unity still prevailed in the mill village. Farmers' houses and barns were scattered among the workers' cottages and resident mill owners often erected a large manor house in sight of their mills. Economy demanded that existing structures be put to new uses; taverns, for example, could become boarding houses or houses could be converted into stores.[30]

The haphazard order of the mill village underlined the absence of a fully industrialized social order. Although the mill bell imposed an unfamiliar discipline on the workers' time, the demands of the factory had not yet completely eliminated more traditional modes of life. Children, with short attention spans, made erratic workers and parents routinely disrupted production by removing their children from the mills whenever they needed them. Both mills and villages remained tied to the domestic economy. Since production was not fully mechanized, mills depended on handloom weaving performed by farmers' wives who had their own domestic priorities. Without cash wages, workers kept animals and grew much of their own food, often trading with neighboring farms. Workers moved back and forth from farm to mill. The rhythm of the agricultural year still made its presence felt; in the summer of 1796, Samuel Slater's workers deserted the factory en masse to pick berries.[31]

At the same time, two separate and opposing points of view about the new industrial system were emerging. Although many Rhode Island mill owners began as workers, ownership and employment increasingly constituted distinct social classes. Mill owners became part of the emerging ruling class while employees, landless and unskilled, composed a new proletariat. Manufacturers justified these inequalities in moral terms, repeating familiar arguments about the virtues of hard work. They cast themselves in the role of benefactors offering long hours of "improving" work to those who, left idle, might otherwise remain "very ignorant or spend time in vicious amusements." Mill owners disapprovingly described their workers' recreational habits as "drunken and debauched" and their job advertisements stressed moral character: "Those who are in the habit of profanity and Sabbath breaking and intend to continue these practices are invited not to make application."[32] They even portrayed the isolation of the mill village as a positive virtue, since it brought "families together . . . [who] must conform to the habits and customs of their neighbors or be despised and neglected by them." This developing ideology allowed Slater's biographer to conclude: "the introduction of manufacturing was thus . . . a harbinger of moral and intellectual improvement on the inhabitants of the vicinage."[33]

No clear philosophy of paternalism emerged from these distinctions. Although the working day was long – a twelve-hour day, six days a week – once it was over, workers were generally left to follow their own inclinations. George S. White's polemic defense of the Slater system, "The Moral Influence of Manufacturing Establishments," rested its claims for the benefits of the mill system more on the improving qualities of hard work than on what White called "beneficial management." Mill owners responding to White's question about village improvements cited their sponsorship of churches as the main evidence of their benevolence.[34] Mill village churches reinforced the work ethic by stressing obedience, industry, and deference as primary religious values. Although Slater established a Sunday School, a secular institution that taught child workers, he abandoned it as soon as churches were firmly established in Webster and Slatersville.[35]

Discussions of the moral implications of factory employment, intended for the middle-class church-going public, meant little to mill workers with more specific grievances. The conditions of employment were heavily weighted in the employers' favor. Workers signed contracts specifying wages and working conditions, setting their house rent, and requiring a pledge not to strike; these were easily broken or arbitrarily enforced by mill owners. Inside the mill, workers were at the mercy of the foreman's unrestricted power, and the machines themselves posed a constant danger of injury or even death. Workers resisted the unfamiliar impositions of work and authority both in and out of the factory. The most common protest against factory discipline was simply not to work, and absenteeism and turnover among workers was high. Occasionally workers took more extreme measures; mill fires were often attributed to arson and a contemporary document describes workers cheering as their employer's mill burned to the ground.[36] Spontaneous protests against attempts to cut wages often broke out, but organized conflicts were rare. Isolated in remote villages, unskilled mill workers remained outside the labor organizations urban artisans were forming.[37] The uneasy peace between capital and labor was instead maintained on an ad hoc basis, and the Slater system continued to expand without a formalized system of labor relations.

THE CORPORATION CITY

Until 1820, towns like Slatersville remained the prototype for the fledgling industry. But, even as these mill villages multiplied, they were already being superseded by a more advanced system of textile production invented in Waltham, Massachusetts. Like Samuel Slater, Francis Cabot Lowell created a reproducible industrial unit based on technical innovation; just as Slater had duplicated the power spinner, Lowell reinvented the power loom. This breakthrough – the final step in mechanizing the entire clothmaking process – produced the first fully integrated textile factory in America. Unlike Slater, however, Lowell was also financially innovative; he organized the Waltham mill as a corporation, the Boston Manufacturing Company, initially capitalized at 300,000 dollars, an enormous jump in scale from Rhode Island mills, which could be started with as little as 30,000 dollars. After five years, Waltham's capital was equal to the amount Hamilton had envisioned for Paterson.[38]

By 1821, however, Lowell's mill in Waltham was moribund. The slow-moving Charles River produced barely enough power to propel the existing machinery. In order to expand, a group of Waltham investors located an ideal mill site along the Merrimack River, one of the largest and fastest rivers in New England, with 32-foot falls that could produce over

30,000 hp – enough for fifty mills the size of Waltham.[39] The firm bought 400 acres and named the new town after Frances Lowell, who had died in 1817. At Lowell, the Waltham system created a town after its own image, reorganizing mills and housing into a new spatial order that reflected the changed financial, technical, and social conditions in the industry. This produced a new type of company town: the corporation city.

In spite of its ambitious aims, Lowell was not a model company town. Although equal in scale to Paterson, Lowell had no Pierre L'Enfant to provide it with a conceptual order. Kirk Boott, the Merrimack Company's resident agent, trained as an engineer and surveyor at Sandhurst, acted as the sole developer, town planner, and architect. Although the initial investors envisioned a city with sites for fifty mills, they did not create a formal town plan. Instead, Boott organized a single industrial unit for the Merrimack's mills and housing, leaving the land outside the factory boundaries, labeled "town," to be subdivided into lots and sold for commercial development. Subsequent mills bought sites and duplicated Boott's prototype, with each new mill settlement expanding the series of industrial enclaves surrounding the power canals in the eastern end of the city.[40] Even in comparison to tiny Rhode Island hamlets, the mill settlements were incomplete; Lowell's founders, satisified with control over their machines and workers, had no "urban vision" of a coherent community.[41]

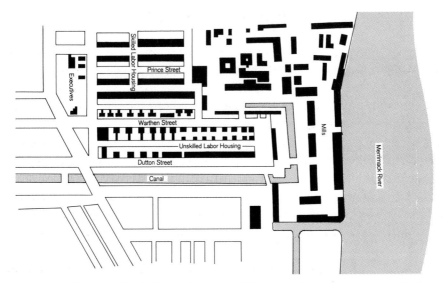

The mills and houses of the Merrimack Textile Corporation at Lowell. The order of the mill settlement replicates that of the factory hierarchy, with the executives' and superintendents' houses located nearest the town and the areas near the factory allocated to boarding houses for mill girls and duplexes for skilled workmen. The rigid geometry and tight spacing echo the increasing regularity of the textile production process.

Boott's organization of the Merrimack mill development followed the same logic as Rhode Island industrial landscapes, while responding to far more complex and rigorous technical needs. The demands of the production processes now controlled the totality of experience in the mill settlement; its rigidly geometric organization, rather than expressing a new concept of planning, reflected the new level of control and regularity imposed by the Waltham system. Set within rectangular boundaries, the long narrow site, located for maximum hydraulic efficiency, ran from the river to the main street of the town to minimize expensive river frontage. Isolated at the river end, a complex of mills, printing and dye works, storage buildings, and a counting house enclosed a central mill yard. The standardized mill buildings were geometrically ordered for the efficient coordination of the flow of

Above: View of Dutton Street, Lowell, Massachusetts, 1849. The main street of the Merrimack Manufacturing Company's industrial enclave. Organized into straight streets lined by rows of identical housing, Lowell's ensemble of mills and housing introduced a new level of order and discipline into textile settlements. On the left are two generations of boarding houses, the mills are at the end of the street and at the right, behind the trees, is the Merrimack Canal. Courtesy of the University of Massachusetts, Lowell.

Left: Plan of a Lowell boarding house at 22 Dutton Street, around 1825. The ground floor, containing the matron's rooms, allows surveillance of the mill girls' comings and goings. The dining room, where the girls ate three meals a day, is the only common room. On the upper floors, four to six girls occupy each bedroom.

industrial operations which transformed raw cotton into printed cloth; an order structured by the sequence of processes necessary for vertically integrated textile production.[42]

The Waltham system's expanded scale and complex technology required a new labor force. Operating power looms demanded more dexterity, intelligence, and discipline than children possessed, forcing Lowell's mill owners to hire more skilled workers. They discovered an untapped source of labor – the daughters of rural New England farmers – who, like children, were only temporary workers. These young women, already trained in domestic spinning and weaving, would stay in the mills for several years then return home with savings that could be used as a dowry, for an education, or as a contribution to the family income. In order to induce respectable families to allow their daughters to come to Lowell, the mills had to assure them of suitable living and working conditions. In 1825 the Merrimack mills provided the answer with the boarding house system. This required mill girls to live in supervised boarding houses and delegated control of their non-working hours to a housekeeper with an impeccable reputation. The corporations supplemented her power with contracts enforcing obedience. Their rules demanded everything from "propriety at all times" to regular church attendance.[43]

This type of corporate supervision, while continuing the employer's role *in loco parentis*, differed considerably from Humphreys's direct paternalism. Rather than inventing a new model of paternalistic labor relations, the mill owners did the minimum necessary to recruit their female labor force. Their system emphasized control without benevolence. Once parental expectations of adequate social standards were satisfied, the mills displayed little interest in improving their employees' morals or their lives. The mills girls' intense participation in cultural and educational activities was on their own initiative, sponsored by the independent urban institutions of church and Lyceum rather than by corporate philanthropy. The mills' motives were fundamentally economic, as even favorable descriptions of the labor system emphasized:

> The productiveness of these works depends on one primary and indispensable condition, the existence of an industrious, sober, orderly, and moral class of operatives. Without this the mills in Lowell would be worthless. . . . Public morals and private interests, identical in all places, are seen here to be linked together in an indissoluble connection. Accordingly, the sagacity of self-interest, as well as more disinterested considerations, has led to the adoption of moral police.[44]

"Moral police" conveys the exaggerated emphasis on control that dominated both mill and boarding house. Designed to duplicate parental supervision, the necessity of imposing a standardized morality on hundreds of workers inevitably rationalized and systematized discipline far beyond the rules that prevailed in even the strictest family. Disobedience was punished by immediate dismissal and blacklisting. In the mills, the total organization of production subjected the mill girls to a far more complete industrial discipline than in the Rhode Island mills or in virtually any other workplace of the period. Enforced by strict supervision, integrated textile production imposed a standardized work routine on the girls. With the exception of a few skilled jobs, tasks were repetitive. Although the machines ran slowly at first, their discipline was inexorable.

The zoning of the mill settlement both reflected and reinforced this control. In stark contrast to informal Rhode Island villages, the spatial order of Lowell's mill settlements mirrored precisely the division of labor in the factory; the owners, corporate investors, lived elsewhere; a small number of resident executives occupied the area closest to the town, dominated by Kirk Boott's large house; workers lived in the sector adjacent to the mill, divided between rectangular blocks of houses for skilled workers and their families and boarding houses for the mill girls. Each block included a foreman's house, to ensure continual supervision of the workers.[45] The predominantly Irish laborers who built the mills and the town were excluded from this purely industrial order, living in shantytowns that sprung up just outside the mill's boundaries.

The housing in the mill settlements followed vernacular prototypes, adjusted to reflect the factory's hierarchy of status and control. Lowell's basic four-square house-type, adapted to the rank of its occupants, could be used as a single family house, surrounded by gardens, for executives. The same house, subdivided into duplexes or a smaller tenement, was rented to skilled workmen with families or configured as a boarding house for mill girls. Inside the boarding house, the layout of rooms made the housekeeper's constant surveillance over her charges easier. Communal bedrooms, sleeping from four to ten girls, made immorality virtually impossible. Even more than in Rhode Island, proximity enforced conformity, and group pressure reinforced the power of the moral police. One observer wrote that "a girl merely suspected of immoralities at once loses caste."[46] However, Lowell mills removed one important element of control employed by Rhode Island mills: the company store. For workers, the payment of cash wages was one of Lowell's biggest attractions. The mill girls took full advantage of Lowell's stores, and often surprised visitors with their fashionable clothes and accessories.[47]

The textile corporations exploited the paradoxical image of powerful machinery operated by demure maidens, using it as a central feature in a promotional campaign advertising Lowell as the economic and social marvel of America. Like Paterson and Humphreysville, Lowell promoted itself as the definitive answer to the "factory controversy." Although its female workers presumably arrived at the mills with their morals intact, their employers attributed their subsequent lack of degradation to the positive influences of factory life. More importantly, they presented their female workforce as a unique method of avoiding the creation of a permanent industrial class. In spite of their heavy workloads and the controls imposed on them, the mill girls also asserted their social equality with their employers. Their perception of their social and economic independence was based not only on their origins as "daughters of freemen" but also on their status as *temporary* workers. Since they could always return to their family, they were never completely dependent on their employers.[48]

Lowell's unique social order was its main selling point. As corporate guides carefully led eminent visitors through the town, the outsiders were invariably fascinated by the sight of genteel female workers, so unlike the degraded proletariat typically associated with manufacturing. Encouraged by lavish corporate hospitality, influential visitors heaped exaggerated praise on Lowell's neat brick mills and its attractive and fashionable young workers. Foreign visitors agreed that Lowell was "one of the most extraordinary towns in this extraordinary country."[49] Although Europeans were shocked by the long hours the girls worked, they attributed this to "Yankee enterprise" and accepted it as part of what otherwise appeared to be a workers' paradise. Charles Dickens's visit to Lowell in 1841 aroused his enthusiasm as had nothing else in North America. He was most astonished by the mill girls' literary journal, the *Lowell Offering*,[50] produced by operatives who managed to find time to write after long hours in the mill. The *Offering*, funded and promoted by the corporations, presented a positive portrait of factory life filtered through the determinedly genteel sensibilities of its writers.[51]

Even as Dickens and others were praising the *Offering* as the ultimate evidence of Lowell's success, rapidly changing industrial conditions were challenging its conventionalized depictions of factory life. When increasing competition threatened profits, the corporations responded by lowering wages and increasing productivity with "speed-ups" to cut costs.[52] In 1834 and 1836 women workers, outraged by wage cuts that undermined their sense of dignity and social equality, organized massive protests that closed the mills. By the 1840s, permanent labor organizations such as the Lowell Female Labor Reform Association appeared for the first time, rejecting the outdated "uplifting" rhetoric of the *Offering* in favor of an alternative discourse based on the actual conditions of work. Their struggles focused on the demand for a ten-hour day. This signaled the end of Lowell's evasion of the class system. The mill girls could no longer see themselves as exceptional, but recognized that they had become full-fledged members of the working class.[53]

During the next decade, however, even organized protests had little effect on conditions in the mill. By 1850, the Waltham system had been transformed. Once the first waves of European immigration eliminated the chronic shortage of low-wage labor, Irish men and children first joined then gradually replaced Yankee women in the mills. Since they no longer depended on young female workers, the mills abandoned the boarding house system and the "moral police," and left workers to find their own housing. After 1848, no new company housing was built in Lowell; the corporations converted their boarding houses into family tenements or sold them as investment property.[54] As improvements in steam engine technology, using coal as cheap fuel, released mills from dependence on water-power, the center of the textile industry relocated to seaports like New Bedford and Fall River, which were closer to sources of raw materials and immigrant labor. There, employers still maintained some family tenements, but took little interest in their workers' lives outside the mills. Corporation cities like Lowell, no longer pioneers, gradually decayed, becoming grimy industrial cities.

THE DISCOURSE OF INDUSTRIALIZATION

Once industry became a dominant way of life in New England – by 1840 Massachusetts was a predominantly manufacturing state – the heated debates generated by industrialization were abandoned in the face of new economic realities.[55] The overwhelming evidence of industry's material success silenced the voices that had raised ethical, humanitarian, or democratic objections to its development.[56] The triumph of economic rationality, how-ever, demanded a concomitant adjustment of ideology. The "opinion which . . . prevailed extensively, that occupation in manufactories were less favorable to morals than other manual labor," was replaced by new social theories that supported industrial growth. Henry Carey, a Pennsylvania businessman and political economist, argued that capitalistic enter-prise was not antithetical to Christian doctrine as long as capitalists acted as stewards of wealth on behalf of the community. If this maintained hierarchical relationships between employer and employee, these were amply justified by the social, moral, and spiritual ben-efits that came with economic growth and an improved standard of living.[57]

Carey's theory of Christian capitalism, emphasizing the responsibilities of the capitalist and setting definite social limits to business ethics, remained a minority position. More pop-ular ideologies accepted the working conditions and social relations imposed by industrial capitalism, with the proviso that they were only temporary. The myth of upward mobility posited, instead of the permanent proletariat already evident in Europe, an American class system in which "the elements of society, like the particles in a mass of boiling liquid, are constantly changing places."[58] Belief in such unlimited possibilities easily led to Social Darwinist notions that riches and success were the rewards of the "fittest," and poverty the lot of those who had failed to measure up. The ethos of individuality relieved the capitalist of any larger social responsibility other than the creation of wealth.[59] With the contradiction between industrial progress and human development eliminated, a new discourse of indus-trialization emerged. Having demonstrated the power of industrialists by seemingly inexorable growth and increasing wealth, industrialists could now take an aggressive stance and dictate their own premises rather than responding to the doubts of their opponents.

2

THE COMPANY TOWN IN AN ERA OF INDUSTRIAL EXPANSION

In 1840, New England's industrial cities and mill towns were anomalies in a predominantly agricultural society. Between 1850 and 1880, the rest of the United States began to be transformed into a fully industrialized economy with unprecedented speed and thoroughness. Development expanded westward along newly laid rail lines that supplied factories with raw materials and created an integrated national market. The first wave of nineteenth-century industrialization, propelled by the New England textile industry, was followed by a second, far more dramatic wave led by the expanding iron and steel industries, fueled by vast quantities of raw materials extracted from the earth. Lowell's large-scale, efficient corporate organization prefigured the increasing size and concentration of American industry. Corporate consolidation expanded the size of factories and dehumanized them even further.[1]

This rapid growth generated new industrial settlements reflecting the diversity of the American economy. The search for available land and resources moved the industrial frontier south and west, closely followed by immigrant labor. Manufacturing initially concentrated in large cities, but, as new extractive and manufacturing districts developed in unsettled areas, the construction of new towns became an essential part of industrial investment.[2] Physically, these towns followed no single pattern. Like the towns produced by the Slater and Waltham systems, the production processes and labor force in each region interacted to produce distinct industrial typologies. Each industrial district established its own standards for working conditions and community life that shaped a characteristic physical and social order. Some company towns, direct descendants of older types of communities, continued traditional practices. In Johnstown, Pennsylvania, the Cambria Iron Works extended the mining and forging activities of the pre-industrial iron plantation into a modern form of vertical integration.[3] Even after the introduction of steampower, conservative New England textile firms continued to locate near sources of waterpower. In other towns the nature of the local labor supply dictated living and working conditions. In Tennessee and Alabama iron towns, a large local supply of black workers enabled employers to offer low wages and poor housing, while in the Michigan copper belt, skilled Cornish miners were able to impose their own mining techniques, payment system, and social customs on their employers.[4]

Within these parameters, the social organization of each town varied with the individual circumstances of ownership and management. The prevailing climate of moral pragmatism left the balance of control and benevolence in each town to the discretion of the individual capitalist. Differences could be extreme. Isolation, for example, encouraged near-feudal control, such as the phenomenon of the "closed town" found in mining regions. In the 1870s, a group of Tioga County, Pennsylvania coal towns were notorious private fiefdoms, operated as a profitable sideline to mining activities. The mine operators claimed these towns, including the roads and railways that led into them, as their private property, forbidden to outsiders. They exercised total authority, imposing a system of arbitrary rules the violation of which was punishable by heavy fines. If a miner refused to pay, he would be dismissed, his family evicted from their company house, and "sent down the road." Even contemporaries were astonished by the extent of the companies' power – an outraged state official declared the town to be "absolute personal government in the midst of a republic."[5]

Once a convenience provided by the management, the company store was often turned into an instrument of abuse. To protect the monopoly of the company store, Tioga County miners were forbidden to buy from outside merchants or peddlers. Employees who did so were fined, discharged, "or else forced to carry back the goods to where they got them."[6] Company stores were a constant grievance to workers: as early as 1848, company store practices triggered a strike in the anthracite coal region of Pennsylvania.[7] In 1854, Maryland became the first state to outlaw the company-owned store.[8] The company store not only produced profits, but also functioned as a crude method of reducing labor turnover. The combination of available credit and infrequent pay days often produced chronic indebtedness, effectively tying the worker to his employer. As late as 1930, federal investigators found workers who had received no cash wages for fifteen years.[9] Some employers dispensed entirely with cash payments, paying wages with "scrip" that, if not spent at the company store, could be redeemed for cash only at an enormous loss of value.

Not all company towns employed such dramatic forms of social control. Industries that needed to attract skilled workers found it to their advantage to create towns where their power was less evident. In upper Michigan, the Calumet and Hecla Copper Company built company houses to rent for nominal sums, but also leased land for residents to build their own houses. Instead of opening a company store, Calumet and Hecla encouraged independent merchants and professionals to settle in Calumet and, in spite of company policies against drunkenness, allowed numerous privately owned saloons to operate there.[10] Johnstown's business district housed not only Cambria Iron's enormous company store, the largest in town, but a host of smaller independent stores, restaurants, and businesses. The company also took an active role in developing the city's residential neighborhoods, building houses to rent to its workers, but also selling building lots to workers and townspeople.[11]

Even in "open" towns, however, the companies still retained a significant control. Calumet and Hecla dominated the county government and discouraged local self-government in its villages. Company executives ran for county offices, almost always successfully. Since balloting was not secret, few of Calumet's miners dared to vote against the company's wishes. The company's myriad ways of asserting its control led one writer to call it "a benevolent octopus."[12] The extent of a company's control became explicit when it was threatened by strikes or labor organizing. The 1870s brought the first wave of labor activity to many company towns and owners fought back with all of their power. In 1872, when miners struck at Calumet and Hecla demanding more pay and an eight-hour day, the outraged management sent for a company of infantry from Detroit and hauled strike leaders into court. Two years later, after another strike, the superintendent vowed to shut the mine permanently rather than be dictated to by workers.[13] In 1874, Cambria Iron Works, faced with a newly organized union, closed the plant rather than recognize the union. After refusing to negotiate, Daniel J. Morell, the general manager, deputized and armed one hundred "special policemen" to keep the peace. The lockout continued until workers agreed to a new contract that prohibited union membership and imposed stringent controls on their behavior.[14]

THE NEW PATERNALISM

The forms that paternalism took changed to meet new conditions. Since the discourse of modernization had eliminated the need for moral supervision, many capitalists avoided unnecessary efforts toward their workers' well-being. Certain types of firm continued to practice paternalism; usually only well-established and successful firms could afford to introduce extensive improvement programs. The paternalist tradition first introduced in New England textile towns still served as an important point of reference. Although located in a remote part of Michigan, Calumet and Hecla's close ties to its elite Boston stockholders – the same group that had first invested in Lowell – linked them to this tradition. Occasionally, competition between firms could express itself through paternalism, resulting in clusters of "benevolent" company towns, as nearby firms competed to outperform their neighbors. In northern Michigan, local firms followed the example set by the dominant firm of Calumet and Hecla, and significantly raised the standard of living in the mining towns.[15]

Since paternalism could not be applied *in loco parentis* to adult workers and their families, more specific practices and more complex justifications appeared. Notions of Christian stewardship still retained considerable power – the individual motivation of many paternalistic employers can be traced to their religious affiliations, particularly among denominations, such as the Quakers, that emphasized social responsibility. But increasingly, the dominant ideology of *laissez-faire* individualism shaped the nature of paternalism. The employer's rhetoric began to emphasize self-interest, justifying good works in terms of economic rationality. In practice, this produced schemes that stressed self-reliance and promoted entrepreneurial virtues of thrift and hard work over direct charity. Many employers saw education as the best way of helping workers to help themselves. Any form of education could potentially reinforce this ethic of improvement: Calumet and Hecla built a large and well-equipped school for miners' children where it introduced the progressive Froebel system of kindergarten teaching;[16] the Ludlow Associates founded a textile school to train workers' sons for managerial jobs;[17] and Cambria Iron Works established a Scientific Institute, a night school where employees could study technical subjects related to iron-making, such as mathematics, metallurgy, and mechanical drawing.[18]

Other popular programs focused on improving the employees' physical well-being. Hospitals, health insurance, and better housing were portrayed as essentially self-serving measures designed to increase productivity. Descriptions of these programs underlined the employer's concern with the workers' productivity rather than their comfort. Healthy workers translated directly into less absenteeism from sickness. In 1868, Calumet and Hecla built the first industrial hospital in the country, at least in part as a compassionate response to the hazards of copper mining. Criticized by other mining corporations for foolishly pampering their employees, the company claimed that "well-doctored" employees directly improved production figures.[19] The Cheney Brothers Company of South Manchester, Connecticut introduced similar humanitarian reforms, including pensions to elderly employees, while insisting that they were "only conducting our business on business principles," not indulging in charity.[20]

Beginning in the 1870s, the growing tension between labor and capital, expressed in an increasing number of strikes and the development of new labor organizations such as the Knights of Labor, provided further impetus to paternalistic projects. Employers hoped that healthy and contented workers would be not only more productive, but, more importantly, less prone to strike. They began to promote the doctrine of mutual advantage, claiming that the improved living and working conditions achieved by paternalism would produce economic advantages for both employer and employee.[21] This ideological unity of interest was intended to smooth over the increasingly visible contradictions between capital and labor. Profit-sharing, a program that awarded workers a yearly bonus payment representing a share of their employer's profits, made the same point in practice. Monetary rewards not only improved workers' performance by involving them in the efficiency and success of the firm, but also encouraged stability, since the size of the bonus depended on length of employment. Profit-sharing was the most popular and well-publicized form of the new corporate paternalism and more than fifty firms introduced plans between 1869 and 1896.[22]

By the 1880s paternalism had adjusted to the problems produced by labor unrest, but increasing immigration presented more difficult obstacles. The first waves of immigration, from English-speaking and Western European countries, brought skilled workers who posed few problems for paternalistic efforts. Often, previous experiences with European paternalist traditions made workers willing participants in American versions. After 1880, a new wave of Southern and Eastern Europeans without skills or English confused and strained the relationship between employer and employee. The language barrier and unfamiliar customs stretched the social gulf between employer and employee so far that paternalism, which depended on a personal bond, became impossible. As a result, whenever large numbers of "unassimilated" immigrants were present, employers usually abandoned paternalistic efforts or limited them to skilled or English-speaking workers. In Johnstown, no welfare "outside of medical and hospital service" was given to unskilled immigrant workers.[23]

THE "IMPROVED" TOWN

In spite of this generally unfavorable climate, old-style paternalism continued to flourish in a small group of New England textile towns: Whitinsville, Hopedale, and Ludlow, Massachusetts; Peace Dale, Rhode Island; and Willimantic and South Manchester, Connecticut. Although these towns became highly publicized advertisements for paternalism, they owed their prominence to a unique set of circumstances. Founded before the Civil War, all these factories had been located in isolated rural areas to obtain waterpower. From 1850 to 1880, they grew rapidly; only Peacedale had fewer than one thousand employees. In each town, the owner and his family lived in the midst of their workers, although in much better quarters. William F. Draper occupied Hopedale's most elegant house, the Hazard family of Peacedale resided on their estates, "Oakwood" and "The Acorns," and fourteen families of Cheneys lived in "handsome residences" in South Manchester. The

A street in Willimantic, Connecticut. By 1900, the town had developed into one of New England's model company towns. The paternalistic owners, the Willimantic Linen Company, built large individual houses in a variety of styles set along landscaped and paved streets, all rarities in most company towns.

unusual circumstance of resident owners isolated with employees who, if not native-born, were English-speaking, in a remote area, increased the potency of the personal bond between the two. The intensity of this relationship cemented paternalism while undermining the development of solidarity among the workers. This kept the towns free of labor disputes until the first decade of the twentieth century.[24]

The benefits these employers offered their workers were impressive – hospitals, libraries, profit-sharing, numerous "improving" organizations – but were not unique. What attracted national attention was their physical appearance. Calumet, Michigan, offered its residents a similar array of paternalistic programs, but was still, according to one observer, "a large sprawling village with only a few streets drained and paved . . . notable only for its long rows of pineboard miners' cottages."[25] In contrast, these New England villages, tidy and well-kept, were anomalies. The manufacturers built clusters of orderly white-washed cottages set in natural landscapes, which consciously led visitors to recall the rural mill towns of early New England. As in Lowell fifty years earlier, visitors enthusiastically described the neat houses, extensive landscaping and impressive public buildings: *Harper's Weekly* declared South Manchester "an epitome of industrial and social development during this century," and British reformer Budgett Meakin later called it "inviting" and "idyllic," redolent of the "peaceful charms of New England."[26] Labor economist Carroll Wright found Willimantic "one of the grandest moments of the day."[27]

Good housing became the most pragmatic element of these towns. In order to attract workers to such out of the way locations, companies had to offer high quality housing at low rents – only 12–15 percent of a worker's monthly wage – and rarely realized more than a 3 percent return on their investment. The quality of the housing won much praise but produced no innovations. The Ludlow Associates experimented with large tenements and expensive, architect-designed cottages before finally settling on inexpensive, single-family frame houses whose low rents and simple exteriors satisfied their occupants.[28] Oakgrove, a group of forty houses built by the Willimantic Linen Company, was particularly admired by visitors. The houses – six-room dwellings on large lots – were not only larger than most company houses, but, even rarer, were finished in a variety of styles, so that each house in a row looked different from the next.[29] The Cheney Company also followed changing architectural fashions, constructing picturesque cottages with varied plans and styles, with design features such as asymmetrical porches and gingerbread detailing.[30]

Although industries in these towns grew rapidly, supporting massive factories using the latest technology, their owners cultivated a pastoral image. In the midst of industrial development, they used extensive landscaping and conservation programs to maintain the appearance of a natural landscape Like the quasi-feudal manor houses of the resident owners, this bucolic setting, evoking the image of an older and more unified community – the rural village – made a conservative point that reinforced the ethos of paternalism. In South Manchester, where the Cheney Brothers employed over two thousand workers, the

One of the picturesque cottages the Willimantic Linen Company built for its workers. Vernacular styling with picturesque details and landscaping created the image of an earlier, more organic community.

mills and housing were scattered over a thousand acres of open terrain, which conserved most of the original trees. To Budgett Meakin, the town resembled a vast, well-kept park rather than a factory town.[31] In Hopedale, the Draper Company prohibited fences, street signs, and mailboxes and provided extensive parkland and garden plots to preserve the town's rural character.[32]

In these towns, elaborate public buildings were paternalism's crowning achievement. Peacedale's "Hazard Memorial Hall," South Manchester's "Cheney Hall," and Whitinsville's "Memorial Building" offered visible testimony to the philanthropy of the resident owners. Designed in the latest style – Cheney Hall was Italianate, Hazard Hall, Richardsonian Romanesque – by architects from Boston or New York, these impressive structures advertised the benefactors' wealth, success, and generosity. Dedicated to the workers' cultural entrancement, they housed "improving" educational and recreational activities. The Memorial Building had an auditorium, music room, library, and meeting rooms, and Hazard Hall contained libraries, reading rooms, a lecture hall, and club rooms for company-sponsored activities such as sewing clubs and manual arts and dancing classes. These "gifts" often brought a measure of control with them. The Hazard family bequeathed their building to the community, but with the proviso that its use was prohibited to any purpose "not in the better interest of the village."[33] Whatever their donors' intentions, monumental community buildings significantly altered the symbolic order of the company town,

Hazard Memorial Hall, donated by the Hazard family to the inhabitants of Peacedale, Rhode Island, with conditions to ensure its "appropriate" use. Such monumental structures – hallmarks of "improved" company towns – housed "uplifting" activities such as libraries, concert halls, classrooms, and clubrooms.

establishing an alternative focus in the living sphere that challenged the domination of the factory and the workday in the workers' lives.[34]

In an era when chaotic physical growth invariably accompanied industrialization, these towns were distinctive, but contributed little to the discourse of paternalism. Without a consistent social or managerial philosophy or a coherent ethos of design, they followed a cumulative logic of piecemeal improvements and effectively demonstrated the existing repertoire of paternalism. In spite of the positive publicity they received, their owners remained curiously ambivalent about their benevolence. The Cheney family denied any good intentions, claiming that "it's our town and we like it to look nice, that's all."[35] In the 1890s, the Willimantic Company abandoned its entire program with the exception of the library because the workers seemed unappreciative.[36] The Ludlow Associates, after selling houses to employees, later bought them back when the employees were unable to maintain the company's high standards of appearance and maintenance.[37]

PULLMAN'S PARADISE

By 1880, when Chicago industrialist George Pullman began planning his new company town, the improved housing conditions and "improving" paternalist institutions in New England towns were widely publicized. For Pullman, proprietor of the Pullman Palace Car Company, the deteriorating labor situation was a more pressing issue. The previous decade had been turbulent, with labor unrest erupting in spontaneous and sporadic revolts all over the country. The 1873 panic brought a wave of strikes and the subsequent depression led to the "Great Upheaval" of 1877, the first mass strike in America. Although these strikes were generally unsuccessful, they revealed the growing power of the workers to disrupt production and led many capitalists to fear popular revolt. To avoid this, Pullman decided to build a model company town outside Chicago, named after himself. Replacing Chicago's "baneful influences" with a rational and aesthetic urban environment, he claimed, would elevate his workers' lives while ensuring a stable and problem-free workforce for himself. Optimistically, he asserted, "the building of Pullman is very likely to be the beginning of a new era for labor."[38]

In planning his new town Pullman borrowed from a number of current ideas. Like the paternalist employers of New England, he provided his workers with extensive welfare programs, including accident insurance, a company doctor, an excellent school system, athletic clubs, a company band, and social and educational clubs. Insisting that improving living standards for his workers should not preclude a 6 percent return on his investment, he followed the principles established by the philanthropic housing movement in New York

City.[39] Physically, the town of Pullman resembled Saltaire, the model company town established by Sir Titus Salt outside Bradford, England. Like Sir Titus, Pullman broke with precedent by locating his town at the far edge of a large industrial city. Rejecting the picturesque image of the rural "model" village, Pullman followed Sir Titus in creating a new urban model, with a geometric plan unified by a single building material and architectural style.[40] Pullman's only innovation was his stress on aesthetics – he constantly asserted his "faith in the educational influences of beauty and beautiful and harmonious surroundings." His insistence on beauty came from his own business experience: the success of Pullman sleeping cars depended on the passengers' willingness to pay extra for beauty and luxury.[41]

A view of Pullman in 1881 shows the town's substantial brick buildings laid out in a grid to the south of the factory. Surrounded by a picturesque park and its own lake, Pullman surpassed earlier company towns by its size and the coherence of its design. Courtesy of the Chicago Historical Society.

Technology, whose difficult imperatives had dominated the planning of earlier company towns, was less evident at Pullman – a fact symbolized by Pullman's purchase of the world's largest engine, the Corliss turbine. Exhibited at the Philadelphia exhibition, it was similar to the engine that would provoke Henry Adams's famous reflections on the Virgin and the Dynamo.[42] At Pullman, displayed behind a plate glass wall, it supplied clean power for the entire plant. George Pullman shifted his interest to the living sphere, where his aesthetic principles, which he called the "commercial value of beauty,"[43] constituted the town's ideology. To ensure that the town's aesthetic reflected his own tastes, he hired the same designers, architect Solon S. Beman and landscape architect Nathan F. Barrett, who had remodeled his own Chicago town house and laid out the gardens on his New Jersey estate.

Closely following Pullman's directives, Beman and Barrett designed a town that was both functional and beautiful. Built of red brick in the American Queen Anne style, the town, in spite of its small size, conveyed considerable urbanity. Monumental structures such

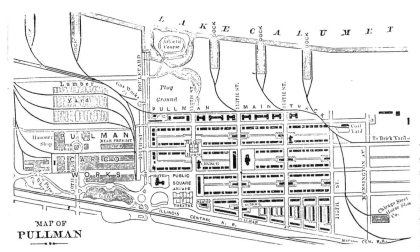

The plan of Pullman shows the industrial area separated from the town by 111th Street. The grid layout is varied by the siting of public buildings – the Arcade Building, the Market House, the school, and Greenstone Church.

as the Florence Hotel (named after Pullman's daughter), the block-long Arcade Building, containing shops, post office, bank, a theater, and library, the Market House Square selling local meat and produce, the large Greenstone Church, intended to serve all denominations, and a three-story school punctuated a grid of lower two- and three-story blocks. Industry, although inescapably present in the massive industrial buildings at the northern end of the town, was separated from the community by a picturesque artificial lake, fed by exhaust water from the Corliss turbine, and a series of small parks. A winding drive intended for Sunday outings looped around the park. The rest of the town had wide, macadamized streets with cobblestone gutters. Except for areas of expensive houses directly across from the plant and blocks of tenement apartments on the edge of town, the residential area consisted of neat rows of brick houses given a variety of façades and roof lines to relieve monotony.[44]

By 1893, Pullman had 12,600 inhabitants. It was the largest company town in the United States and the most famous. As at Paterson and Lowell, observers interpreted Pullman's innovative physical order as a compelling demonstration of a new industrial system. Most observers found Pullman at least "as handsome as any wealthy suburban town" if not, as a London newspaper claimed, "the most perfect city in the world."[45] An 1885 report prepared by the chiefs of the state bureaus of labor statistics, experts on industrial conditions all over the country, passed quickly over Peacedale, South Manchester and Willimantic to heap effusive praise on Pullman: "For comprehensive plan, for the beauty of the executed plan, for the financial and social success thereof, Pullman City stands at the head."[46] Economist

A view of Pullman from Arcade Row looking west toward the Arcade Building. The neat rows of brick houses, substantial public buildings, and well-kept streets made Pullman an object of much admiration. Even the most critical visitors conceded that the town was the equal of any middle-class suburb. Courtesy of the Chicago Historical Society.

Richard Ely, a more critical observer, noted that "No other feature of Pullman can receive praise needing so little qualification as its architecture."[47] Even the workers in their later strike plea acknowledged that "our town is beautiful."[48]

Although impressed by Pullman's architecture, Ely expressed concern about the price that had to be paid for the town's beauty. Obsessed with the town's aesthetic unity and order, George Pullman took extreme measures to preserve it. Residents, while certifiably "of good character," had little control over their rented dwellings; the company inspected, painted, repaired, and maintained all buildings and yards; all horses had to be kept in the town stable. In order to protect the town's visual coherence and maintain its high standards, George Pullman refused to sell any land, even to congregations wishing to build churches. His control exceeded even that of "closed" mining towns: he not only banned liquor, but restricted tobacco smoking and imposed a curfew. As a result, Ely observed, "nobody regards Pullman as a real home, and, in fact, it can scarcely be said that there are more than temporary residents of Pullman." As soon as workers could afford to, they usually moved to one of the communities that grew up around Pullman, where, although they lacked "improvements," they were free from Pullman's rules and could purchase their own homes.[49]

THE PULLMAN STRIKE

Pullman had experienced a number of labor disputes and two or three short strikes during the mid-1880s, but the hot summer of 1894 put additional pressure on the town's already strained labor/capital relations. Across the country, a series of strikes, beginning with a steel strike at Homestead, Pennsylvania, followed by confrontations with silver miners in Coeur d'Alene, Idaho, coal miners in Tennessee, and railroad switchmen in Buffalo, New York, demonstrated the growing tension between increasingly unionized workers and newly concentrated industrial corporations. The panic of 1893 led to widespread layoffs and, for those still employed, wage cuts. "Coxey's Army" of the unemployed marched on Washington, confirming widely held fears that full-scale class war was on the verge of breaking out. 1894 surpassed the previous record holder, 1886, in the number of labor disputes, involving more than 750,000 workers.[50] Compared to these bitter struggles, the Pullman strike was still notable. It began in May, with a peaceful walk-out by Pullman workers in the model town. By July, provoked by George M. Pullman's absolute refusal to negotiate, the strike had escalated into a national railroad boycott.

Troops from the Illinois National Guard lined up in front of the Arcade Building. The town was occupied during the 1894 railroad strike. Courtesy of the Chicago Historical Society.

The American Railway Union joined Pullman workers in a sympathy strike, its 125,000 members refusing to handle Pullman cars or equipment, a move which effectively tied up all rail traffic moving in and out of Chicago. The General Managers Association, an organization representing the twenty-four railroads based in Chicago, backed George Pullman.

The entry of both groups into the dispute raised the stakes further. Without trains, Chicago was virtually sealed off from the rest of the country. Although only sporadic violence had occurred, on 4 July, President Grover Cleveland sent Federal troops from nearby Fort Sheridan into the city, a move that provoked riots. A mob of 10,000 attacked the railroad yards, and fires broke out all over the city. By 19 July, when order was forcibly restored, twelve people were dead and five hundred were under arrest. On 2 August, a Federal injunction resulted in the strike leaders' arrest and finally forced the formal abandonment of the strike. The Pullman strike was the most expensive and far-reaching labor dispute of its time.[51] The railroads claimed property damages of nearly 700,000 dollars as well as a 4,000,000-dollar loss of earnings. Railroad workers lost over 1,600,000 dollars in wages.[52]

Recognizing the strike as a watershed in labor relations, President Cleveland ordered an unprecedented investigation into its causes. In November 1894, after taking the testimony of 107 witnesses, the Strike Commission published an exhaustive report. Although the Commission concluded that the strike's broadest significance lay in the increasing concentration of capital and the resulting organization of labor, the report blamed its specific outbreak on George Pullman's attempt to be, in his own words, "both landlord and employer. That's all there is of it."[53] Pullman regarded his town as a "strictly business proposition." Even after the depression of 1894 reduced orders, forcing him to lay off workers and cut wages, he insisted on this position. Asked by workers to reduce rents on company-owned houses, he refused, claiming that the roles of employer and landlord were completely separate. The Strike Commission later identified this action, which could easily have been avoided, as the immediate cause of the strike. The amenities that Pullman was so proud of did not impress the Commission. Observing that "aesthetic and sanitary features aside, rents at Pullman are from twenty to twenty five percent higher than in Chicago or surrounding areas for the same accommodation," they concluded that "the aesthetic features are admired by visitors, but have little money value to employees, especially when they lack bread."[54]

After Pullman's adamant refusal to negotiate with the strikers, many observers interpreted his past behavior in the town in a new light. Although Pullman's management had followed the usual pattern of paternalism, combining benevolence with control, his actions now appeared excessive. Pullman had carefully monitored activities in the town. To ensure propriety, he had even selected the plays performed in the town's large and elaborate theater. The stern librarian, Pullman's cousin, and a 3-dollar fee kept membership in the library low, just as high prices and an intimidating atmosphere kept workers away from the hotel, the only place in town where alcohol could be purchased. Pullman was expensive; residents had to spend as much as 30 percent of their wages on rent. Jane Addams, who had personally pleaded with Pullman on behalf of the Chicago Civic Federation during the strike, now characterized him as "a modern Lear," whose benevolence had crossed the line into dictatorship.[55] These negative opinions were supported by an Illinois Supreme Court decision that the Pullman Company's ownership of the town violated its charter of incorporation, and the state ordered the company to dispose of all property not required in manufacturing. By 1898, Pullman had begun to dismantle his model town, thus dramatically terminating the first chapter in the history of the American company town.[56]

THE LESSONS OF PULLMAN

What were the lessons of Pullman? To many of George Pullman's fellow capitalists the Pullman strike amply confirmed their suspicions of benevolent undertakings. In 1882, William Vanderbilt, head of the New York Central Railroad and the rival Wagner Sleeping Car Company, had ridiculed Pullman, stating that the town "smacks too much of the old-country landlord system." Charles Elliot Perkins, of the Chicago, Burlington and Quincy Railroad, had also forecast disaster for the project, since "he [Pullman] has got to keep doing more and more or else there is bound to be discontent."[57] Even before the town was completed, Pullman stock was announced on the floor of the New York Stock Exchange with the derisive call, "how much for flower-beds and fountains?"[58] Asked for advice by Harley Procter, who was considering building a similar model town near the Procter & Gamble factory outside Cincinnati, George Pullman had warned against housing workers. This suggests that, as early as 1883, he had serious misgivings about his own enterprise.[59]

To other factory owners, Pullman provided an object lesson in how to avoid paternalism in their own company towns. In 1895, Apollo Steel hired a landscape architect to plan the town of Vandergrift, Pennsylvania, but offered lots for sale and made a point of not regulating the character of the buildings. At Ambridge, Pennsylvania, the American Bridge Company laid out a town and built houses, which they immediately sold to employees.[60] In 1906, the giant US Steel Corporation, planning an enormous plant and town on the Indiana shore of Lake Michigan, just across the state line from Pullman, took explicit advantage of its experience. The president of the Indiana Steel division, Eugene J. Buffington, wrote in *Harper's Weekly*: "fresh in the minds of all of us is the failure of the Pullman Company to maintain its authority." Claiming that American workers preferred independence, he felt that "the most successful attempts at industrial betterment in our country are those furthest removed from the suspicion of domination or control by the employer."[61]

Anxious to prove this at Gary, US Steel did not consult a professional city planner, but developed their own "rule of thumb" plan, a relentlessly uniform grid intended to reduce

Advertisement for land in Gary, Indiana. Developed by US Steel, Gary was an attempt to avoid the mistakes of Pullman. Gridiron planning and densely packed housing was intended to eliminate the amenities for which Pullman was famous.

building costs. The company dispensed with amenities such as parks and recreation facilities. Steel officials donated land for libraries, schools, and churches, but expected the community to build these for themselves.[62] To avoid becoming a landlord, the company established an independent development company, the Gary Land Company, managed by Armanis Knotts, who, in 1894, had been the Pullman strikers' lawyer, and was thus presumably well aware of the dangers of paternalism. The company sold lots to both employees and outsiders and later built a variety of houses for skilled workers and management. The housing of unskilled workers for the most part was left to speculative builders, who produced acres of "barrack-like shacks." By 1910, private developers seeking quick profits, aided by the town's elected politicians, who allowed virtually unregulated growth, had turned the town into a dreary and chaotic industrial city.[63]

Another, ultimately more influential, evaluation emerged, which drew the opposite conclusions from the débâcle at Pullman. A small group of government experts and urban reformers continued to assert that many of Pullman's principles had been correct and that comprehensive planning and architecture should be used to improve living conditions in company towns. They were still convinced that a well-designed environment, properly administered, could serve both capital and labor, providing employers with a stable workforce and workers with a quality of domestic and community life that they could not acquire on their own initiative.[64]

They saw the town's fatal flaw as George Pullman's excessive and outdated paternalism, which was no longer appropriate in a large-scale corporate economy. To them, the scale on which the strike had been conducted, pitting the giant Pullman firm (which employed over 14,000 people in 1893) against the American Railway Union (with over 150,000 members), demonstrated that personal control was no longer possible or desirable. They cited the fact that one of the strikers' major complaints had been Pullman's rule of personal authority without personal knowledge, "Just as no man or woman of our four thousand toilers has ever felt the friendly pressure of George M. Pullman's hand so no man or woman . . . can ever hope to own one inch of George M. Pullman's land."[65] As an alternative, government observers like Carroll Wright, and social reformers such as Jane Addams, Graham Taylor, and Richard Ely, concluded that model industrial towns would only succeed if independent professionals, acting as buffers between capital and labor, took a larger role in their conception and planning.

Thus, the Pullman strike, rather than sounding the death knell for model company towns, as many historians have claimed, initiated a new chapter in their development.[66] Over the next thirty years, a new generation of company towns appeared all over the country, as professional designers assembled a body of specialized knowledge. Industrialists increasingly abandoned older models of paternalism in favor of modernized bureaucratic methods, producing a completely new version of the model company town. Like Paterson and Humphreysville one hundred years earlier, these towns were models intended to represent physical and social ideals. Architects, landscape architects, and city planners tried to translate new concepts of industrial relations and social welfare into new physical forms. Capitalists, anxious to avoid George Pullman's experience, willingly sponsored their efforts. In his 1905 survey, Budgett Meakin found only fifteen planned industrial communities in the United States, all of which had been built before Pullman.[67] In 1939, the Urbanism Committee documented over seventy planned industrial settlements built after 1900, almost all designed by professionals.[68]

3

WELFARE CAPITALISM, HOUSING REFORM, AND THE COMPANY TOWN

By 1900 the social and environmental ideals behind Ely's and Addams's assessment of Pullman had become standard tenets of the Progressive campaign to reform urban and industrial life. In the 1890s, Ely's admiration for Pullman's systematic and scientific order and Addams's rejection of Pullman's oppressive paternalism were controversial; ten years later the reform movement that had formed in opposition to the dislocations of rapid industrialization easily accepted both principles. The Progressives' programs reflected the growing concerns of the urban middle class, a group that had increased both numerically and in influence during the 1880s and 1890s.[1] Their position, as articulated by intellectuals such as Ely and Addams, regarded the hostile stand-off between big capital and big labor, demonstrated by the Pullman strike, as cause for alarm. If, like Addams, they feared the unfettered power of huge corporations, they also rejected the growing strength of militant labor organizations.

Instead, they attempted to occupy a middle ground, urging cooperation between capital and labor in the interests of a greater social good. In 1894, the Progressive economist Graham Taylor, founder of the Chicago Commons settlement, protested "against the extreme attitude of either side" claiming "one should stand for the rights of the public as the third and greatest party in industrial struggles."[2] Similarly, Jane Addams saw the labor movement "not merely as a class struggle," but as "a general social movement concerning all members of society."[3] The Progressives replaced class conflict with a vision of social harmony under the leadership of the "competent." By the end of the 1890s, a decade of dramatic labor upheavals, these middle-class reformers increasingly identified themselves as both the "public" and the "competent." Their goal was an orderly and stable society that fostered individual achievement, in opposition to both Social Darwinist notions of the "survival of the fittest" in a free market and the socialist ideal of the collective unity of the

46

masses. Instead, the middle class championed the enlightened individual as the primary agent of social change.

As the Progressive Movement developed, the identity of this enlightened individual gradually changed from an ordinary citizen motivated by religious and humanitarian concerns into a professional expert trained to reorganize society on a rational basis. In the 1890s the Progressive Movement had been closely linked to a drastic reorientation of organized religion. Faced with evidence of the wretched conditions in which the urban poor lived, many Protestant clergymen had abandoned the prevailing doctrines of "Christian capitalism" for a new "social gospel" that channeled religious impulses into urban social reform. Washington Gladden, a Congregational minister from Columbus, Ohio, was one of the first to preach the social gospel. Gladden condemned both unbridled capitalist competition and the radical communalism of socialism. His book, *Applied Christianity* (1885), argued for the practical as well as the spiritual mission of Christianity. Under his influence, many Protestant churches began to reach out to the urban masses, offering them social services such as nurseries, libraries, and community programs. Middle-class women, attracted by the movement's religious orientation and with leisure time for volunteer activities, served as the backbone of the movement.

Although Protestantism remained an important strand in Progressive ideology, after 1900 the reform movement became increasingly secularized. As reformers developed more systematic approaches, rationality succeeded religion as the movement's defining value. Under its influence, Progressives shifted their emphasis from improving the individual's moral condition to improving the social and environmental conditions that produced the individual. Addressing this larger goal required a scientific reorganization of the social environment, a task that demanded full-time, organized, and skilled efforts. Inevitably, this expanded the realm of middle-class professionalism. For example, as reform-minded women increasingly trained as social workers, teachers, and nurses, they transformed female volunteer efforts into new "helping" professions. Once trained professionals dominated reform movements, they rationalized and institutionalized their efforts, a tendency that culminated in widespread interest and enthusiasm for Frederick Winslow Taylor's "scientific management" movement.[4]

THE FACTORY AND THE SLUM

By the first decade of the twentieth century, professional administrators, social workers, architects, and economists began to translate general ideas of industrial and urban reform into specific programs. Two separate reform movements shaped the development of the "new" company town: the "industrial betterment" movement, focused on improving the industrial environment and the campaign for housing reform, aimed at upgrading living conditions in urban slums.[5] The muckrakers' vivid descriptions of squalid tenements and inhumane workplaces had already identified the factory and the slum as social problems of the first magnitude. Few questioned the threat both posed to a stable social order. According to historian Roy Lubove, urban reformers regarded slums as "potential volcanos, [their] inhabitants the willing recruits of the demagogue and revolutionary."[6] Increasingly, professionalized reform groups responded by reorganizing haphazard individual paternalist and philanthropic "improvements" into systematic social programs. Under their supervision, new methods of "social engineering" – a popular phrase of the period – were invented and applied in the hope of transforming slumdwellers and factory workers into respectable American citizens.

Industrial betterment or welfare work was an updated version of paternalism. Rather than improving individual morals, welfare work instead attempted to create a new sense of identification between employer and employee. To demonstrate this commonality, welfare programs attempted to integrate the workers' lives into the functioning of the corporation. Unlike *laissez-faire* capitalists, firms undertaking welfare work assumed a degree of responsibility for their workers' safety and well-being, hoping to receive increased loyalty in exchange. A 1916 government study defined welfare work as "anything for the comfort and improvement, intellectual and social, of the employees, over and above wages paid, which is not a necessity of the industry nor required by law."[7]

Although a few pioneering firms, such as Filene's Department Store in Boston and the National Cash Register Company in Dayton, Ohio, started extensive welfare programs in the 1890s, the organized industrial welfare movement began in 1898, when Josiah Strong, a social gospel minister, organized the League for Social Service and appointed William H. Tolman, another ex-minister, as Director of Industrial Betterment.[8] Tolman spread the new gospel of systematic welfare work. He toured the country extolling its benefits to employers and produced a steady stream of publications, including a weekly newsletter sent to firms interested in welfare work. In 1904, the National Civic Federation (NCF), under the direction of Ralph Easley, a school teacher and journalist turned reformer, created its own Employers Welfare Department. The NCF, an organization composed of "responsible" corporations, conservative unions, and academic and political theorists, who represented "the public," was dedicated to restoring social stability. Denying class interests, the organization pursued conciliation between capitalist and workers through a variety of programs. The NCF set up its Welfare Department with the specific purpose of bringing anti-union companies into the Federation.[9] Unlike other sections of the NCF, which welcomed union representatives, only employers were allowed to join. Easley and his assistant, Gertrude

Beeks, a social worker and close friend of Jane Addams, supplied expert information about welfarism to interested employers.[10]

Both organizations sought to institutionalize and professionalize welfare work. A new professional appeared – the specialist welfare secretary – defined by Tolman as

> one who can devote his whole time to become acquainted with the employees and promoting their general welfare; one who looks after sanitary conditions, seeks to increase the general intelligence, fosters a healthful social life and strives to improve the general morale."[11]

The NCF offered consultation to its members and operated an employment service for welfare secretaries. By 1906 it had placed more than twenty welfare secretaries in firms. In spite of the masculine pronoun Tolman used, women, recruited from the helping professions, dominated the new field. Initially, there was no specific training, "no one science or art which can be mastered in preparation for all kinds of welfare work."[12] But in 1906, Graham Taylor opened a class in industrial welfare work at the Chicago Commons settlement house and, by 1916, over one hundred engineering schools were offering courses in "industrial service work."[13]

One of the welfare secretary's main tasks was to act as a personal link between the company and the individual employee. Large corporations, afraid of losing touch with their employees, used welfare workers to restore the personal relationships that had existed in smaller firms. Isabelle Nye, an early New York welfare worker, observed, "our real vocation is rather that of a diplomat in endeavoring to bring the employer and employee to a point of view which will lead to mutual trust and satisfaction." To do this, welfare workers acted as troubleshooters, disciplinarians, and role models. When Gertrude Beeks began her career as MacCormick Harvesting's welfare secretary, her only assignment was to "adjust" the workplace problems of the firm's four hundred female employees. Other secretaries followed the workers home and became involved in their private lives. Mary Gilson of Joseph and Feiss visited working girls at home to discuss appropriate clothing, advising them against the "demoralizing effects" of elaborate clothes, jewelry, and make-up. Another welfare worker, Elizabeth Wheeler, even investigated her employees' fiancés to confirm their good character and reputation. Welfare workers extended their attentions to the workers' families, instructing mothers on how to bring up their children, prepare foods, and furnish their homes. Above all, the welfare worker was intended to embody middle-class virtue. As one manager put it, "she influences the employees to be honest, to keep well and strong and to live right."[14]

The League for Social Service and the NCF Employers Welfare Department both functioned as clearing houses, documenting the increasing number of welfare programs. Handbooks and guides to industrial welfare work proliferated, including works by advocates

NATIONAL CASH REGISTER COMPANY
DAYTON, OHIO, U. S. A.
INCIDENTS OF OLD AND NEW FACTORY LIFE.

The Old Way—Luncheon in the Work Room.

The New Way—Young Women's Dining-Room.

Young Women of the Factory Among the Canna-Beds on the Lawn.

The National Cash Register Company developed one of the earliest and most extensive welfare programs. With a large female workforce, the firm took great pains to publicize its concern for its workers.

such as Tolman and Beeks, Nicholas Gilman, Edwin Shuey and Budgett Meakin.[15] The Federal Government also studied betterment programs – the Bureau of Labor Statistics published full-scale surveys of employers' welfare work in 1913 and 1919, while other government studies covered welfare work in specific industries.[16] These studies reveal a clear pattern to welfare activities. Although by 1914 the NCF listed over 2,500 firms that practiced some form of welfare work, three types of firm dominated welfare activities: firms that employed large numbers of women – textile mills, department stores, and food processing plants; firms located in geographically isolated company towns, who found it necessary to attract workers; and firms that relied on skilled workers, whom employers considered difficult to find, hard to keep, and susceptible to unionism. Within firms, employers used welfare programs selectively, often limiting them to skilled workers or a designated category of favored employees.[17]

Welfare programs, although widespread, addressed a limited number of situations. The earliest campaigns focused on improving working conditions. Manufacturers redesigned their factories for greater cleanliness and hygiene and opened them up to sunlight and fresh air. Safety training and improved equipment reduced the dangers of industrial accidents, while company-owned hospitals and infirmaries provided health care and first aid. Lunchrooms, bathhouses, lockers, changing rooms, and restrooms for women made factory life more tolerable and encouraged workers to regard the workplace as a home away from home. To emphasize this, companies "beautified" their factories, planting shrubs and flowers in their grounds. A New Jersey manufacturer even hung lace curtains at the factory windows and placed potted plants throughout the factory.[18]

Other programs aimed at improving employee morale. Company newspapers and magazines encouraged "team spirit" within the "corporate family" by publicizing welfare programs, reporting factory news and gossip, and promoting company social events and outings such as parades and picnics. Suggestion boxes encouraged worker participation and improved communication between workers and management. Companies also encouraged employees' financial self-improvement: savings plans, profit-sharing, group insurance, and mutual benefit associations rewarded thrift and promised financial security. Many employers provided extensive athletic and recreational programs and facilities. Offered as substitutes for the pleasures of the saloon, employers hoped that sports would improve health and morale, and thereby increase efficiency. Company teams also encouraged loyalty. As one observer noted, "nothing strengthens the bonds of fellowship more than mutual devotion to a game." Most companies justified welfare programs strictly in terms of economic rationality. Consciously avoiding the paternalistic rhetoric of benevolence, Joseph Patterson, head of National Cash Register, summed up the rationale behind his extensive welfare program with the succinct slogan: "It pays."[19]

In comparison to other types of welfare programs, the "model towns" and industrial housing projects described by these surveys were far less impressive. Budgett Meakin's survey, *Model Factories* (1905), G.W. Hanger's Bureau of Labor report, "Housing of the Working People by Employers," and Tolman's 1910 study, "Workmen's Cities," cited nearly identical lists of American company towns. According to these authors, the American towns ranked far below English and Western European examples, in both number and quality. All three experts evaluated the older group of New England textile towns, such as Hopedale and its neighbors, as the outstanding American examples of workers' housing. However, these old-fashioned towns, built before the advent of systematic welfare work, were precursors, rather than demonstrations of the industrial betterment movement.[20]

A new group of steel mill towns, built after the Homestead strike of 1892, when steel companies first began to provide houses for their workers, drew mixed reactions. Steel towns varied greatly: Meakin evaluated Pratt City, Alabama, as "below our ideals" and "not beautiful;" he considered Sparrow's Point, Maryland, and Roebling, New Jersey, if "not beautiful" at least neat and substantial. Only Vandergrift, Pennsylvania, designed by the noted landscape architect Frederick Law Olmsted, met his standards. He described the town as "clean, healthy, and beautiful."[21] The steel companies' major innovation was to sell houses to their workers. In Vandergrift, Ambridge, and Wilmerding, Pennsylvania, Gary, Indiana, and Granite City, Illinois, steel workers could buy houses at below-market prices or with special mortgage plans.[22] Such programs were part of a campaign to retain skilled workers. The welfare director of a steel firm summarized the companies' logic: "get workers to invest their savings in their homes and own them. Then they won't leave and they won't strike. It ties them down so they have a stake in our prosperity."[23] This program excluded other groups of workers. Although Apollo Steel advertised Vandergrift as the "workingman's paradise," they reserved the town for skilled workers, clerks, and professional employees. This left unskilled, mostly immigrant workers to fend for themselves in Rising Sun, a ramshackle settlement on the other side of the railroad tracks from Vandergrift.[24]

The reports mentioned housing in isolated mining and textile towns only as a "distinct improvement of conditions that had previously been far worse." In spite of their very different regional settings, the minimal houses built by Colorado Fuel and Iron for their mining camps closely resembled those of cotton mill workers in Graniteville or Pelzer, South Carolina – identical rows of wooden frame cabins lining unpaved roads. These surveys demonstrated that corporations and welfare workers were giving housing and town

Mining houses in Segundo, Colorado. An example of the Colorado Fuel and Iron Company's attempts to improve living standards in western mining towns. Better quality housing, however, was rarely accompanied by town planning or community services.

Workers' housing built by the Bethlehem Steel Company at Sparrow's Point, Maryland. The uniform rows of identical houses maintained the traditional company town image. The size and upkeep of these large houses impressed observers as an improvement on earlier conditions in steel towns, but, with little concern for aesthetics or amenities, they did not measure up to the best industrial towns of the era.

planning more attention, but taken as a whole, the towns they singled out as "models" did not offer any new ideas. A few towns, such as Vandergrift and Echota, New York, had been designed by professionals, but few writers identified this as a significant fact: Meakin noted in passing that "a landscape gardener was employed to plan Vandergrift's wide streets," but apparently no one noticed that Stanford White, one of the country's best known architects, had designed Echota's "tasteful" houses. Moreover, all the experts agreed that none of the towns equalled Pullman's comprehensive design or aesthetic clarity.[25]

THE NEW FACTORY

Professional welfare work was only one of many attempts to create a more systematic industrial order. During the last two decades of the nineteenth century, manufacturers, recognizing the growing size and complexity of the factory, began to replace time-honored methods of shop organization with newly coordinated systems to manage production. Before this, most factories had operated in an improvised fashion, relying heavily on inherited practices that had often been introduced and directed by skilled workers and foremen. As trained engineers took over management as well as technical tasks, they took control of the entire factory. With mechanical engineers directing them, factories introduced more systematic management and production techniques, codifying methods of cost-accounting, production and inventory control, and departmental coordination into standardized procedures. Professional organizations such as the American Society of Mechanical Engineers and technical journals such as *Engineering* and *System* devoted increasing attention to the managerial aspects of industrial production.[26]

After 1901, systematic management's drive for greater efficiency was superseded by a far more comprehensive system of technical organization – scientific management. Introduced by a mechanical engineer, Frederick Winslow Taylor, scientific management synthesized existing systematic management methods into a total rationalization of factory work. Taylor's system was based on a "scientific" analysis of the production process. This had two major aspects. First, engineers broke down each task into components, then reorganized these components in the most efficient order. This established a norm – the shortest possible time for each operation – the time each task *should* take. Wages were then set according to the norms. "Piece rate" wages were based on how close a worker came to the norm. This system allowed management to operate the factory on a supposedly "objective" basis, but entailed a considerable loss of the worker's control over his job. Taylor argued that his plan would solve labor problems by greatly increasing output, but labor unions saw the individual nature of the "differential" piece work wage as an attack on collective bargaining. As a result, labor unions became Taylorism's main opponents.[27]

Although Taylor himself regarded welfare work as "a joke" and welfare advocates condemned Taylorism's lack of concern for "the human element,"[28] in practice no real barriers separated scientific management from industrial welfare work. Scientific management focused exclusively on production tasks while betterment work was concerned with working and living environments. Although the two competing doctrines occasionally clashed in specific firms, increasingly manufacturers found it to their advantage to employ both systems and, by 1915, the two rival factory reform systems coexisted in many companies.[29] Both brought new system and order to industrial management, and together, they dramatically extended the managers' control over the workers and their environment. Yet those involved in these reforms saw them from very different perspectives.

The employers were clearest about their goals. Although a few still subscribed to philanthropic or religious motives, their concerns were primarily pragmatic. Most agreed with Augustus P. Loring's assessment: "as we approach the purely philanthropic we get further away from usefulness."[30] They preferred to emphasize economic considerations. According to the National Industrial Conference Board, "the individual employee represents a definite investment, and sound business principles require that the investment be capably handled in order that it may yield a fair return." Thus, welfare work was "not a frill or a vehicle for the fulfillment of philanthropic impulses, but a natural and businesslike method of dealing with the work force to secure results."[31] What were these results? The employer's main goal was to gain control over what they viewed as the most difficult and unstable variable in rationalizing the industrial process: the worker.

In a period when turnover rates were high and retaining workers difficult, employers, asked why they provided housing, answered "to control the labor supply," "to insure a stable workforce," and "to decrease the floating element."[32] They hoped that benefits such as housing, pension plans, and profit-sharing would give workers a specific stake in their job. Once the worker was on the job, welfare work was intended to reduce his anxiety about accidents and injuries and thereby improve his efficiency. One manager urged, "we must find ways and means to help our workers get their worries out of their minds so they can get on the job rarin' to go."[33] According to its advocates, the entire welfare effort would engender the workers' contentment and loyalty.

If welfare programs did not achieve these objectives, firms could always use them for advertising. As at Lowell and Pullman, welfarism and public relations were closely linked. One large employer admitted that his stock ownership plan was a failure, but rather than change the program, he planned to advertise it widely as a way of cultivating public approval.[34] Gaining public support was an important aspect in maintaining the employers' power and independence, which had come under increasing attack by restrictive legislation and the growing strength of the unions. To enhance their public image, companies distributed lavishly illustrated books or special issues of plant magazines containing glowing accounts of their welfare work, sponsored elaborate displays at world fairs, and cultivated sympathetic journalists. They made special efforts to impress influential groups: National Cash Register, for example, sponsored all-expenses-paid tours to its Dayton plant for interested faculty members from the University of Chicago.[35]

Public approval was particularly important in combating what, for employers, was the workers' most troubling characteristic: their tendency to organize and strike. The economist Sumner Schlicter claimed that industrial welfare programs "are one of the most ambitious social experiments of the age, because they aim, among other things, to counteract the effect of modern technique upon the mind of the worker, to prevent him from becoming class conscious and from organizing trade unions." This concern, far more than considerations of humanity, efficiency, or publicity, motivated welfare capitalism.[36] As a result, employers adjusted welfare programs to fit the current labor situation. Programs were tailored for specific groups of workers and specific industrial problems: home ownership and financial incentive programs aimed at skilled workers came first; later, "Americanization" efforts tried to assimilate unskilled immigrants into industrial life; and in the 1920s employee representation plans and company unions offered alternatives to the labor movement. Welfare programs also reflected the prevailing labor climate, proliferating during times of labor militancy and lagging during periods of calm.

The workers' reactions to welfare work was less easy to document. Initially, conservative labor leaders like AFL President Samuel Gompers, although excluded from the NCF welfare committee, supported the organization's advocacy of welfarism. Later, after much criticism from the left wing of the union movement, Gompers changed his stance, and, testifying before Congress, castigated "hell-fare" programs. Most union leaders were antagonistic to industrial welfare, attacking its anti-union motivations, which were clearly enunciated by plain-speaking capitalists, such as the Plymouth Cordage executive who asserted that "the greatest argument for welfare work is that the professional labor leader is opposed to it. He hates it."[37] They also objected to specific practices, such as home ownership programs intended to reduce workers' mobility and independence. After Apollo Steel developed the town of Vandergrift, a union official complained, "the system of this company in the lot and building line has many really good men tied up."[38]

The workers themselves criticized welfare programs as poor substitutes for higher wages. They particularly resented the welfare secretary's intrusion into their private lives. Many responded to welfare work with open hostility. When Jean Hoskins, a newly hired welfare secretary, arrived at a Maine textile factory with a well-publicized mission of "social uplift," the workers gave her "hard suspicious glances" and nicknamed her "Sanitary Jane." Later, angry workers refused to submit to physical examinations or take off their shoes and stockings, claiming that they were just as clean as she was. After a National Tube Company playground worker told a child to ask her mother to wash her dirty hands, the child returned, answering, "She said 'you go to hell'." A factory questionnaire circulated in the mid-1920s showed that of five incentives – job security, wages, advancement by ability, and opportunity for promotion – welfare work scored lowest. On a scale from 1 to 5, with 5 indicating "extremely favorable," workers rated welfare at 2.[39]

Contrary to the hopes of employers and reformers, welfare programs were rarely the decisive factor in establishing a worker's relationship with the firm. As historian Gerald Zahavi has pointed out, the real test of the employer's concern occurred on the shop floor.[40] Even in companies offering extensive welfare programs, workers did not hesitate to strike over wages or working conditions, as demonstrated by strikes in the coalfields of Colorado, West Virginia, and Pennsylvania, the Michigan copper mines, and the steel industry in 1919. Their extensive welfare programs did not spare firms such as National Cash Register and International Harvester from major strikes during the first decade of the twentieth century.[41] Will Herford's "Welfare Song," written in 1913, sums up labor's view of welfarism:

> Sing a song of "Welfare,"
> Forty 'leven kinds,
> Elevate your morals
> Cultivate your minds

Kindergartens, nurses,
Bathtubs, books and flowers,
Anything but better pay,
Or shorter working hours.[42]

Its middle-class advocates saw welfare work very differently. Although they undertook industrial reforms in the spirit of rationality and efficiency, their goal was a larger one: the eradication of class differences and the creation of social unity. The literature of welfare work continually extolled the theme of social harmony. Reformers from Ida Tarbell to Lincoln Steffens invoked what Tarbell called the "Golden Rule of Business – the interests of the employer and the employee were identical." Steffen's "Theory of Scientific Christianity" argued that society could be improved simply by asking "the big bad men of business" – those who held the real power in society – to be magnanimous and to show them that magnanimity paid.[43] Even Frederick Winslow Taylor claimed that "scientific rate fixing made each worker's interest the same as that of his employer."[44]

Those who recognized the difficulties inherent in welfarism still advocated a middle ground. In 1904, Gertrude Beeks cautioned employers about the dangers of both "direct" paternalism and "democracy": "The spirit of welfare work must not be that of condescension, nor rob the worker of self-respect . . . . Going to the other extreme, even the so-called democratic idea is also to be avoided."[45] A more critical observer, Richard Ely, called for a similar synthesis between "industrial benevolence and industrial democracy," rejecting "extreme forms of industrial paternalism and extreme forms of democracy," specifically Marxist socialism. Ely, however, expanded the democratic side of the equation, preferring democracy even with its necessarily "painful adjustments" to the "government of a private corporation." Ely pointed out, with anti-paternalistic logic, that "children can never learn to walk if they have no opportunity to stumble." Ely sought industrial reform through state intervention rather than, as Beeks urged, by "reforming" private interests through exhortation and example.[46] However, as long as welfare work remained under the direct control of corporate management, its most conservative interpretation inevitably dominated.

THE SLUM AND THE SUBURB

Although the housing reform movement shared many of welfare capitalism's concerns, it followed its own course. Initially, the movement focused on attacking a single problem: housing conditions in urban slums. The movement's initial impetus came from a typically Progressive source – middle-class outrage at the desperate living conditions in crowded tenement districts, dramatically exposed by sensational accounts such as Jacob Riis's *How the*

Other Half Lives. Middle- and upper-class reformers organized philanthropic pressure groups to eliminate slum housing – the most visible manifestation of the social costs of industrialization and urbanization.

Like welfare work, housing reform began with a few exemplary amateur exponents, then became increasingly professionalized. Early experiments, like Alfred White's Home and Tower Buildings, built during the 1870s, were directly modeled on English philanthropic housing. White's buildings were "well-ventilated, convenient and agreeable" and earned him a steady 7½ percent profit. In spite of White's proselytizing articles and pamphlets and the support of important Progressives like Theodore Roosevelt, he found few followers. White, however, established the basic principle of subsequent reforms. He claimed that reformers could do good and still make a modest profit without challenging the workings of the free market. As Jacob Riis put it, "it was just a question whether a man would take seven percent and save his soul or twenty five and lose it."[47]

In the 1890s, the first housing professionals appeared, transforming amateur philanthropy into an organized movement. In 1895, E.R.L. Gould, a political scientist specializing in municipal affairs, produced the first systematic survey of housing reforms in Europe and the United States, the massive study, *The Housing of the Working People*, sponsored by the Department of Labor. Gould analyzed urban housing and "small model houses" in company towns in great detail, discussing Pullman, South Manchester, and Willimantic along

Bandit's Roost, 39½ Mulberry Street, a New York alley between two tenements, from Jacob Riis's *How the Other Half Lives*. Such graphic depictions of slum conditions led middle-class reformers to attack the housing problem.

with well-known European examples, such as the Meunier factory settlement at Noisel-sur-Marne and the Krupp colonies in Essen. Gould's extensive research led him to the same conclusion that White and Riis had reached earlier: "that proper housing of the great masses of working people can be furnished on a satisfactory commercial basis."[48]

In order to prove this in practice, the next year Gould became president of the newly formed City and Suburban Homes Company. The Committee on Improved Housing – whose secretary was welfare advocate William Tolman – sponsored C and S Homes as a philanthropic endeavor, "a business investment tempered by justice," with dividends limited to 5 percent. Over the next decade, C and S Homes built model tenements across New York City. The tenements were supervised by "friendly rent collectors," a method pioneered by London housing reformer Octavia Hill. A corps of women agents, similar to welfare secretaries, visited each tenant weekly to collect the rent, and, if necessary, offer advice about work and personal problems. Their constant surveillance of the apartments and insistence on high standards of upkeep and deportment kept C and S Homes in top condition. In spite of such evident success, Gould considered urban apartments to be only a temporary solution. His ultimate goal – the "acme of achievement" – was the single family suburban house. This led C and S Homes to invest most of its capital in Homewood, a tract of small cottages in suburban Brooklyn. This allowed better-paid workers to "leave the promiscuous and common life of the ordinary tenement" for the "dignified and well-ordered life of the detached home."[49] Gould hoped that single family dwellings in suburban surroundings would transmit the values of middle-class America to workers and immigrants.

Lawrence Veiller further expanded the professional role Gould pioneered, transforming housing reform into a national movement. Knowledgeable about technical problems and an outstanding administrator, Veiller efficiently reorganized housing reform. He created new standards with which to evaluate hygiene, space, and economic viability and then, collaborating with Progressive politicians like Theodore Roosevelt, made sure they were enforced through restrictive laws, such as the New York Tenement House Law of 1901. Veiller took on a variety of public and private roles, first leading the New York Tenement Housing Commission of 1900, then becoming the director of the Charity Organization Society's Department for the Improvement of Social Conditions and, after 1910, heading the National Housing Association. Veiller understood the importance of public relations. In order to focus public concern on the "tenement evil," he organized a tenement exhibition that attracted more than ten thousand visitors. Maps, charts, diagrams, and more than a thousand photographs graphically conveyed the severity of New York's housing problems and demonstrated Veiller's solutions.[50]

In spite of his efforts to improve slum conditions, Veiller felt that urban decentralization was the only long-term solution to the housing problem. Like Gould, he called for a suburban solution, "an organized effort to distribute the population and set the tendency back to rural or semi-rural communities." He believed that this would help re-establish the moral ethos of the small town, which had been destroyed by the modern industrial city. Similarly, although Veiller had fought for restrictive legislation to curb housing abuses, he felt that government interference in the housing market should go no further. In spite of his admiration for the advances made in Europe, where the state increasingly financed and built working-class housing, he rejected similar initiatives in the United States. Instead, he believed that housing improvement should depend on private investment. As a result, he became an early advocate of company-sponsored industrial communities, urging "far-sighted employers of labor [to] develop their community in such a way that it will not only furnish a delightful dwelling place for their workers but will be a real asset to the community."[51]

Thus, by 1910, welfare capitalism and housing reform were both organized movements actively promoting conservative interpretations of progressive ideals. Their rejection of state intervention and advocacy of private efforts to solve social problems forced them to look to corporate benefactors for support. Searching for scientific solutions to the urgent problems of the slum and the factory, both movements drew the same conclusion: away from the bad influences of the city, a socially engineered environment could offer a *tabula rasa* on which capital and labor could renegotiate their differences. The "new" company town, a decentralized settlement of single family houses, would serve as an ideal venue for demonstrating these shared ideas. If these concepts resembled George Pullman's plans of twenty years earlier, there was one critical difference: the "new" company town would develop under the direction of "disinterested" professional experts.

4

DESIGNERS AND THE "NEW" COMPANY TOWN

After 1900, design professionals – architects, landscape architects, and urban planners – began to join reformers in attacking urban and industrial problems. In large cities such as New York, Boston, and Chicago, their professional aspirations converged increasingly with Progressive reform agendas. Design professionals and urban reformers, both demanding a stronger voice in setting the nation's social and political priorities, were natural allies. In New York, prominent architects like Ernest Flagg, I.N. Phelps-Stokes, and Grosvenor Atterbury were active housing reformers, designing new prototypes for model tenements financed by philanthropic supporters.[1] In Chicago, the settlement movement became a focus for the exchange of ideas between designers and reformers. Allan Pond, president of the Chicago American Institute of Architects, served as a design consultant to Jane Addams's Hull House, while Jane Addams, in turn, gave lectures at the Chicago Architectural Club. Herbert Croly, the editor of the *Architectural Record*, became a prominent spokesman for Progressive causes, using the pages of his journal to apprise architects of their stake in current social and political issues.[2] Encouraged by growing public awareness of urban problems, the design professions became advocates of decentralization and supporters of the "new" company town.

THE DESIGN PROFESSIONS

For design professionals, redesigning the company town offered an ideal opportunity to expand their professional domain. Like other occupations, the design professions were emerging from a social struggle in which the educated middle class gradually established a "monopoly of competence," over a range of specialized services. Newly organized professionals now claimed exclusive rights to what had previously been an unregulated marketplace. Control over this professional territory – necessary to separate professional designers from other groups providing similar services – depended on demonstrating both technical and social qualifications. First, they had to meet contemporary standards of rationality, efficiency, and technical expertise. Second, they had to establish an ethical claim of social disinterest, appearing to operate independently of any particular class or economic allegiance. More visible institutional indicators of professional status, such as licensing or formal education requirements, depended on satisfying these conditions.[3]

Although architecture was an ancient activity, its qualifications as a modern profession were limited. Architects began to organize themselves just before the Civil War, founding a professional organization, the American Institute of Architects (AIA) in 1857, followed by academic degree programs at Massachusetts Institute of Technology (1868) and Cornell University (1871). The final validation of professional exclusivity, a legal definition provided by the state, however, was still in question at the turn of the century. Illinois had instituted the first licensing requirement in 1897, but this gave architects control only over large structures, such as churches, apartment houses, and public buildings.[4] Thus, in spite of its institutional gains, the profession was still having difficulties in maintaining its professional legitimacy. This was complicated by the profession's inherited identity. Architecture's long history as an artistic endeavor limited its more recent claims of technical rationality, already challenged on one side by the technical superiority of engineering, and on the other by the empirical efficiency of the building industry.

The absence of a broad social base supporting architectural activities constituted another inherited weakness. The architect's traditional dependence on elite patronage undermined the profession's new claims of social disinterest. The lavish commissions prominent architects had executed for robber barons like Vanderbilt and Frick were visible reminders of the many debts architecture owed to wealth and power. The profession's aesthetic capabilities constituted its only undisputed professional asset. At the turn of the century architectural styles, following the conventions established by the Ecole des Beaux Arts in Paris, functioned effectively as a communicative medium. Through their command of diverse stylistic vocabularies, architects could invest built forms with a broad range of values and meanings, using historical styles as a repertoire of clearly defined and widely accepted meanings. The popular success of the elaborately neoclassical White City at the World's Colombian Exhibition of 1893 illustrated the power of Beaux Arts aesthetics, demonstrating that the cultural messages expressed in architecture could be read, understood, and appreciated by large numbers of people.

Beginning in the 1890s, architects made attempts to recast their professional identities. The Exhibition's architects claimed that the White City had transcended its commercial sponsorship by invoking a larger public ideal. Other Chicago architects contested the profession's elitist legacy with democratic rhetoric. In 1891, Dankmar Adler claimed, "our architecture will never be the expression of the wants and desires of any small class but of the American people as a whole."[5] Herbert Croly confronted the issues facing American architects more directly. During the thirteen years he wrote for the *Architectural Record*, he proposed a radical professional reorientation. Believing that professional experts were the natural leaders of society, Croly urged the architectural profession to assume a major role in reforming the social and aesthetic chaos of the American built environment. In order to "be formative in a large way," he believed that architects had to strengthen their professional authority by creating "exclusive technical standards." Only a profession defined by "expert competency" and "uncompromising technical excellence," rather than by the support of wealthy patrons, he argued, could achieve the autonomy and independence necessary to make a significant social impact.

Croly outlined a paradoxical strategy to achieve these goals. Convinced that insignificant projects with "low budgets and uneducated clients" were a waste of time, he urged architects, now confident in their professional expertise, to invert their existing relationships with wealthy clients. Rather than simply serving their patrons, architects should use important commissions with large budgets for their own ends, as opportunities to develop new ideas and forms that eventually could be adapted to projects with broader social goals. Croly anticipated that elite professionals, free to experiment, would agree on a set of coherent formal values that could serve as the basis for standardized architectural solutions. This "nationalized" norm of good design could then be applied to large-scale projects across the country, thereby eliminating the architectural confusion that provincial individualism had brought about during the last decades of the nineteenth century.[6] In 1907, at the end of his tenure at *Architectural Record*, Croly published *The Promise of American Life*, expanding the principles he proposed to architects into an argument for the total reform of American life. Leading political figures such as Theodore Roosevelt and Woodrow Wilson began to adopt his ideas of expert leadership and centralized organization, and Croly became an important figure on the national political scene.[7]

The new industrial communities being proposed by welfare and housing reformers meshed neatly with Croly's version of top-down architectural reform. The company town offered architects a laboratory situation that they could use, as Croly urged, to satisfy both professional goals and social responsibilities. Emphasizing the need for scientific standards of housing, site planning, and social organization, reformers described these towns in terms that matched the profession's new self-definition – "systematic," "rational," and "socially efficient." The technical demands of designing an entire town encouraged architects to go beyond traditional definitions of architectural services. Croly's call for standardization and national norms easily lent themselves to the company town's need for large numbers of housing units and a unifying aesthetic. By adopting the mediating role proposed by middle-class reformers, architects could claim at least rhetorical independence from their wealthy clients. Although industrialists continued to finance company towns, architects increasingly saw themselves as serving a larger vision of social harmony.

Architects were not the only professionals attracted to this fertile professional territory. Landscape architecture, although a much younger profession, had been engaged with public design since before the Civil War. Although designing gardens for the estates of the rich still supported many landscape designers, the public park was an equally significant professional concern.[8] In comparison to architecture, landscape design had even fewer professional advantages. The American profession had been created by two dominant figures, Andrew Jackson Downing and Frederick Law Olmsted, who were both essentially self-taught. Well into the twentieth century many landscape designers followed their example, acquiring skills through apprenticeships or work in landscape nurseries. This lack of institutionalized training limited the profession's claims to technical expertise. In addition, like architecture, many of its technical tasks were also claimed by civil engineers. Despite these difficulties, landscape design, like other occupations, gradually moved toward greater professionalization. In 1899, a small group of Boston and New York landscape architects, mostly alumni of Olmsted's office, organized the American Society of Landscape Architecture and, one year later, sponsored the first professional curriculum at Harvard University.

The new profession continued the social orientation of its founders. Early advocates of urban parks, Downing and Olmsted transformed the English picturesque landscape style from an aesthetic into a force for moral regeneration. Both discussed the urban park in therapeutic terms, as a work of art that served a civilizing mission by explicitly imposing the cultivated values of an educated elite on the urban masses. For Downing, parks worked "to raise up the working man to the same level of enjoyment with the man of leisure and accomplishment," while Olmsted claimed that Central Park's naturalistic beauty "exercised a distinctly harmonizing and refining influence upon the most unfortunate and lawless classes of the city – an influence favorable to courtesy, self-control and temperance."[9] This point of view privileged a single experience – the contemplation of the landscape – over the demands of working-class and immigrant groups for more active and varied recreation, such as competitive sports and popular entertainments, which Olmsted banished from Central Park. In order to enforce these values, Olmsted recommended drilling the park keepers in crowd control to protect the park against "the shock of an untrained public."[10] Central Park's apparently natural landscape was, in fact, a highly artificial and romanticized design, calculated to convey an exaggerated contrast between its rural beauty and what Olmsted perceived as the evils of the city. Downing claimed that naturalistic landscaping acted as an effective antidote to what he called "America's spirit of unrest," bringing rural virtues of order, security, and repose into the city. Olmsted emphasized the pastoral landscape's power to counteract the oppression of city life. By soothing the senses, the park would alleviate discontent among the urban masses, a safety-valve necessary to moderate social and class conflict.

Olmsted considered the suburb, characterized by "picturesque, sylvan tranquility," to be the ultimate refuge from the city's chaotic activities and crowds. Convinced that domestic life should be physically separate from the industrial and commercial world, Olmsted noted that "the more intelligent and fortunate classes" are increasingly seeking the "special charms of rural life."[11] In 1869, Olmsted created a new visual identity for suburban settlements by transposing Central Park's picturesque style into a residential environment in his design for Riverside, Illinois, nine miles west of Chicago's central business district. Enhancing the natural topography by planting forty thousand trees and an equal number of shrubs, Olmsted transformed a featureless prairie into a romantic sequence of forest groves punctuated by clearings for large houses set back a designated distance from the road. A complex network of winding streets and a riverside park that meandered through the town gave Riverside what Olmsted called a "wholly untownlike" character.[12] The first of fourteen suburbs that Olmsted and his partner Vaux laid out, Riverside's curving, tree-shaded streets, open lawns, and informal public spaces defined a new ideal for the American suburb. Since this image depended on landscape elements more than on the architecture of individual houses, landscape architects gradually assumed the professional responsibility for designing suburbs. Over time, changes in urban politics and social demands increasingly altered Olmsted's ideal park, but his model suburban landscape maintained its power, constituting an enduring legacy to the landscaping profession. This gave landscape architects, in spite of their professional weaknesses, an ideology of social and moral improvement and an aesthetic vocabulary that could easily be applied to the design of company towns.

Landscape architecture was closely linked to another newly professionalizing field – city planning. The two groups' professional responsibilities and social interests overlapped so much that, in 1909, the Landscape Architecture Department at Harvard had introduced the first American university course in city planning. City planning, however, rapidly differentiated itself from landscape architecture. The two professions reflected the social values of two different eras: landscape architecture emerged from the elite reform programs of the Gilded Age while city planning reflected the newer progressive values of rationality, efficiency, and functionalism. City planning's emphasis on technical and administrative rather than aesthetic skills attracted landscape architects hoping to broaden their professional opportunities. In contrast to the modest domain that landscape architects claimed, city planning from its beginnings asserted ambitious goals, not only subsuming many of landscape architecture's tasks, but claiming the comprehensive organization of the city as its professional responsibility.

The first National Conference on City Planning and the Problems of Congestion, held in 1909, brought design professionals together with urban reformers, public officials, social workers, and economists to address the problems of the American city. The majority agreed that aesthetic solutions, such as those identified with the Olmsted landscape tradition or the City Beautiful movement, were simplistic. Instead, the "City Functional" approach dominated the conference. Attempting to rationalize and standardize the study of the city and its problems, the City Functional advocates defined city planning as an objective and primarily technical endeavor. This necessarily involved an enormous range of legal, physical, economic, and social considerations. One of the conference organizers, Frederick Law Olmsted, Jr, now a partner in his famous father's firm, declared that he felt overwhelmed by the "complex unity, the appalling breadth and ramifications of real city planning." Planners were "dealing . . . with the play of enormously complex forces which no one clearly understands and few pretend to."[13]

In the absence of the public powers necessary to tackle such an immense job, city planners initially occupied themselves with detailed analysis of urban problems. Anxious to demonstrate their mastery of "scientific" methods, they collected statistical data to describe the social and physical characteristics of the city and to analyze municipal finance and taxation. This factual information, aimed at attracting potential supporters in the business community, was couched in the language of scientific management, then at the peak of its popularity. In a 1913 article, "Efficiency in City Planning," architect George F. Ford claimed that the use of survey procedures in city planning was a "method of work, systematized, standardized, 'Taylorized' that appeals strongly to the businessman and convinces everyone that the experts have real knowledge and are not presenting mere dreams."[14]

In spite of these assertions, few municipal entities were willing to sponsor such expensive and untested procedures. Cities rarely hired planners – in 1914, Harlan Bartholomew was the only municipal planner employed full time in the United States – and the few cities that commissioned plans rarely implemented them. Although the city planning profession continued to urge the necessity of state intervention, many planners realized that, in its absence, private patronage could help them fulfill more realizable goals. This made private planning commissions, such as company towns, attractive alternatives to non-existent public projects. Compared to the complexity of large cities, the small scale of the company town offered a manageable site where planners could develop techniques that might later be used for more comprehensive social and physical planning. Moreover, financing and control by a single company eliminated most of the obstacles, such as individual ownership, real-estate speculation, and conflicting political demands, that typically plagued large-scale planning projects. As a result, many of these plans had a good chance of being implemented.

As the design professions' interest in company towns grew, their differing concerns produced an approximate division of professional labor, with tasks allotted by professional specialization. Although architects specialized in designing buildings, by the end of the century many had answered Croly's call to work on a larger scale, and had designed group housing and even subdivisions. Landscape architects and planners, rarely involved with building design, concentrated on site planning. In addition to laying out town sites and "platting" lots, they provided planting plans and outlined detailed requirements for grading, drainage, and infrastructure. Architects and landscape designers focused on aesthetic and functional considerations while city planners emphasized analytical and organizational tasks. Such professional differences did not produce conflict. Instead, all three professions agreed that, since the scope and complexity of an entire town required a broad range of skills, a collaborative approach was best. Ideally, the comprehensive design of a company town should be a team effort, pairing architects with landscape architects or planners.

When dealing with clients and users, even minor professional differences vanished. All three design professions depended primarily on wealthy individual and corporate clients for their livelihood. Although landscape architects had grappled with the complexities of urban politics while designing public parks, elite patrons usually had been their primary supporters. Landscape architects identified themselves with what Olmsted called "the class that has had the opportunity of educating their tastes in constructive activity."[15] Lacking state or municipal sponsorship, city planning, even though it defined itself as a "public profession," acknowledged the local businessman – "the man who has to pay the bills," as one planner put it – as the fundamental supporter of the planning process.[16] In spite of their rhetorical commitment to the public good, none of these groups displayed any interest in the opinions of the actual users of their designs. Convinced that they knew best, whether designing house-plans, laying out a neighborhood, or landscaping its streets, the expert professional's abstract concern for "the people" rarely translated into respect for the values or aspirations of working-class communities or the individuals for whom they designed.

ARGUMENTS FOR THE "NEW" COMPANY TOWN

By the end of the first decade of the twentieth century, public opinion favoring "scientific" industrial towns had grown significantly. Several important events during the decade increased public awareness about the severity of urban problems and the possibilities of solving them. In 1907, a group of prominent New York reformers, led by Lillian Wald and Florence Kelly of the National Consumers League and the representatives of thirty-seven other civic and philanthropic organizations, formed the Committee on the Congestion of Population. In 1908, their executive secretary, Benjamin Marsh, organized an enormous exhibition at the Museum of Natural History to publicize the evils of congestion. Graphically illustrating the social and economic costs of urban overcrowding, the "congestion show," like Veiller's earlier tenement show, functioned as thinly veiled propaganda for planning and reform. As alternatives to crowded tenements and teeming streets, Marsh endorsed a variety of decentralizing solutions, including cheap public transportation, zoning, and more parks and open space. One of the most popular exhibits was a model of an industrial village of single family houses, a compelling visual argument for Marsh's policy of transplanting factories and housing to unsettled parts of the city, where land was still cheap. This, he asserted, was the only way to improve living conditions for the working class.[17]

Other revelations about living conditions in industrial communities added weight to arguments for decentralization and resettlement. As the Progressive Movement evolved, factual analyses replaced the flamboyant but unsystematic exposés of the muckrakers. The Pittsburgh Survey's exhaustive investigation of urban and industrial conditions in the city graphically expanded on Lincoln Steffen's earlier indictment of Pittsburgh's political corruption and wretched living conditions, *The Shame of the Cities*, published in 1904. Organized by the New York Charity Organization Society and financed by the Russell Sage Foundation, the Survey comprehensively documented Pittsburgh's urban problems, surveying employment and wages as well as working, housing, and living conditions.[18] The facts uncovered by the Survey's team of expert investigators painted a grim picture of life in a city dominated by the steel industry, describing typhoid-ridden neighborhoods and exploited workers who, after working twelve hours a day, seven days a week, had little time to do anything but eat and sleep. These findings, widely disseminated in the popular press, appalled many Americans.[19] The New York *World* accused the steel companies of operating "a man-killing system."[20]

Like the Tenement and Congestion exhibitions, the Pittsburgh Survey alerted the public to the seriousness of the social and urban problems which rapid industrialization had produced. In 1910, the Survey's fourth volume, *Homestead: The Households of A Mill Town*, focused on the steel town of Homestead, fourteen miles south of Pittsburgh. Its author, Margaret Byington, described the community in devastating detail. To avoid responsibility for housing its workers, Carnegie Steel had located its plant outside the town limits, allowing real-estate speculators to develop the town without any controls. Housing expanded as

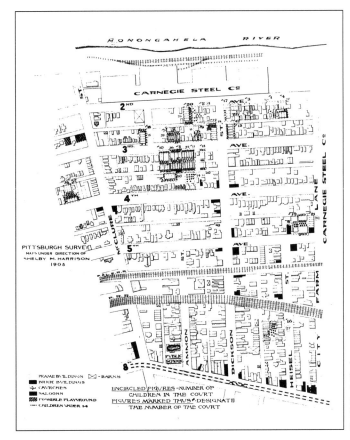

The Pittsburgh Survey's careful evaluation of Ward 2 in Homestead, Pennsylvania, done in 1908. The Survey studied the area in detail, mapping the number of children under fourteen, the location of churches and saloons, and the absence of playgrounds.

the mill grew, and dense rows of cheap frame houses spread haphazardly across the hills and ravines above the plant. "Slavs," unskilled Eastern European workers, crowded together in squalid tenements and shanties in "Hunkytown." After the 1892 strike, Carnegie Steel began to provide housing for skilled workers. The company developed Mulhill, an area adjacent to Homestead, constructing neat cottages with lawns and trees that Byington called "the best houses for the money in town."[21] Homestead itself had amenities such as a Carnegie library and two parks, but railroad tracks ran directly through its streets and open sewers compromised the residents' health. The largest green space in town was the lawn of the mill superintendent's mansion. Horrified by the conditions the Survey uncovered, the Charity Organization Society asserted that "it raises a great, grimed question mark as to whether this is the type of community example which the leading industrial center of the country is to set," and demanded, "What are American standards anyway?"[22]

GARDEN CITIES, INDUSTRIAL VILLAGES, AND GARDEN SUBURBS

The English Garden City Movement offered a solution to these urban problems, proposing a strategy for decentralizing large cities along with a compelling physical model for the decentralized community. Reacting to similar conditions in England, Ebenezer Howard invented a new urban form – the garden city – as an alternative to urban industrial society. Disturbed by the featureless sprawl and desperate overcrowding he saw in London, Howard envisioned a new way of life that would combine the best features of city and countryside. His book *Tomorrow: A Peaceful Path for Reform*, published in 1898 and reissued in 1902 as *Garden Cities of Tomorrow*, described this new form of decentralized urbanization. Its density would be low enough to maintain a healthy contact with nature, while its population would be large enough to support urban institutions such as hospitals, libraries, and concert halls. Economically and spatially self-sufficient, the garden city would provide a balanced way of life, blending industrial pursuits with agricultural activities. A practical thinker, Howard formulated detailed plans for the new town's social and economic organization. Its economy would balance public and private control. Agriculture and industry would be private enterprises, but, to avoid speculation, private landownership would gradually be replaced with collective community ownership. Tenants would pay rent to a trust, the sole owner of land in the garden city, which would use any surplus funds to support hospitals, schools, and charities.

Determined to build a garden city, in 1901 Howard founded the Garden City Association to mobilize financial and political support. Two of the Association's earliest members were the industrial philanthropists George Cadbury and William Lever. Motivated by religious convictions, both men had built model industrial villages during the 1890s, in the tradition of nineteenth-century paternalism. By 1900 Bournville, sponsored by Cadbury's Chocolate, and Port Sunlight, named after Lever Brothers' most successful product, Sunlight Soap, had become, like Pullman, world-famous examples of town planning and industrial betterment. Although aware of George Pullman's mistakes, Cadbury and Lever shared many of his inclinations. Like Pullman, they placed a premium on order, cleanliness, and beauty, and did not hesitate to impose these preferences on their workers. These qualities, however, took on a completely different physical form from Pullman's. Bournville and Port Sunlight were both "garden villages," self-consciously rural and "English" alternatives to urban and industrial life. Instant recreations of vernacular settlements, these industrial communities belonged to an English tradition of manufactured villages. Beginning in the eighteenth century, romantically designed rural villages, such as John Nash's picturesque cottages at Blaise Hamlet, served as substitutes for traditional villages, which were increasingly modified by economic and social changes. Like Olmsted's parks, they embodied a benign myth of rural life counterposed to the wickedness of the city. Transposed to the company town, this idyllic vision of the unchanging order of English village life, unified yet hierarchical, offered comforting illusions to capitalists and workers entering the twentieth century.[23]

George Cadbury, objecting to "the unwholesomeness of city life," moved his factory to the rural fringe of Birmingham. Like Olmsted, Cadbury believed in the moral benefits of the natural landscape. To maintain Bournville's bucolic image as its population grew, he kept housing at low densities and heavily landscaped the town, planting trees and shrubs in quantities large enough to justify the slogan "the factory in a garden." Convinced of the therapeutic benefits of physical exercise and gardening, Cadbury urged them on his employees as natural antidotes to industrial labor, providing both economic and health benefits. The town was well provided with sports grounds, a swimming pool, and all kinds of parks, each house had a large garden, and the company sponsored gardening classes and issued seeds free to encourage residents to produce their own food. Often, they had little choice; leases required tenants to maintain trees and shrubs, and Cadbury expected workers to join in the calisthenics offered during lunch breaks.[24] In spite of this, Cadbury worried about the dangers of paternalism. To avoid company domination of the town, he encouraged outsiders to settle in Bournville and by 1895, non-employees constituted 50 percent of the town's inhabitants.[25]

William Lever maintained much stricter control over Port Sunlight, prompting British trade unions to continually attack the town. One union official complained that "no man of an independent turn of mind could breathe for long in the stifling atmosphere of Port Sunlight."[26] Obsessed with perfecting the town, Lever focused on architecture. Sparing no expense, he employed a number of well-known architects to design "artistic" groupings of cottages. Seeking an image of pre-industrial permanence, Lever favored retrospective styles and even constructed replicas of well-known Tudor and Elizabethan buildings, such as Ann Hathaway's cottage. Port Sunlight's housing was notable for an almost exaggerated attention to materials, texture, and detailing. Since the individual units were small, the architects grouped them together in volumes that resembled large, middle-class houses, then organized these volumes into compositions that defined the edges of superblocks. Such careful design produced a somewhat artificial effect, leading many observers to note the town's stage-set quality. However, as Walter Creese has pointed out, the ultimate result was an environment whose visual richness and spatial unity were the polar opposites of the prevailing image of English industrial life – the dull and oppressive cities of the industrial North.[27]

Port Sunlight and Bournville transformed the image of workers' housing. After visiting Bournville, the architect of the Krupp's workers' villages at Margaretenhohe, near Essen, gradually transformed the Krupp projects into garden villages. Port Sunlight regularly attracted royal visitors. In 1903 King Albert of Belgium was so impressed by the town that he asked Lever to build settlements in the Congo. After the Garden City Association met at Bournville in 1901 and at Port Sunlight in 1902, the two industrial villages were absorbed into the developing ideology of the movement as important precursors of garden city ideas. In spite of the important social and economic differences between the company town and the garden city, this connection established a powerful institutional link between the two types of town.

In 1903, Lever and Cadbury provided important financial backing to First Garden City, Ltd, allowing the firm to begin construction of Letchworth, the first garden city. Although Ebenezer Howard had provided a detailed economic and social outline for the garden city, an architect was necessary to give it physical form, so the firm commissioned the young architects Barry Parker and Raymond Unwin. While sympathetic to Howard's goals, Parker and Unwin had already developed their own town planning aesthetic. The previous year, they had designed a model industrial village, New Earswick, for the Quaker chocolate manufacturer, Joseph Rowntree. Parker and Unwin's design for New Earswick adapted the picturesque imagery of towns like Bournville and Port Sunlight, transforming it into a highly sophisticated planning and architectural style.

Parker and Unwin used several of New Earswick's design features, the street picture, the court, and the cul-de-sac, as fundamental elements of garden city design. To create street pictures, Parker and Unwin adjusted the spatial relationships between housing and street, establishing a rhythmic sequence of open and enclosed spaces. Site planning configurations

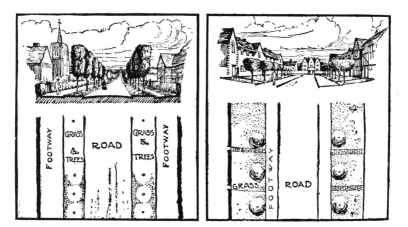

Parker and Unwin's methods of varying streets and groups of houses – by subtle changes in scale, landscaping, setbacks, and road patterns – established the image of the garden city. From *Town Planning in Practice.*

such as the court, a three-sided group of houses facing the street, and the cul-de-sac, a group of houses reached by a dead-end street, varied these sequences, while other techniques, such as removing the corner house on a block, emphasized the spatial relationships. These innovations produced subtle changes in street patterns, alternatives to both the monotony of the grid and what Unwin called the "aimless wiggles of picturesque planning." The small scale of the groupings created a sense of intimacy and community that evoked the traditional English village in a less overtly self-conscious way than Bournville or Port Sunlight.[28] Still, Parker and Unwin's idealization of the aesthetic virtues of village life brought with it a visible nostalgia for pre-industrial times that was absent from Howard's more future-oriented concept of the garden city. Unwin hoped that the garden city would "give life just that order, that crystalline structure it had in feudal times."[29] Parker and Unwin's town planning style, emphasizing "organic unity," infused the tradition of picturesque village design with new life.

Letchworth's planning elaborated this idea on a much larger scale. Organized as "a group of connected villages around a civic center with a factory district on the outskirts," Parker and Unwin's plan achieved a level of naturalism that, according to historian Robert Fishman, has kept many visitors and even some of its inhabitants unaware that it was consciously designed.[30] Letchworth's plan combines a formal center with informal residential areas; a central axis with a symmetrical group of municipal and cultural buildings spreads out into a loose network of roads lined with houses. Unwin literalized Howard's metaphorical garden city, creating site planning and landscape principles that carefully avoided both the formality of Beaux Arts planning and the convolutions of the picturesque style. The entire plan was adapted to the contours of the site, then subtly adjusted between straight streets and gently curving roads. Density was set at twelve or fewer houses per acre. Existing trees were left on the site, and each street planted with a different species of tree. Parker carefully arranged trees and shrubs to frame views of the surrounding landscape, a technique he called "driftways." As Howard specified, Letchworth was surrounded by an agricultural greenbelt three times as large as its built area, blending the town into the countryside.[31]

Unlike the picturesque company towns, Howard wanted Letchworth to grow naturally over time, as residents and local builders gradually built housing and other structures. Parker and Unwin designed much of Letchworth's early working-class housing, sponsored by Garden City Tenants, Ltd, a cooperative building society. They replaced the historicism of Port Sunlight's cottages with a simplified version of the Arts and Crafts style that still evoked the vernacular cottage tradition. The exteriors of their houses at Letchworth, with their clean volumes, tiled gable roofs, and rough-cast white stucco surfaces, resembled the work of contemporary architects such as Voysey and Baillie Scott. The interiors, however,

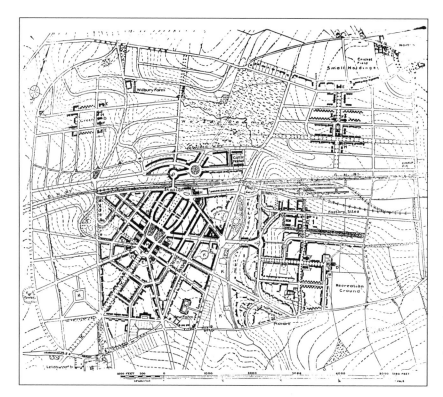

Plan of Letchworth, the first garden city, located in Hertfordshire, 34 miles north of London. Designed by Parker and Unwin, Letchworth combined a formal town center with informal residential areas, an attempt to balance town and country, nature and architecture.

demonstrated Parker and Unwin's active desire to transform existing ways of living. Beginning with their 1902 project for "Cottages Near a Town," the architects had attempted to improve working-class life, designing healthy and functional interiors that provided better ventilation, more sunlight, and more efficient circulation. At Letchworth, they aligned the houses to face the sun and eliminated the working-class parlor, considering it a "useless luxury." They designed a more efficient open-plan combination kitchen-living room organized around the stove, which they believed was the real center of working-class life.

The cooperative quadrangle was their most radical housing proposal, although, like all of Unwin's ideas, it clothed innovation in an idyllic representation of the feudal past. In 1901, Unwin first suggested a communal living arrangement for Yorkshire workers, modeled after college quadrangles at Oxford or medieval cloisters. He proposed grouping kitchenless dwellings around a central court, with a "common room," where residents could gather in the evening, shared laundry and drying rooms, and cooperatively organized cooking and dining.[32] Following Unwin's suggestion, Homesgarth, the first cooperative quadrangle at Letchworth, was built in 1909, designed by A. Clapham Lander.

Adopting Unwin's physical plan but not his cooperative ideals, Homesgarth provided child-less, middle-class residents with a common garden, dining hall, tea room, and reading and smoking rooms, maintained by a shared staff of trained servants. The most famous res-ident was Ebenezer Howard himself, an enthusiastic proponent of cooperative housekeeping. Cooperative housing projects became one of the essential elements of the English garden city, and Homesgarth inspired similar projects at Letchworth, Welwyn Garden City, and Hampstead Garden Suburb.[33]

Letchworth had an immediate and world-wide impact. In the United States, architects, planners, and urban reformers rapidly adopted the garden city as a new ideal. In 1906, a group of prominent urban reformers, including E.R.L. Gould and Christian Socialist William D.P. Bliss, founded the Garden City Association of America. Before dissolving a year later, the group had proposed plans for a series of garden cities to be built in New York, New Jersey, and Pennsylvania. Benjamin Marsh's influential planning text, *Introduction to City Planning*, published in 1909, discussed the garden city at great length, offering it to American planners as a model for decentralizing settlement. Howard's ideas for limiting size and density inspired planners while Parker and Unwin's site planning techniques and group housing designs intrigued architects and landscape designers. Once American writ-ers began to praise garden cities, Letchworth, Port Sunlight, and Bournville became necessary stops for American designers and reformers touring Europe. After seeing Port Sunlight, an American social worker exclaimed that she had "not known that there was any-where in the world a village in which there was nowhere to be found one ugly, inartistic, unsanitary, or other demoralizing feature."[34]

American garden city enthusiasts defined the garden city in a very general way, often ignoring the most radical aspects of Howard's program, such as cooperative ownership, economic self-sufficiency, and innovative living arrangements. Used carelessly, the terms garden city, model industrial village, and garden suburb became interchangeable. Many housing reformers, already proponents of decentralization, adopted the garden city as a model for physical planning rather than as a new form of social and economic organiza-tion. Lawrence Veiller, then head of the National Housing Association and an early supporter of the garden city movement, interpreted the garden city in terms of his own concern with housing improvement. In 1909, he convinced the Russell Sage Foundation to sponsor the construction of an American garden suburb on the outskirts of New York City. The Foundation's intentions were also contradictory. Forest Hills Gardens was to be both a "model town" and a "business proposition." The Foundation, founded in 1907 to "improve social and living conditions in the United States," envisioned the town as a demonstration project to educate the public about the benefits of decentralization, com-prehensive planning, and good housing.[35] However, the Foundation's charter also specified that its 2,000,000-dollar capital investment must produce a 3 percent profit.[36]

These goals came into conflict immediately after the Foundation bought a farm in Queens, 8 miles from Manhattan on the Long Island railroad, as the site for the new settlement. First, the choice of a suburban location precluded self-sufficiency, leaving the town dependent on Manhattan's economic and cultural resources. The Foundation originally intended Forest Hills Gardens to be a community for those of modest means, but the high costs of land so near the city immediately altered the town's social composition. Since the Russell Sage Foundation had to earn 3 percent on its investment, it passed on these high costs to buyers. This drove up housing prices at Forest Hills, making them prohibitive for anyone without a middle-class income. Moreover, the Foundation's need for an immediate return on its investment precluded long-term financing alternatives, such as co-partnership. The town's real success was its outstanding design. The architect, Grosvenor Atterbury, and the planner, Frederick Law Olmsted, Jr, successfully adapted English garden city design to an American suburban setting. Once the town was begun, the high quality of the architecture and planning attracted wealthy buyers, pushing prices up even further and definitively transforming the settlement from a social experiment into an exclusive suburb.[37]

Two years later, the Massachusetts Homestead Commission, a unique state agency specifically created to improve working-class housing conditions, began to plan its own version of the garden city, to be called Billerica Garden Suburb. Prohibited by law from directly spending public money for housing, the Commission organized the project as a limited profit investment, with dividends limited to 5 percent, an arrangement similar to Forest Hills Gardens and other philanthropic housing projects in New York. Like Forest Hills Gardens, Billerica was a demonstration project, but the Homestead Commission, more willing than the Russell Sage Foundation to experiment with new forms of ownership, provided zones for rental, purchase, and co-partnership. Unlike Forest Hills, economically dependent on Manhattan, the Homestead Commission intentionally located Billerica Garden Suburb in an isolated area near a large industrial employer, the Boston and Maine Railroad Shops, from where it hoped to draw its residents. The landscape architects Arthur C. Comey and Warren Manning sketched out a plan for a 57-acre model settlement, based on what they called "advanced garden suburb lines." However, the novelty of the project made it difficult to find investors, so the Commission was able to build only a few houses before the agency was abolished in 1919.[38] The failure of Forest Hills Gardens and Billerica Garden Suburb as alternative models of development pointed out the difficulties of using the limited dividend system to finance suburban settlements that working-class families could afford. Even by limiting profits, new settlements providing low-cost housing for workers could not be built within existing housing markets.

For many designers and reformers, the "new" company town suggested a way out of this dilemma. Planned industrial communities, financed by employers and designed by professionals, appeared to offer a comprehensive solution to urban and industrial problems, Employers, acknowledging their social responsibilities, would upgrade working and housing conditions for their workers. Designers, using the garden city as a model, would create new types of communities away from urban areas. The resulting decentralization of industry and housing would reduce urban congestion, thus improving living conditions in cities. In 1910, landscape architect Warren Manning, speaking at the Second National Conference on City Planning, restated the premises of the "new" company town from the designer's point of view:

> I would say that much of the improvement of city conditions is to come through the construction of manufacturing villages for the lowest priced labor with all essential pipes, stores, schools, playgrounds, reservations, houses and gardens and with enough home character to attract different nationalities and to keep the cost within their income limit.[39]

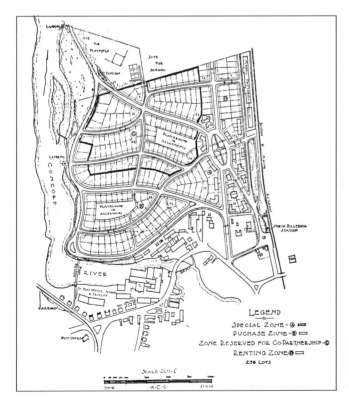

Plan for Billerica Garden Suburb by Arthur C. Comey and Warren Manning. Although inspired by the English garden city, only part of Billerica was reserved for co-partnership ownership.

5

THE SEARCH FOR A STYLE

In order to take control of the "new" company town, designers needed to claim a much stronger role in the design process. This required major readjustment to the roles of both designer and client. The company town, after all, was not a new design problem. Professional designers had been intermittently engaged with company towns since the 1880s. Pullman had been the first company town designed by professionals, but George Pullman's strong opinions and dominating personality overshadowed the contributions of his design team. During the 1890s, other professional attempts to design company towns had encountered similar difficulties with industrial clients. In 1892, one of the most prominent architects in the country, Stanford White, of the firm of McKim, Mead, and White, designed an industrial complex for the Niagara Power Company at Echota, New York.

While White designed massive Romanesque buildings housing corporate offices and the electric powerhouses, the company's engineers laid out streets and installed utilities for a workers' village on a level site nearby. White then produced plans for a series of neat colonial houses, ranging from single family dwellings to group houses of three or four units. Clad with wooden shingles or clapboard and sparingly detailed with Georgian motifs, each house was a variation on a common theme – miniature versions of the shingle style the firm had perfected during the 1880s. The houses were small but carefully planned, with particular attention paid to cross-ventilation and interior circulation. However, once built, their architectural variety could not counteract the monotony of the engineers' gridiron planning. Lined up in rows, and set back uniformly from the road, the houses reproduced the repetitious order that had become a hallmark of the company town.[1]

Other firms employed landscape architects to plan their towns. In 1896, toward the end of his career, Frederick Law Olmsted designed a picturesque plan for Vandergrift, Pennsylvania, a town owned by the Apollo Steel Company. Avoiding the gridiron monotony of Echota's plan, Olmsted laid out a street pattern consisting of long meandering curves,

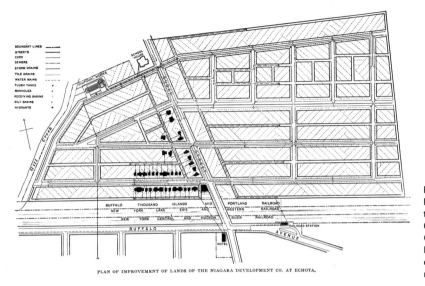

BOUNDARY LINES
STREETS
CURB
SEWERS
STORM DRAINS
TILE DRAINS
WATER MAINS
FLUSH TANKS
MANHOLES
RECEIVING BASINS
SILT BASINS
HYDRANTS

PLAN OF IMPROVEMENT OF LANDS OF THE NIAGARA DEVELOPMENT CO. AT ECHOTA.

Engineer's plan for
Echota, New York, built by
the Niagara Power
Company in 1892.
Gridiron streets, laid out
by company engineers,
ensured a repetitious and
monotonous urban order.

the same style he had used in upper-middle-class suburbs such as Riverside. However, accustomed to working with large parcels of land, Olmsted had difficulty with the small lots that the sponsor specified and the circuitous routes imposed by the curvilinear plan were incompatible with the daily needs of steelworkers and their families. After half of the town had been built, Apollo Steel, dismayed by the high land costs of curvilinear planning, abandoned Olmsted's plan.

In 1896 and 1904, the Draper Company enlarged the textile town of Hopedale, Massachusetts, commissioning Warren Manning and then Arthur Shurtleff, both Olmsted alumni, to lay out two new subdivisions, Bancroft Park and Lake Point. Both designers sited streets and lots in relation to the contours of the land, transforming Hopedale's grid into loose and informal curves. Contour planning as practiced by Manning and Shurtleff extended the repertoire of naturalistic site planning, and, like Parker and Unwin's nearly contemporary design for Letchworth, was more functional than Olmsted's land-consuming picturesque style. The Draper Company hired several prominent Boston architects to design housing for the new areas. However, since the company insisted on building high density housing to justify the expense of developing the land, this forced the architects to design box-like duplexes that destroyed the subtlety of the land planning.[2]

The limits of these projects pointed out the difficulties of designing company towns. Although the companies employed professional designers, they still maintained total control over their projects. They did not hesitate to ignore, alter, or abandon their designers'

FRONT ELEVATION.   SIDE ELEVATION.

KITCHEN
12'0" X 12'0"

LIVING ROOM
12'0" X 14'0"

BED ROOM
12'0" X 18'6"

BED ROOM
10'6" X 15'0"

FIRST FLOOR.   SECOND FLOOR.

ELEVATIONS AND PLANS OF ONE OF THE SMALL HOUSES AT ECHOTA.

Colonial revival cottage designed by Stanford White for Echota, New York. Although small, these houses were unusually well-planned and carefully detailed.

plans if they strained budgets or challenged conventions too radically. As a result, none of these towns was designed as a whole; White had to work within the constraints of the factory engineer's plan, while Olmsted had no control over Vandergrift's speculative housing. Contractors, in fact, overbuilt many of Vandergrift's narrow lots, leaving only a few feet of space between houses.[3] Thus, the few professionally designed towns built between 1890 and 1910, although more attractive than similar towns developed without professional advice, did not change the image or ideology of the company town. Asked to design company towns, White and Olmsted simply adapted their existing styles to a new problem, while Manning and Shurtleff's work, innovative on a small scale, did not address more comprehensive planning.

LABOR AND THE "NEW" COMPANY TOWN

By 1910, the balance of power between designers and clients had shifted decisively in the designers' favor. Facing major labor problems, industrial clients began, for the first time, to value professional expertise. If many industrial employers had remained equivocal about making substantial and permanent investments in company towns, the changing labor climate convinced them of the need to rethink their position on welfare, housing, and town planning. The situation had begun to change after 1905, when a seven-year "honeymoon" between labor and capital ended with a new series of strikes. Beginning in 1909, each year brought at least one major outbreak; the garment workers strike of 1909, the Philadelphia general strike of 1910, the Harriman railroad strike the next year, the 1912 textile strikes in Lawrence and Paterson, followed by miners' uprisings in West Virginia, Colorado, and the Upper Michigan copper fields. Unionism grew rapidly, not only among conservative AFL craft unions, but also with the appearance of more militantly radical labor organizations such as the Western Federation of Miners and the Industrial Workers of the World. The IWW brought new groups into the labor movement, organizing women, immigrants, unskilled workers, and even the unemployed into "one big union."

On the defensive, capitalists fought back with increasingly violent means. In isolated company towns, the tension between capital and labor escalated. Old-style paternalism proved to be a weak defense against newly militant labor. Strikes even hit the idyllic New England textile towns: Ludlow Manufacturing had a major strike in 1909; in 1912, the IWW organized the Draper Company at Hopedale as part of their campaign to unionize the textile industry, and in 1913, inspired by the IWW's victory in the Lawrence strike, Draper workers began their own four-month strike. That same year, the Western Federation of Miners organized Michigan copper miners and led them in a bitter strike against Calumet and Hecla. Acknowledging the company's extensive paternalism, a Labor Department investigator concluded after the strike, "Only one thing appeared to be lacking and that was the right of the workers to be free men in every sense of the word."[4]

Colorado Fuel and Iron also operated its mining camps with absolutist control; according to one miner, the absentee owner, John D. Rockefeller, Jr, was "invested with what is virtually the power of life and death over twelve thousand men and their families." When the miners finally struck against poor working and living conditions, the mine owners demonstrated their power by bringing in a private army made up of company guards, private detectives, and the state militia. Armed with machine guns, detectives roamed the countryside in a special armored car with a Gatling gun mounted on top, known as the "Death Special." On 20 April 1914, the company forces attacked a tent colony inhabited by strikers at Ludlow, Colorado. Raking the miners and their families with machine guns and high-powered rifles for an entire day, the troops completely destroyed the colony, finally burning it to the ground. Thirty-two people were either shot or burned to death.[5] The "Ludlow Massacre" and similar incidents of employers' violence increased public sympathy for labor and focused national attention on living and working conditions in isolated company towns. Alarmed, state and Federal agencies launched investigations. *The Survey*, a journal sponsored by the Charity Organization Society, questioned a group of social workers, philanthropists, and college professors about industrial conditions, then summarized their conclusions: "Actual class warfare exists in the United States and the conditions leading to such warfare have to be changed."[6]

The crisis in industrial relations worked to the advantage of the design professions. Under attack, capitalists began to seek new methods of improving their relations with their workers and upgrading their public image. Already involved in industrial betterment, they began to look to the "new" company town as a possible solution to their labor problems. For the first time, many employers were willing to listen to and accept direction from professional designers. As historian Burton Bledstein observed, the culture of professionalism flourished in an "atmosphere of constant crisis – emergency – in which practitioners both created work for themselves and reinforced their authority by intimidating their clients."[7] At the same time, however, the employers' priorities did not necessarily coincide with the views of housing and urban reformers. Industrial employers continued to make a distinction between unskilled, usually immigrant, workers and skilled, English-speaking workers. Concerned with attracting skilled workers and avoiding unionization, employers hoped that professionally designed communities would build loyalty and stability and thus head off

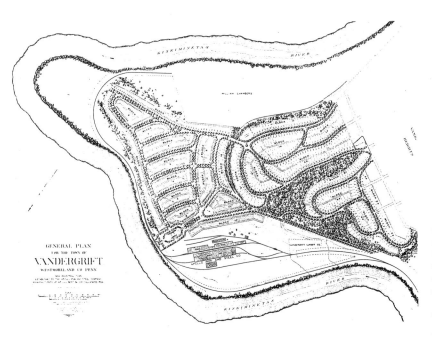

Plan of Vandergrift, Pennsylvania, designed by Frederick Law Olmsted. A late example of Olmsted's curvilinear and picturesque planning style, adapted to an industrial town.

more strikes. Seeking new and more effective ways of addressing these persistent problems, manufacturers accepted the design profession's claims to have mastered the industrial environment and relinquished physical control of the company town to them.

THE SEARCH FOR A STYLE

The outlines of the "new" company town emerged with three very similar towns built between 1909 and 1913: Fairfield, Alabama; Torrance, California; and Goodyear Heights, Ohio. Although none of these towns was completely successful as a design, as a group they established the social and aesthetic criteria for a new generation of company towns. These commissions validated the claims of architects, landscape designers, and planners to the same systematic rationality that characterized industrial and urban reform. In all three towns, the clients selected well-known practitioners, rather than local designers. This reinforced professional aspirations to establish nationally accepted norms of good design. Arriving with standardized and generalizable solutions, these professionals rarely addressed local traditions or conditions in their designs. Similarly, the sponsor's willingness to incur the additional expense of hiring both architects and landscape designers acknowledged the importance of professional specialization and demonstrated a commitment to comprehensively designed environments. Encouraged by the degree of authority these firms gave them, company town designers began to assert their autonomy.

Hiring professional designers also served the clients' interests. In spite of the aesthetic freedom they allowed the designers, the clients' instructions reflected their current preoccupations. The sponsors of all three towns were responding to severe labor problems that plagued many large industrial employers. The struggle was taking place on a national scale, with unions conducting well-publicized campaigns to organize entire industries and regions. Large corporations, under increasing public scrutiny, exploited the experts they imported to demonstrate their good intentions and lack of paternalism. They incorporated the designers and their designs into corporate publicity, focusing national attention on the company's efforts to improve their employees' living conditions. At the same time, concerned about protecting their investments, employers refused to take risks, preferring to follow existing precedents rather than experimenting with new ideas or methods. Attempting to attract stable families and skilled workers by offering them homes to buy, employers had to address their workers as consumers as well as employees. As a result, they took great pains to give workers the type of housing they preferred, instructing their architects to design model houses with prices and styles that would appeal to them. This gave the workers a significant role in evaluating the company town. With the company's large investments at stake, the workers became the final arbiters of a town's success.

FAIRFIELD, ALABAMA

The US Steel Corporation's decision to build Fairfield, Alabama exemplifies the dramatic shift in employers' attitudes toward company towns. During the first decade of the twentieth century, US Steel, mindful of Pullman, consciously avoided any comprehensive or professional planning, allowing towns such as Gary and Aliquippa to develop free of company control. However, in 1910, only three years after they established Gary, the Corporation, which had just taken over the Tennessee Coal, Iron and Railroad Company, reversed its position and began planning Fairfield, the most ambitious new town since Pullman. This change in policy reflected a major transfer of power within the giant steel corporation – Judge Elbert H. Gary's victory over the old-line ironmasters, unrelenting in their dealings with labor, who controlled the company's local subsidiaries. Gary's supporters were financiers who, more conscious of public opinion, favored industrial welfare rather than coercion in dealing with workers. In 1909 Gary introduced a comprehensive welfare program, including pension plans, voted over a million dollars for improved housing, and set up a corporate Bureau of Safety, Sanitation, and Welfare to oversee welfare work in individual plants.

In spite of Gary's efforts, US Steel continued to be a major target for reformers and labor unions. In 1909, the IWW launched a major campaign at US Steel subsidiaries in Hammond, Indiana, McKees Rock, Butler, and New Castle, Pennsylvania. For the first time, skilled American workers joined unskilled immigrants to protest against eighty-hour working weeks. Further dramatizing the inhuman living and working conditions brought to light by the Pittsburgh Survey, the strike attracted national attention. In 1911, the corporation's own stockholders, shocked by the exposés, demanded an investigation into labor practices in the steel mills. The same year, a House of Representatives committee began an investigation into US Steel's activities, the government instituted an anti-trust suit, and the Department of Commerce and Labor released a four-volume study, *Labor Conditions in the Iron and Steel Industry*, which further highlighted abuses in US Steel plants. Desperate to change its public image, US Steel used Fairfield as visible evidence of its new welfare policies and concern for its employees.[8]

Anxious to demonstrate the Corporation's changed outlook, US Steel's local developer, Robert Jemison, visited a number of industrial towns across the country before hiring Boston landscape architect George H. Miller and New York architect William Leslie Welton. Although Jemison and US Steel gave the designers complete aesthetic freedom, their economic and industrial decisions had already decisively shaped Fairfield. Hoping to attract local businesses to invest in the town, Jemison discouraged innovation, emphasizing the need for practicality and feasibility. The corporation imposed its own requirements. As the town would house employees from several US Steel plants, providing pedestrian access to the factories dictated the town's location and plan. More importantly, like all of US Steel's housing projects, Fairfield was restricted to skilled workers who could afford to purchase houses, for US Steel had no interest in housing lower-paid, mostly black, and recent immigrant workers who were forced to rent accommodation in neighboring towns such as Ensley, which Graham Taylor compared to an industrial barracks.[9]

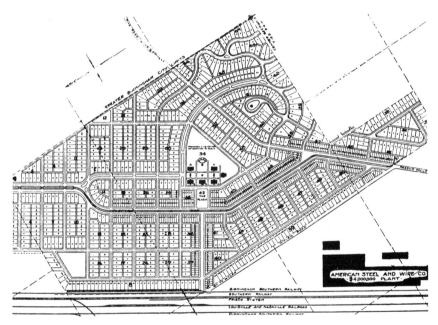

Fairfield, Alabama, designed by landscape architect George Miller. The town, entirely separate from the American Steel and Wire Company plant, combines a grid of small blocks with curvilinear streets. A landscaped parkway forms a spine through the center of the town. The center of the town is marked by a plaza with an elaborate fountain. To the north, a formal group of symmetrical buildings housed civic facilities, schools, and the headquarters of the corporation's welfare programs, surrounded by a large park. At the southern end, the main streets are lined with small lots for independent businesses. Housing surrounds the central core – four zones, from small blocks to the south to curving streets on the hillside in the upper part of the plan.

Miller produced a detailed and complex plan to accommodate a projected population of more than 1,600 people. Miller used three different planning styles to separate the town into three visually distinct zones. The civic area, at the center, was an axial Beaux Arts composition with formal buildings symmetrically arranged around a large open park. The commercial district consisted of a functional grid of small lots lining the two main streets.

For the residential areas Miller considered introducing the grouped housing favored by garden city designers, but, after Jemison convinced him to respect local customs, he subdivided the residential area into standard rectangular lots. These were zoned according to cost. The cheapest houses, 1,250 dollars, were relegated to a grid of small lots south of the business district. North of this, the cost of housing rose with the elevation; in the hilliest and most expensive area, the grid turned into a pattern of curving streets and large, irregular lots.[10] Residential zoning, a concept borrowed from expensive suburban developments, was intended to protect the workers' property values, but in the context of the company town, took on less positive connotations. While not as explicitly segregated as housing in early nineteenth-century textile towns, zoning still functioned as an obvious indication of rank within the company.

Miller used landscaping to soften these distinctions, balancing the plan's controlled order with an informal setting. Following garden city practice, he planted each street with a different species of tree, along with shrubs and flowers coordinated by color and growing season. As it curved up the slope through the main residential area, a broad avenue turned into a parkway landscaped with local plants with a pedestrian path running down the center. The parkway linked the town's parks, connecting the formal green surrounding the civic center to a hilltop park that overlooked the town. Recognizing the importance of landscaping to Fairfield's image, Jemison started a city-run nursery to provide the town with plant materials and supply residents with free plants to encourage them to beautify their property.

Intending to make a profit by selling houses and lots, the Jemison Company asked William Leslie Welton to design model homes that would attract working-class buyers. Avoiding the standardized company house, Welton adopted the popular craftsman style as the architectural image for a wide variety of one-story bungalows and two-story duplexes. Walton embellished basic four- and five-room houses with detailing that encompassed the entire range of craftsman decorative features. Protruding eaves and beams, porches, dormers, shingle and wood surfaces differentiated and individualized each dwelling.[11] To ensure that Fairfield would maintain its craftsman image, Miller imposed restrictions on the style and materials of future housing.

Widely popularized through Gustav Stickley's *The Craftsman* magazine, the craftsman aesthetic communicated many of the same values as the picturesque and arts and crafts styles used in Port Sunlight and Letchworth. Many reformers identified its emphasis on natural building materials with rebellion against industrialism and materialism. To others, the simple forms and complex detailing of the craftsman bungalow, heavily laden with nostalgia for pre-industrial times, embodied concepts of stability and democracy.[12] For workers, the craftsman style conveyed flattering associations with upper-middle-class individualism,

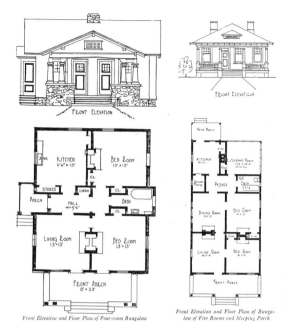

Front Elevation and Floor Plan of Four-room Bungalow

Front Elevation and Floor Plan of Bunga-low of Five Rooms and Sleeping Porch

Two of the many bungalow types used at Fairfield. Although plans are similar, detailing individualized the bungalows, a notable effort to alleviate the monotony and uniformity of company housing.

while, at the same time, its proponents advertised it as a "civilizing influence" on working-class taste and behavior. These associations symbolically counteracted, in the home, the realities of the industrial worker's daily activities in the steel mill. The style's innumerable variations were an obvious antidote to the repetitive nature of the company town.

The beneficial associations of the style had limits, however. Fundamentally domestic, the craftsman aesthetic was difficult to adapt to urban and public uses. This forced Welton to adopt a squared-off classical style for Fairfield's commercial and civic buildings. This not only reduced the town's architectural unity, but was at odds with the informal character of the residential areas. Even the lush greenery Miller recommended could not disguise the bulk of heavy commercial blocks. The town's most popular elements, its craftsman bunga-lows and lavish planting, were suitable only for domestic purposes and could not be adapted to the scale of comprehensive planning. Thus, neither Fairfield's architecture nor planning could provide the town with a unified identity.

Designers using the craftsman style for industrial housing encountered a problem that had little to do with its merits as a style – the aggressive competition of prefabricated build-ing companies. Firms such as the Aladdin Company, Ready-built Homes, the Gordon Van-Tine Company, and Sears, Roebuck and Company had mastered a simplified version of the craftsman style and were mass-producing bungalows at bargain prices. Aware of the growing interest in industrial housing, prefabricated housing suppliers mounted a marketing campaign aimed directly at their main competitors – the architectural profession. Advertising in a trade publication, Aladdin dismissed the "theoretics of professional experts," and boasted that, on the basis of their extensive experience, they could erect an entire town in twenty-six days. Sears' catalogues marketed simple, inexpensive models as industrial housing, claiming that they were "a type of cottage being put up in large numbers by factory or mine owners who furnish their employees with cottages." These houses could be purchased for under 400 dollars, clearly undercutting even the cheapest architect-designed house. As companies began ordering houses by the dozen, firms like Aladdin began to provide plans for complete industrial communities. Organized in simple geometric forms, models such as the deluxe "Sovereign City" could house a population of three thousand in bunk houses or substantial bungalows "suitable for foremen or superintendents."[13]

One of the Aladdin Company's many varieties of inexpensive prefabricated houses, offered as a cheaper and more practical alternative to architect-designed housing. Aladdin advertised its houses as a means of improving the workers' efficiency.

In order to distinguish themselves from commercial competition, architects turned to their most secure professional skill: aesthetics. Focusing on workers' housing, they designed small and inexpensive houses in distinctive architectural styles. They searched for architectural styles with associations, like the craftsman style, that counteracted industrial images. Scaling down proportions, they adapted many of the features that were already standard in middle-class houses to a smaller scale, replanning interior space to improve function and privacy. Other architects began to investigate concrete and other new materials to lower costs and speed up construction. Collaborating with landscape architects and planners, they looked for ways of combining planning, landscape, and architecture to give the company town a new coherence. The garden city was an important source for planning techniques, but earlier English-style company towns such as Bournville, Port Sunlight, and New Earswick provided equally useful models of comprehensive design.

Adopting the theoretical arguments of industrial betterment and housing reform, designers began to synthesize ideology and form into a new rationale for the company towns. They expanded the logic of environmental determinism to the scale of an entire town and, arguing that an improved environment produced better workers, used it to justify the additional expense that professional design required. Applying the rhetoric of industrial betterment, architects and planners asserted that their designs produced improved industrial efficiency. Fairfield's planner, George H. Miller, for example, pronounced that "every feature in such a town is designed to have some constructive influence for specifically benefitting the workman for his work."[14] However, in spite of increasing agreement about the advantages of the professionally designed company town, no consensus about the specific form it should take had emerged.

MODERNIST IMAGES: TORRANCE, CALIFORNIA

A year after Fairfield was started, another equally ambitious industrial town offered an alternative solution using the architectural vocabulary of modernism. As in Fairfield, the impetus for founding the new town of Torrance, California came from continuing labor struggle in the steel industry. In Los Angeles, this struggle took a particularly intense form. Local anti-union forces, led by General Harrison Grey Otis, owner of the *Los Angeles Times*, were determined to keep Los Angeles an open shop town, while union leaders all over the West were equally determined to organize the city's workers. The International Association of Bridge and Structural Iron Workers' strike, in June 1910, escalated the situation. As the conflict intensified, membership in the city's Central Labor Council doubled from six thousand to twelve thousand men, and violence broke out. Two metal trades unionists were arrested for planting dynamite under the Hall of Records construction site where the virulently anti-union Llewellyn Iron Works was working. On 1 October 1910 an explosion destroyed the Los Angeles *Times* building. On Christmas Day, Llewellyn Iron Works was wrecked by another blast. By May 1911, when James and John McNamara and Ortie McManigal, members of the Iron Workers Union, were indicted for the bombings, the case had become a national *cause célèbre*. The union hired Clarence Darrow, America's most famous criminal lawyer, to defend the MacNamaras. Later brought to trial for attempting to bribe jurors in the case, Darrow's summation caught the country's mood:

> The McNamara case came like a thunderclap upon the world. Everybody who sympathized with the corporations believed it was dynamite; everyone who sympathized with the workingman believed something else. There was a direct cleavage in society. Those who hated unions and those who loved them. The fight was growing bitterer day by day. It was a class struggle, filled with all the bitterness and venom born of a class struggle. These two great contending armies were meeting in almost mortal combat. No one could see the end.[15]

Shortly after the *Times* explosion, Llewellyn Iron, the Union Tool Company, and the Pacific Electric Railway, all adamantly anti-union employers, began planning a new town 15 miles southwest of downtown Los Angeles.[16] Describing their decision to leave downtown in the conventional language of industrial location, the companies claimed that decentralization would reduce production costs and improve productivity.[17] Although they did not mention it, relocating would also allow them to escape the city's escalating labor strife and give them the opportunity to renegotiate their relationship with their workers. They named the town Torrance, after Jared Sidney Torrance, a director of the Union Tool Company with a reputation for being civic-minded. The town's sponsors organized Torrance as a completely new type of company town, built by a group of enterprises rather than a single industry. By providing industrial sites and workers' housing, they hoped to attract other manufacturers and create a major industrial district.

From the beginning, Torrance was widely publicized and its sponsors made much of the town's unique attributes. Calling the town "not charity but mighty good business," they stressed its advantages: the absence of paternalism or welfare work, the availability of jobs from different employers, and the benefits of home ownership.[18] In other ways, however, Torrance resembled single-industry company towns. Like Fairfield, it was restricted to skilled labor. Aiming to limit the town's residents to what they called "the better class of workmen," the sponsors explained, "there are some classes of workers of better character than others. Therefore it is desirable to attract the one and discourage the other."[19] Contrary to its advertised claims, Torrance imposed major restrictions on its inhabitants. Like Fairfield, the town was legally segregated. Non-caucasians, barred from renting or buying, could settle only in a "foreign quarter" outside the city limits. The town's charter forbade the sale of liquor in any form and discouraged public loitering.

Professional planning and design were another important selling point. Borrowing the cachet of the English garden city, Torrance's developer, the Dominguez Land Company, promoted the town as "America's first industrial garden city." With great fanfare, they hired Frederick Law Olmsted, Jr, the planner of Forest Hills Gardens, to lay out the new town. The announcement that one of the best-known landscape architects in the country would design Torrance made the front-page of the Los Angeles *Examiner*, which reported that Olmsted would be paid 10,000 dollars for the job.[20] Olmsted was enthusiastic about the town's possibilities. After visiting the 2,000-acre site, the former Dominguez rancho, Olmsted excitedly wrote his partners, "it is a good deal bigger than the Forest Hills job and much more lively."[21] Soon afterwards, he submitted a detailed set of instructions to the developers, listing the new town's economic, technical, physical, and social necessities, and outlining the team of specialists, including planners, a consulting architect, civil engineers, and real estate specialists, he hoped to assemble.[22]

Olmsted's comprehensive plan was similar to Miller's plan of Fairfield. Zoning separated the town into industrial, civic, commercial, and residential districts, segregating the factories at the northeast edge of town, on the far side of the railroad tracks, so that the prevailing winds would blow the noise and smoke away from the rest of the city. Olmsted's plan also resembled Fairfield's in its balance between formal and informal areas. The town center, El Prado, was a symmetrical two and a half block park, lined with civic buildings that terminated at the city hall. A broad boulevard on axis with Mt San Antonio to the east ran through the business district. The residential area was laid out along winding contour streets. Here, the housing was zoned according to price, ranging from 2,500 to 5,000 dollars. Like Miller, Olmsted, concerned with maintaining the town's unity, introduced restrictive deeds to control future building, including a strict design review for all new buildings.[23]

As construction began, the company engineers hired by the Dominguez Land Company increasingly found fault with Olmsted's curvilinear streets, claiming that the irregular lots they produced were impractical and that a rectangular grid subdivision would be more profitable. By the summer of 1912, the difficulties of long-distance supervision from Boston and the hostility of the engineers convinced Olmsted to withdraw from the project. This left the engineers free to replatt Torrance according to their calculations, leaving only a vestige of Olmsted's original plan. Olmsted later complained that the plan was "more or less butchered by the local people."[24] However, before he left California, Olmsted selected San Diego architect Irving Gill as Torrance's consulting architect. While working at the Panama-California Exposition in San Diego, Olmsted had been impressed by Gill's innovative stripped-down interpretation of the Mission style.[25] He also knew of Gill's growing interest in low-cost housing, such as the recently completed Lewis Courts in Sierra Madre, affordable garden apartments designed for blue-collar tenants. However, this was a controversial choice, since Gill's work was highly experimental, both in its simplicity and its regionalism.

In order to establish the new town firmly, the Dominguez Land Company planned to build a core of commercial and industrial buildings and a series of housing prototypes. Addressing the same issue that Weldon had confronted at Fairfield – finding a coherent style to unify the town, Gill proposed a radical answer. His new image for the town was a reductive and abstract style, virtually without ornament, that presented both factories and commercial buildings as pure cubic forms. Only the arched railroad bridge and the domed and colonnaded Pacific Electric depot – both ceremonial entrances to the town – still contained hints of the Hispanic references that had characterized Gill's previous work. Ignoring their diverse functions, Gill applied a vocabulary of austere geometry to factories, hotels, and commercial blocks alike. This undermined Olmsted's careful zoning. His plan had clearly separated the industrial area from the commercial district, while Gill's undifferentiated application of a stark and symbolically functional aesthetic reunited the two areas, accentuating the town's industrial purpose.

A street in Torrance. One of Irving Gill's radically simplified houses is in the foreground; the rest of the street is lined with the bungalows Torrance's residents preferred.

The housing styles were equally reductive. Initially, Gill proposed group houses and gardens. Although this concept had also been developed by Parker and Unwin and other garden city planners, Gill adapted the idea from Mexican architecture, believing that it suited the climate and way of life in southern California. A plan published in *American City* showed five duplex houses grouped around a common court. Instead of a private yard, each unit opened onto a walled patio.[26] Torrance's sponsors refused to build them, claiming that single family houses would attract more buyers. Gill then designed ten small, simple, and economical four-room houses as model homes. Although they were constructed in a conventional technique of plaster over a wooden frame and lath, their undetailed planar surfaces, similar in appearance to Gill's tilt-slab buildings, led many observers to misidentify them as concrete.

These houses incorporated a variety of hygienic and housekeeping innovations. Like Ebenezer Howard and Parker and Unwin, Gill wanted to raise aesthetic standards and improve working-class life. He was especially concerned with the woman's role in the home. According to Gill, a wife "spent ninety percent of her time inside the house." He therefore radically simplified the interiors, eliminating baseboards, beams, and moldings, and used oiled and waxed concrete floors to reduce housework as much as possible.[27] Torrance's prospective residents did not appreciate these efforts. Offered a choice of housing, the working-class buyers quickly rejected Gill's innovative forms. They found their simplicity more suggestive of poverty and austerity than the emancipatory values that Gill intended. Instead, they preferred heavily detailed California bungalows, with their connotations of homeyness, comfort, and individuality.[28]

CONCRETE SOLUTIONS

Although Gill's houses did not appeal to Torrance's working-class homebuyers, other designers continued to pursue the ideal of the simple concrete house as an economical solution for industrial housing.[29] In 1904, Grosvenor Atterbury, the architect of Forest Hills Gardens, began to experiment with precast concrete panels to reduce housing costs. Milton Dana Morrill, a Washington DC architect, developed a more extensive system utilizing panels poured on site. The system was based on reusable steel forms, which could be adjusted for each job. Since costs were reduced each time the mold was reused, Morrill's system was ideal for the serial production of identical company houses. The most extensive demonstration of Morrill's system was a forty-house settlement at Nanticoke, Pennsylvania, built in 1911. Since the housing was for Delaware, Lackawanna and Western Railroad Company employees, Morrill utilized the railroad to speed up the construction process. He laid track in a rectangle, then mounted a mixing plant on a flatcar, followed by other cars laden with sand, cement, and cinders. The train moved from house to house, taking full advantage of the steel formwork to build the houses section by section.[30]

Unlike Gill's stripped-down forms, the straightforward design of the Nanticoke houses, flat-roofed boxes evenly spaced around a rectangular court, did not represent an aesthetic choice, but simply mirrored their efficient industrial production. Morrill's attempts to relieve the boxiness of the houses with canopies over the doors and flower boxes at the windows could not disguise their harsh forms. Builders using the Morrill system often

A model of the concrete houses at Nanticoke, Pennsylvania, designed by Milton Dana Morrill. In spite of their efficiency and economy of construction, concrete walls and flat roofs made concrete houses more practical than beautiful.

recommended planting vines to cover the rough casting.[31] Even favorable observers praised their functional qualities rather than their appearance. Morrill advertised his houses as "germ-proof." One article lauded the Morrill system for being low-maintenance, fireproof, and impervious to the worst abuses of its working-class inhabitants. Another noted approvingly that a bonfire on the living-room floor could do little damage and "the entire house can be literally flushed out with a hose if necessary, making it ideal from a sanitary standpoint."[32]

These virtues encouraged many employers to use concrete for industrial housing, particularly in houses designed for unskilled workers. A 1918 survey of industrial housing projects lists houses built with both monolithic and panel systems at Youngstown, Ohio, Donora, Pennsylvania, Gary, Indiana, Rochester, New York, and Walpole, Massachusetts.[33] The Minneapolis architectural firm of Dean and Dean designed the US Steel town of Morgan Park, Minnesota entirely in concrete. Employing a single material on such a large scale reduced costs enough for the company to provide row houses for unskilled workers. In spite of the town's thoughtful planning and extensive landscaping, the unrelieved use of concrete gave the settlement a grey and grim appearance. Trade journals such as *Concrete, Engineering and Cement World* and companies such as the Atlas Portland Cement Company regularly reviewed industrial housing experiments using concrete, promoting the material for its sanitary nature, durability, and potential for cheaper construction, although the last was not always achieved.[34] In spite of these advantages, concrete dwellings, whether

Morrill's austere blocks or Gill's sophisticated designs, never became part of the architectural vocabulary of the "new" company town. Companies adopting industrial betterment policies were not interested in simply housing their workers, but wanted to convince them of their concern for the quality of their lives. The starkness of concrete, a visible symbol of the economics of industrial efficiency, could not communicate the comforting assurances of welfare capitalism.

CONSENSUS: GOODYEAR HEIGHTS, OHIO

Goodyear Heights, Ohio used the lessons of Fairfield and Torrance to consolidate a new image for the company town. Like Fairfield and Torrance, Goodyear Heights owed its existence to Akron's labor problems. In August 1912, Frank Sieberling, president of Goodyear Tire and Rubber, concerned about a growing housing shortage, bought a tract of land intending to build housing for his workers sometime in the future. The next month, Industrial Workers of the World organizer Elizabeth Gurley Flynn arrived in town. Fresh from victory in Lawrence, she exhorted the rubber workers, "The IWW will lead the war . . . what was done in Lawrence textile mills may be done in Akron rubber shops."[35] Rubber workers in Akron, an open shop town, were ready to be organized. The rubber plants had recently introduced Taylorism, imposing new piecework wages set according to the pace of the fastest worker. To maintain their wages, the other workers had to speed up their pace and work long hours. On 10 February, Firestone tire makers walked out, joined the next day by Goodyear workers. A week later twenty thousand workers were on strike and six thousand had joined the IWW.[36] Sieberling, like other owners, refused to meet with workers, and instead organized local vigilante groups to oppose the strikers. Martial law and vigilante violence finally broke the strike, although a state senate investigation into the causes of the strike acknowledged that the strikers' grievances were justified. Even though the strike was defeated, Sieberling, anticipating future labor problems, decided to start building a new town immediately: this would be Goodyear Heights.[37]

Goodyear Heights followed the pattern that Fairfield and Torrance had established. Looking for an experienced company town planner, Goodyear brought in Boston landscape architect Warren Manning, widely known as an advocate of company-sponsored communities. They also hired the New York architectural firm of Mann and MacNeille, specialists in low-cost housing design. Like Torrance and Fairfield, Goodyear Heights targeted skilled workers who could afford to purchase houses or lots. Manning, like Miller and Olmsted, zoned the town according to the price of the houses and provided restrictive deeds that established minimum house prices, controlled future architectural and landscape development, and prohibited unsightly additions such as fences and garages. Limiting commercial development and prohibiting the sale of alcohol further guaranteed Goodyear Heights' appeal to upwardly mobile workers and their families.

However, unlike the developers of Fairfield and Torrance, Goodyear was not interested in selling houses and lots to make a profit. This gave Manning the freedom to plan Goodyear Heights as a harmonious garden village. He emphasized the community's physical and symbolic distance from the Goodyear plant, a quarter mile away, by building a concrete bridge over the railroad tracks that passed in front of the town. The main street, Goodyear Avenue, on axis with the bridge, led from this dramatic entrance to a town square surrounded by shops, apartments, churches, and a dormitory for women workers.[38] An alternative to Fairfield and Torrance's gridded downtowns, the square provided a physical and social focus for the town, invoking the symbolism of the American town square. The rest of the town was planned informally, following garden city precedents. The street pattern, adapted to the sloping site, combined long straight blocks along the lower boundary with gently curving roads that sloped up the hillside to a reservoir park overlooking Akron's city center, two miles away. Small irregular parks and large stands of existing trees broke up the loose grid of streets. Planting reinforced the image of the garden. Each street was lined with a different shade tree with smaller trees planted in between and each lot came with fruit trees, a grape-arbor, and ornamental plants.[39]

Goodyear Heights offered workers a choice of housing styles. In order to determine which house types the employees preferred, the architects Mann and MacNeille designed ten different styles of five- and six-room houses, priced between 2,000 and 3,000 dollars. The most popular were simple but spacious two-story frame houses. Rather than proposing any new design ideas, the houses resembled contemporary middle-class dwellings. Goodyear sold these houses at cost. Still unwilling to relinquish control completely, they tried to protect their investment by imposing complex financing arrangements designed to eliminate speculation. Mortgage payments for the first five years were based on market values; if the buyer was still employed after five years, the company would reduce payments by 25 percent. Workers could also buy life insurance that would pay off the mortgage in the event of their death.[40]

Comprehensively planned, with housing tailored to the tastes of its working-class residents, Goodyear Heights established a new standard for company town design. Although still largely dependent on English garden city design techniques, the town square at the center of the settlement suggested the possibilities of historic American forms as a source of new imagery. In an article published in *American City*, "A Step Towards Solving the Industrial Housing Problem," Manning described Goodyear Heights' achievements while acknowledging its limitations. As the title suggests, he saw Goodyear Heights as only the first

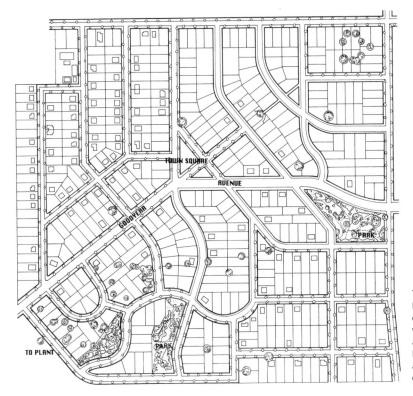

The plan of Goodyear Heights by Warren Manning, 1913. A clear and coherent plan in which the town is entered across a bridge at the lower left. A broad avenue leads to a public square of shops and churches.

step in solving a much larger problem. Towns such as Fairfield and Torrance revealed that high costs limited professional planning and design to the highest paid workers; architects were still not able to design houses that unskilled workers could afford. Dissatisfied with the conventional nature of the housing offered to workers, Manning, like Howard, Unwin, and Gill, wanted to investigate new methods of construction, new forms of housing, and new ways of life. Inspired by the social and design experimentation taking place in English garden cities, he called on the sponsors of industrial housing to break away from established precedents and expand the possibilities of the company town.[41]

Graham Taylor's important book, *Satellite Cities*, published in 1914, echoed Manning's conclusions, but placed them in a broader economic and political context. Taylor, an economist and editor of *The Survey*, was in touch with both Progressive reformers and the growing number of architects and planners interested in industrial communities. Evaluating the evolution of "satellite cities" from Pullman to Torrance, Fairfield, and Goodyear Heights, Taylor concluded that industrial decentralization was irreversible, but that, without proper management, uncontrolled suburban development would inevitably recreate the political, social, and physical problems of the cities it was replacing. Praising the skills of "scientific" city planners, who "have the problem in hand," Taylor called on housing reformers, industrialists, and Progressive public officials to sponsor new satellite cities that would "combine living and livelihood" in innovative ways.[42]

In the final chapter of his book, Taylor surveyed well-known architects, city planners, housing reformers, and Progressive businessmen, asking them how to bring new industrial satellite cities into being. Although all agreed on the necessity of new settlements, two distinct positions on their ownership emerged. Many, like Taylor himself, argued that new industrial settlements should be based on "co-partnership," the cooperative form of ownership used in the English garden cities, with land and houses held in common by a cooperative organization. In addition to encouraging comprehensive planning, Taylor felt that co-partnership would give workers a sense of ownership without tying them down. This would finally resolve the contradiction between democracy and improved living conditions that had always plagued company towns. Another group felt that the employers' involvement was still necessary. Their spokesman, Flavell Shurtleff, secretary of the National Conference on City Planning, asserted that to create new towns, "we must continue to depend on the enthusiastic cooperation of industrial managers."[43]

Shurtleff's assessment proved to be correct, but, once again, changes in the labor market provided the impetus for the cooperation of industrial employers. In 1914, the outbreak of war in Europe exacerbated the labor shortage. The increase in demand for American products stimulated an economic boom that promised unprecedented profits for American industries. Expanding productive capacity, however, depended on the availability of workers, and the war in Europe simultaneously cut off the supply of immigrant labor. The result was a serious labor shortage. The situation gave already militant workers an even greater sense of power, and they joined unions in ever larger numbers. Hoping to divert workers from unionization, employers expanded welfare programs even further. The booming economy provided profits for increasingly elaborate programs.[44] As factories grew, serious housing shortages developed. Wages increased, but the cost of living spiraled out of control. Providing adequate housing became an even more important means of attracting scarce labor. Now firmly in the hands of professionals, the "new" company town promised to solve these problems.

PART II

DESIGNING THE "NEW" COMPANY TOWN

6

AMERICANIZING THE GARDEN CITY: GROSVENOR ATTERBURY AND INDIAN HILL

Built in 1915, the industrial suburb of Indian Hill, Worcester, Massachusetts was the first full-fledged example of the "new" company town. Sponsored by the Norton Company and designed by Grosvenor Atterbury, Indian Hill marked a turning point in the design of company towns. In an effort to deflect unionism, the Norton Company, pioneers in corporate attempts to modernize industrial life, created Indian Hill as a showcase for the company's comprehensive welfare work and personnel policies. Atterbury, a gifted designer with extensive practical experience in low-income housing, exceeded their expectations by transforming the company town's image. Synthesizing picturesque imagery, colonial revival architecture, and garden city planning into an expressive design vocabulary, he invented an identity for Indian Hill: a charming New England village with cozy colonial cottages, tree-lined streets, and a town square. Signifying stability, domesticity, and traditional American values, Indian Hill simulated community in order to encourage social harmony and industrial peace. To employers, Indian Hill's sophisticated planning supported the design profession's claims that aesthetics not only enhanced but expanded the social and economic goals of welfare capitalism. To designers, Indian Hill's picturesque architecture and planning, rivaling the best English and European garden suburbs, opened up new aesthetic possibilities in the design of company towns. Combining comprehensive planning with appropriate imagery, designers could produce a complete, if fictional, environment, that, like the picturesque English villages, offered an alternative to the troubled industrial landscape.

THE NORTON COMPANY

By 1915, events in Worcester had made industrial peace one of Norton's major concerns. The year began with labor struggles, and, by the spring, Worcester's skilled machinists and metalworkers initiated a city-wide campaign for higher wages and shorter hours. Encouraged by union organizers, workers at Norton Grinding joined the struggle. Although some of Worcester's metal trade shops were unionized, Norton was violently opposed to any collective activity. Company director George Alden, president of the local open-shop organization, the Employers Association of Worcester, warned that Norton did "not propose to allow . . . any outside person or interest to interfere with its business, tell us how to run it, or interfere with our honest endeavor to have a happy working family of all of us employed by this company."[1]

In October, even before the workers made a decision to strike, Norton forced a confrontation. The company demanded that each worker sign a card pledging "not to strike or in other ways injure the Norton Grinding Company." When more than three hundred workers refused to sign, the company locked them out. The company ignored the ensuing strike. By recruiting workers from nearby towns to replace the strikers, the plant continued to operate at full capacity. Months later, the strike spluttered to a halt. Although more than three thousand Worcester workers had walked out, they were no match for the powerful Metal Trades Organization.[2] The Massachusetts Board of Conciliation and Arbitration found Norton guilty of discouraging unions, but the company refused to abandon its anti-union policies. Isolated incidents of protest and unrest continued. Norton's turnover rates, once negligible, ran as high as 90 to 158 percent. The firm responded by carefully monitoring discontent and weeding out potential protesters. The Employment Department kept records of malcontents and possible subversives, reported by foremen, and punished efforts to organize with immediate dismissal.[3]

During the same year, Norton's directors had been quietly exploring the possibilities of providing housing for their workers. After meeting with Grosvenor Atterbury, they expanded their ideas and commissioned a plan for a complete settlement. In April 1915, with much fanfare, the company presented its plans for an elaborate new company town, to be called Indian Hill. Announcing the program to its workers, the company did not mention their labor problems but framed their intentions within the conventions of industrial betterment. Claiming "enlightened self-interest," their stated aim was

> to make it easy for the . . . more progressive workmen to obtain for themselves homes of taste and convenience, likely to make the employee happy and contented with his personal work, to improve his taste, stimulate his ambition [and] lead him to assume without terror some of the responsibilities which fall upon men of all stations of life.[4]

Like Fairfield, Torrance, and Goodyear Heights, Indian Hill was intended for the top rank of blue-collar employees: foremen, machinists, and other highly skilled workers.

By emphasizing the lack of any practical need for a new settlement, Clifford Anderson, the company attorney, reiterated the company's claims of disinterest. Asserting that Norton had no difficulties in hiring labor from the "pool of workmen who are continuously attracted to the city," Anderson went on to describe Worcester as a city "without slums" where workers could easily find adequate and affordable housing.[5] In fact, however, in addition to labor unrest, Norton was facing a growing labor shortage. The company's rapid expansion, increasing competition from other Worcester machine industries, and a decline in immigration together had reduced the company's usual sources of labor. In the absence of a real need for housing, Norton intended to use home ownership as a method of attracting a new group of stable employees, both as a reward for loyal service to the firm and as a tangible demonstration of what the company could offer its employees, in contrast to the dubious rewards of union membership.

THE NORTON "SPIRIT"

Providing housing for its workers was a logical extension of Norton's management style. Norton specialized in manufacturing abrasives, and, through its subsidiary, Norton Grinding, machine tools. Founded in 1885, Norton had transformed itself from a traditional New England family firm into a modern corporation. By 1915, the firm was in the vanguard of American science-based industries. Operating with an inclusive style of management, Norton's directors adopted both scientific management and welfare capitalism while searching for other management strategies that would help to modernize production. In a field that demanded constant technical innovations, Norton was one of a small group of science-based industries that rapidly incorporated the most advanced corporate methods developed during this period. Two of the firm's four founding directors, George Alden and Milton Higgins, both mechanical engineers, constantly pushed for technical and managerial innovation.[6]

Without abandoning family ownership and management, from 1910 to 1920 Norton grew from a small shop into a multi-unit and multinational corporation dominating abrasives production. The firm aggressively pursued integration and diversification. Although it operated plants in Arkansas, Germany, and Canada, Norton's management focused most of its attention on its Worcester headquarters, where it employed 3,500 men and women. The firm pursued methods of improving productivity with equal zeal. Early advocates of scientific management, in 1914 the directors brought in a team of efficiency experts from

Western Electric, a leading scientific management firm, to reorganize Norton and Norton Grinding's production tasks. In spite of the workers' strenuous objections, they instituted incentive methods based on piecework. The company created new "Methods" and "Planning" Departments to supervise and continually improve production techniques.[7] The next year, Norton became one of the first firms to establish an Employment Department. Instead of leaving hiring decisions in the foremen's hands, Norton's management centralized personnel functions under the direction of a mechanical engineer. Equally prescient in recognizing the value of public relations, the firm created a professional publicity department, directed by a young New York copywriter who supervised Norton's house journal, *Grits and Grinds*, which celebrated Norton's achievements to the trade.[8] Like other science-based industries, Higgins and Alden also instituted a Research and Development Department. The firm opened its first laboratory in 1889, and in 1912 hired a leading ceramics engineer to systematize testing procedures and product development.[9]

While serving as Norton's president, Higgins expanded his interest in industrial development beyond the boundaries of the firm. Already a pioneer in trade school education – he had helped found Worcester Polytechnic Institute, an early industry-sponsored engineering school – he advocated restructuring the American educational system to respond to corporate needs. In 1907, he became the first president of the National Society for the Promotion of Industrial Education (NSPIE), an organization devoted to incorporating industrial training into public and private education. On a practical level, industrial education programs supplied firms with trained and socialized employees, but, like scientific management and welfare capitalism, they also led toward the larger goal of a more efficient and stable society. Higgins, like other NSPIE members who served on city and state school boards, exerted a considerable influence on public education. In spite of objections from educators who felt that vocational education imposed social and intellectual restrictions on working-class youth, Massachusetts, encouraged by Higgins, became the first state to institute comprehensive vocational education for all children between the ages of fourteen and sixteen. This introduced students to the basic principles of manual and manufacturing trades.[10]

Norton was also in the vanguard of welfare capitalism. Deeply involved in paternalism since its founding, the company's welfare programs changed with the times. The earliest programs had developed from the New England paternalist traditions of such Worcester institutions as Mechanics' Hall, founded by local philanthropists in 1857 to "educate and improve" artisans by lectures and reading. Director John Jeppson, a Swedish immigrant who had started as a skilled worker, expanded these activities to include the large number of Swedes employed by the firm. Serving as a father figure to his fellow Swedes, he helped them with citizenship papers, language problems, and cultural adjustment. By 1900, Jeppson had established a Mutual Benefit Society and enthusiastically organized company social events, such as Christmas Eve dinners that blended Swedish and New England customs, and the annual company excursion, which took place on Swedish midsummer day. By 1902, Norton's paternalism was so extensive that the social work journal *World's Work* singled out the company as an outstanding example of employer concern.[11]

Welfare work was an important element of Norton's strategy to avoid labor organization. In 1901, when the Worcester Central Labor Union had attempted to establish a union at Norton, management condemned the organization and fired several workers for their union activities.[12] The Swedish workers backed up the company's decision and refused to participate. Although Norton continued to cultivate the loyalty of its Swedish workers, the second generation of owner-managers, Aldus Higgins and George Jeppson, replaced John Jeppson's ad hoc activities with modern welfare methods. Reorganizing their programs around the guiding concept of the "Norton Spirit," they redefined their relationship with their employees in "a spirit of co-operation and enthusiasm which inspires everyone to do their utmost on behalf of the Norton interests."[13] Like other corporate liberal firms, Norton, recognizing the crucial links between labor relations, technical development, and productivity, used the "Norton Spirit" to convince workers that the company was a community rather than a workplace. In 1912, Aldus Higgins claimed that "improved plant operations can only be handled successfully through the creation of a real, living, breathing, sympathetic and broadminded spirit – a spirit that is bringing employers and employees closer together every day." The plant newspaper, the *Norton Spirit*, reinforced this ethos, reporting social events, marriages, births, and deaths among workers and managers, offering household hints and constantly reiterating the theme of mutual interest. Employees paraded on holidays carrying the Norton banner, athletes on company teams wore the Norton letter "N," and veteran workers celebrated the anniversaries of ten, fifteen, and twenty-five years on the job with company banquets and medals.[14]

The company offered its workers a full array of welfare activities. These included programs focusing on health, such as the well-equipped company hospital, visiting nurses, and preventive medicine, factory safety and sanitation programs, improvements in factory conditions such as employee dining rooms and cafeterias, and financial benefits such as paid vacations, a credit union, and pension programs. Norton added its own innovative education and recreation programs. Milton Higgins supervised the firm's industrial education and apprenticeship programs. The Education Department offered introductory classes in technical subjects, advised workers about educational possibilities, and rewarded particularly promising employees and their children with scholarships to Worcester Polytechnic. The Recreation Department also offered a wide range of activities: company sports included baseball, soccer, track, rowing, swimming, volleyball, tennis, basketball, and

Norton Company employees parading to open the company folk fest and family outing in 1916. One of the numerous examples of the activities, organizations, and services that Norton provided for their workers in order to foster the "Norton spirit." Courtesy of the Worcester Historical Museum.

trap-shooting; there were clubs for dancing, gardening, photography, and stamp-collecting; in the summer, Norton families flocked to Norton Beach on Indian Lake and Norton Bathhouse on Lake Quinsiganara for swimming and evening outings.[15]

In 1918 all these programs were organized into the Service Department, headed by the company physician, W. Irving Clark. However, recognizing their importance to the company, George Jeppson continued to direct the firm's labor relations and welfare programs in person. Educational programs trained a steady supply of skilled workers to operate and maintain complex machinery, visiting nurses reduced absenteeism, periodic check-ups, preventive medicine, and warnings about smoking, drinking, and late hours reduced accident rates and improved workers' health and efficiency, while medical examinations screened unfit workers as well as identifying their physical capacities for various tasks. Even clubs and recreation contributed to productivity. Clubs reinforced an ethos of self-improvement, and, according to one company official, "healthful, happy play is fundamental in any community that wants to achieve industrial efficiency and social happiness." George Jeppson saw recreation as an opportunity for management to make "healthy contact" with the workers outside of work. This, he hoped, would not only help foremen and other supervisors understand their workers better, but also serve as a "steadying influence" on the workers.[16]

The new settlement at Indian Hill would extend the "Norton Spirit" even further.

Intending to create a model community, the company offered employees the possibility of becoming part of the middle class. This would serve as a visible example to the rest of the workers, demonstrating the rewards that thrift and ambition could bring. According to Clifford Anderson, the community would

> furnish tangible evidence of the thoroughly satisfactory and worth-while things of life which may be secured by diligence and industry, stimulating in them a desire to make themselves more useful, to improve their conditions of living, and to so win for themselves and for their families a bigger share of the truly good things of life.[17]

Thus Indian Hill was addressed not only to the small number of skilled workers who would actually live there, but also to the aspirations of unskilled employees, encouraging them to persevere so that one day they too could achieve this goal. In exchange for loyalty and dependability, Norton would provide at least some of their employees with an ideal living environment.

THE NEW YORK ARCHITECT

To design their model village, Norton hired Grosvenor Atterbury, a prominent architect and well-known designer of model housing. Atturbury's fame reassured Norton's directors, always respectful of specialized expertise. Norton publicity always referred to Atterbury as "the famous New York architect." Atterbury, at forty-six, had made a name for himself as a versatile designer in a range of eclectic styles. A product of New York's upper class, Atterbury graduated from Yale, then studied architecture at Columbia University and the Ecole des Beaux Arts before starting his career in the office of McKim, Mead, and White. Atterbury followed that firm's lead in producing classically correct urban and institutional buildings while perfecting an informal and picturesque design mode for rambling country houses.[18] Atterbury's social contacts provided him with a steady stream of wealthy clients for residential projects, including Norton director Aldus Higgins, who commissioned the architect to design an elaborate English Tudor house in Worcester for his family.[19]

More than just a successful designer, Atterbury was deeply involved in the housing reform and planning movement in New York. A member of Lawrence Veiller's Tenement House Committee and a charter member of the National Housing Association, Atterbury shared Veiller's conservative approach to housing reform. An active supporter of the philanthropic housing movement, Atterbury had designed several innovative housing projects. In 1906, the steel magnate Henry Phipps commissioned him to design the first group of Phipps Tenements and, in 1913, he designed the Rogers Model Dwellings. Unlike many philanthropic housing advocates who felt, like E.R.L. Gould, that model housing should not be "too attractive," Atterbury emphasized the importance of design. His housing designs went beyond minimum standards of sanitation and economy, offering their low-income tenants attractive settings and more amenities than usual. Atterbury organized both the Phipps Houses and the Rogers Dwellings around open courtyards and incorporated public spaces such as reading rooms, roof gardens, and playgrounds. Classical detailing, roof-top loggias, and high quality construction made the buildings indistinguishable from middle-class apartment houses. In spite of these successful projects, like most housing reformers Atterbury supported decentralization as the ultimate solution to urban housing problems.[20]

Through his reform activities, Atterbury had formed close contacts with the Russell Sage Foundation. This made him a logical choice as the architect of the new Sage garden suburb at Forest Hills, along with Frederick Law Olmsted, Jr, another active reformer. Their design accounts for Forest Hills' immediate success as a desirable suburb. The tightly composed ensemble of buildings reflected the urban design lessons of the Austrian architect Camillo Sitte, transmitted through Parker and Unwin's designs for Hampstead Garden Suburb and Unwin's recent book, *Town Planning in Practice*, the first comprehensive treatment of

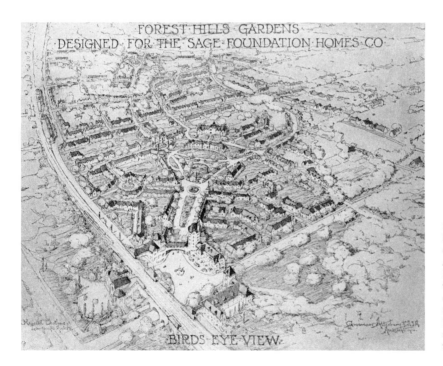

Bird's eye view of Forest Hills Gardens designed by Grosvenor Atterbury and Frederick Law Olmsted, Jr. From the tight urban enclosure of Station Square, the plan moves in a carefully calculated sequence from urban to rural.

Sitte's work in English. Adopting Sitte's technique of defining irregular spatial enclosures by ensembles of buildings, Atterbury and Olmsted orchestrated a sequence of scenographic spaces that created a metaphorical journey from urban to rural. This began at the enclosed space of Station Square, then moved through a village green defined by continuous row houses, to culminate in the open fields of Forest Park. Atterbury's picturesque, loosely Germanic–Tudor architecture, exemplified by the fantastic half-timbered medieval tower and brick arcades of Station Square, worked perfectly with Olmsted's calculated street pictures to create a highly theatrical environment. Like the English picturesque villages, Forest Hills Gardens was a newly created old place. Its vague medieval associations – one writer compared it to "a college or cathedral city" – offered suburban commuters an escape from modern life, only minutes from Manhattan.[21]

Atterbury's work at Forest Hills Gardens confirmed his skill as an architectural designer, and, in spite of its failure as a social experiment, enhanced his reputation as a reformer. In 1912, Atterbury tackled the social, economic, and aesthetic problems of building suburban settlements for the working class in an article, "Model Towns in America," published in the popular journal, *Scribner's*. Citing by now familiar arguments for suburban resettlement and improved living conditions for workers, Atterbury, like other progressives, advocated a middle ground, calling for a distinctly American type of model town that would be neither paternalistic nor socialistic, unlike European state-sponsored housing programs, of which he thoroughly disapproved. However, Atterbury's main interest was in urban design issues, "the science and art of town-planning."[22] Using model New England company towns such as Hopedale and Whitinsville as examples of "harmony and charm" that had evolved over time, he outlined techniques for comprehensive planning and what he called "collective design" that could produce the same sense of unity in new settlements. Atterbury proposed innovative block layouts like those he had designed for Forest Hills. Influenced by garden city courts and cul-de-sacs, Atterbury reconfigured standard blocks of single family houses, grouping houses around common gardens or clustering lots to create parks in the interior of the blocks.

INDIAN HILL VILLAGE

Atterbury hoped to take comprehensive planning even further at Indian Hill. Although he had previously expressed reservations about paternalism, the Norton Company's modernized welfare programs met with his approval. Already experienced in negotiating with philanthropic sponsors to improve design standards in low-income housing, Atterbury intended to use the commission as an opportunity to reinvent the company town.

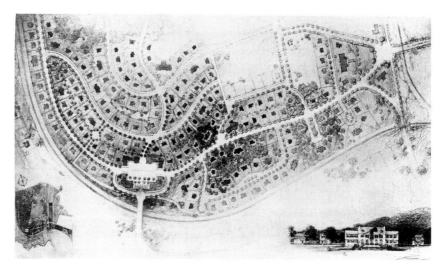

Plan of Indian Hill. Anchored by formally composed entrances to the south and east, the street plan forms a loose grid that moves across the slope of the hill. The first houses were built on the right hand side of the plan. Atterbury elaborated the street plan with cul-de-sacs, landscaped islands, and footpaths, which lead into parks within the blocks. The plan is organized around two entrances: the main entrance is a long bridge from Holden Street, halfway up the hill, while a second bridge at the eastern edge of the hills crosses the Norton plant to the east. These function as the "front and back doors" to the settlement. The first presents a formal and public face to the town, while the second provides the daily route to work.

Confident in Atterbury's abilities, Norton accepted his suggestions for the project's financial and social organization and left Indian Hill's design completely in his hands. Indian Hill was a tiny settlement – only 150 lots were initially planned – but Atterbury imbued it with a complex and distinctive identity. Like Forest Hills, Indian Hill was a sophisticated effort to simulate community. Drawing on an eclectic set of sources and influences that ranged from New England company towns and picturesque colonial cottages to English and German garden city designs, Atterbury invented a newly Americanized image for the company town, expressed through specific techniques of site planning, urban design, and architecture.

Indian Hill was to be built on a steep, wooded site to the west of the Norton plant on the outskirts of Worcester, where the Norton Company had bought a 116-acre plot overlooking Indian Lake. Atterbury's first decision was to locate the settlement on the southwest slope of the hill, literally turning its back on the plant, which was barely visible in the distance. Although near Norton recreation facilities, its steep elevation and a deep cut for the Boston and Maine railroad tracks isolated the site from the rest of the company property. Streetcar lines at the foot of the hill connected the area to the rest of Worcester. The site's location and its distance from "Greendale," the community on the far side of the plant where many Norton workers lived, clearly indicated the distinctive role the new community was to play in the company. Physically isolated from both the industrial activities of the Norton plant and the workers' culture of Greendale, from its beginning Indian Hill declared its separate identity.

The earliest site plan, of April 1915, established Indian Hill's basic features. Acting as both architect and planner, Atterbury adopted many of the ideas Unwin described in *Town Planning in Practice* as well as the techniques Olmsted had introduced at Forest Hills Gardens, adapting them to a far steeper site and a much smaller scale. Taking advantage of the steep hill, Atterbury planned a bridge as the entrance to the settlement. The bridge, the formal entry into the town, follows Parker and Unwin's rule of delineating strong boundaries as a way of defining the identity of a settlement. As at Goodyear Heights, this worked to separate the town definitively from its surroundings. Like Forest Hills Gardens, circulation organized the plan, with roads structuring a sequential passage through the town. After crossing the bridge the main road divides and winds up the hill to meet again at the town square, which is set on the shoulder of the hill on axis with the bridge. The town square, a formal and symmetrical enclosure framed by four identical buildings, was the focus of the community. As Camillo Sitte specified, the square provided a sense of defined and enclosed space, reinforced by a colonnaded terrace with a carefully designed vista framing views of the bridge and Indian Lake below.[23]

Radiating out from the formal town center, Indian Hill's residential streets meander informally across the hillside, establishing a strong contrast between formal and informal – another Unwin maxim. The steep slope of the hill necessitated a long, loose grid of parallel streets running east–west across the side of the hill with few cross-connections. Atterbury employed numerous garden city site planning devices to vary the basic street pattern. Road widths vary according to function, with a few broad thoroughfares alternating with much narrower side streets. A separate network of pedestrian footpaths cut through the middle of the long blocks to provide direct routes down the hill, leading, along the way, into small landscaped parks enclosed in the interior of the blocks. Irregular intersections, streets terminating in cul-de-sacs, landscaped islands, and parks with cut-off corners added to the variety. The locations of the houses on the lots alternate, with one house facing the street and the next perpendicular to it. Atterbury carefully adjusted the curve of the roads to the hilly topography, composing street pictures that framed views of Indian Lake below. At the east end of the site, two lots, intended for large boarding houses, define a second, less formal square. From here, an elevated footbridge leads across the railroad tracks to the plant. The northern part of the plan is incomplete, so that streets could be extended as the town grew.

"AS IN THE CHARMING VILLAGE OF WHITINSVILLE"

Atterbury overlaid the site plan with a self-consciously "American" urban design image, analogous to Parker and Unwin's English cottage vernacular. An increasing national emphasis on "Americanization" made Forest Hills' Germanic imagery less appropriate than it had been only five years earlier. Americanization – a reform movement whose goals paralleled and often combined with welfare work – was becoming an important social force. Aimed at counteracting the changes brought about by mass immigration and the industrialization of cities, the campaign to assimilate the immigrant became part of employers' efforts to acquire and retain an adequate labor supply. Employers arranged English lessons, classes in citizenship, American history and civics, and preparation for naturalization to encourage immigrant workers to become "good" Americans.[24] Cultural Americanization took the form of a self-conscious mythification of the Anglo-Saxon and colonial heritage. Simulating the architectural styles of the colonial period allowed industrial managers to affirm their allegiance to pre-industrial cultural values and simultaneously repress the multicultural social reality on which the industrial economy depended. Searching for a regional source for an earlier American urban identity, Atterbury discovered the nearby company town of Whitinsville, only 15 miles south of Worcester, which, he thought, "provided a picture of considerable architectural harmony and charm."[25] Whitinsville's identical white clapboard houses, evenly spaced along tree-lined streets, recalled the early nineteenth-century villages of southern New England, although the town was actually begun after the Civil War. Atterbury condensed Whitinsville's visual qualities into a single image: "white walls seen among the trees, roofs, grey-green to unify the composition."[26]

Atterbury adopted this visual image as a unifying device, subordinating the individual houses to the larger theme of the town. Convinced that "only by this and similar evidence of collective design can there be produced dignity and carrying power in an aggregation of which the units, taken singly, must be too small or too insignificant to be effective," he used a single roofing material, grey-green slate, and a single color, white, for wall surfaces.[27] As at Forest Hills, collective design produced a highly coherent image. The consistent use of a roofing material was a basic tenet of garden city urban design. According to Raymond Unwin, "by keeping to tile roofs, a unity of effect is produced which in no other way could be so easily or completely attained."[28] Charles May, describing Indian Hill in an early article, associated the white-painted surfaces with the New England tradition and claimed that white, unlike other colors, can be repeated in a great number of cases without becoming tiresome, "as in the delightful village of Whitinsville."[29] Landscaping completed the image. Indian Hill's streets would be lined with shade trees, framing the white walls of the houses with greenery.

"O'ERTWINED BY CLINGING VINES"

If Atterbury hoped to pursue the principle of collective design in his housing designs, he encountered a series of obstacles. First of all, the Norton Company imposed strict cost guidelines. Although the company did not intend to make a profit on Indian Hill, it was unwilling to subsidize any additional costs. Since Indian Hill's housing was directed at a specific strata of workers, prices had to match their budgets. However, Atterbury's experience in philanthropic housing had trained him to maximize design with limited funds. Interested in new forms of housing, he proposed innovative schemes for group housing and lot division similar to his designs for Forest Hills Gardens. In his first presentation to the Norton Company's workers, Atterbury promoted group housing for its economic and aesthetic advantages. He argued that group houses, already popular in English and German garden cities, offered far more architectural flexibility and more interesting urban design possibilities than blocks of single family houses on separate lots. He also stressed the economic rationality of group houses, which were far cheaper to build than single family houses. The money saved by excavating one hole and building one foundation, fireplace wall, and back wall instead of two made it possible to provide more and larger rooms. Grouping houses would also produce more open space and larger lawns.[30]

The architect's arguments failed to convince Norton's workers. Presenting a semi-detached, two family house he had designed for Indian Hill, he met opposition. Objecting to group houses, which they associated with urban slums, and concerned about the lack of clear property boundaries in the common gardens, Norton's employees made it clear that they preferred standard single family dwellings. Whatever their architectural advantages, multiple units did not accord with the workers' concept of "home." Only two double houses were ever built at Indian Hill, and the company brochure describes these as being "principally for architectural effect."[31]

In spite of such limitations, Atterbury's housing designs added yet another level of meaning to Indian Hill, a comforting and convincing image of "home." Although a puzzled *Norton Spirit* writer described the style of the houses as "a modification of the bungalow type of house, not very often seen in Worcester," a more accurate characterization might be a colonial revival cottage.[32] The colonial revival style, increasingly popular since the 1876 Centennial Exhibition, provided an appropriate cultural symbol for a New England village intended to reinforce "American" values. At a time when rapid social changes were altering living and working conditions in Worcester, the use of colonial styles conjured up reassuring images of New England's tightly knit communities.[33] To suggest even earlier local roots Norton changed the site's original name – Mt Ararat – to Indian Hill and borrowed street names, such as Nashoba and Sautucket, from Worcester's Indian history.[34]

· SINGLE·FAMILY ·
· DWELLING ·
· 6·ROOMS·AND·BATH ·
· SALE PRICE $3285 ·

Grosvenor Atterbury
Jr. A.

· SECOND·FLOOR ·

· FIRST·FLOOR ·

The single-family cottage was Indian Hill's basic housing type. Atterbury developed six sub-types, with five, six, or seven rooms. The houses all had two floors – the upper floor was concealed behind a pitched roof with dormer windows – an attic, full basement, and at least one porch. Solidly constructed, using the highest quality materials available, including brass piping and copper flashing, they also included up-to-date amenities such as steam heating, gas, and modern appliances and plumbing. Prices ranged from 2,800 to 3,500 dollars.

Still maintaining a colonial theme, Atterbury replaced the reductive forms of Whitinsville's housing with a less regionally correct variation of the colonial revival style – the Dutch colonial. Unlike Whitinsville's boxy colonial houses, with their suggestion of industrial austerity, Dutch colonial lent itself to the intensely detailed surfaces Atterbury preferred. Its most distinctive element, a gambrel roof with dormers, suggested a cottage rather than a dignified Georgian revival house. If colonial styles symbolized the stability of an established social order, the cottage served as an equally powerful symbol of domesticity, associated with coziness and family life. Atterbury also used detailing to individualize several standard models. Buyers could select houses with steeply pitched gable or gambrel roofs; with fieldstone or brick basements; with different types of porches and entries added on to or cut into the house. The houses could be clad in stucco, clapboard, shingles, or various combinations of these materials.

These details gave Indian Hill a romantic and picturesque quality not usually associated with the colonial revival style, but recalling the cozy cottages of Port Sunlight and New Earswick. The architect's pencil sketches emphasize this by reducing the scale of the houses and breaking up the severity of the white walls. Exaggerating the textured surfaces of the slate shingles, clapboard and shingle siding, shutters, and latticework trellises, and adding details such as white picket fences, quaint street lamps, and signposts, Atterbury suggested

A typical street scene in Indian Hill. Careful planning, picturesque architecture, and extensive landscaping produced a convincing image of a stable New England community.

what one observer called "the domesticity, intimacy, and hint of aloofness that belong rightly to cottage surroundings."[35] Surrounded by flowering shrubs and covered with "the plentiful use of ivy or some other form of climbing vine," the drawings illustrate a storybook version of an idyllic cottage. In its wooded setting far above the busy Norton shops, Indian Hill was to be the antithesis of "industrial housing." The company, recognizing the value of this compelling image, adopted it to promote the project. Even the normally staid *Norton Spirit* became poetic when it described the houses as: "cozy and attractive . . . backed by tall trees, surrounded by a green well-kept lawn, and o'ertwined by clinging vines which give [them] the quaint air that lends distinction to what would otherwise be commonplace."[36]

The Norton Company took pains to guarantee that Indian Hill's unity and homelike character would be more than just a design image. They attempted to create a model community. The shops that surrounded the town square would allow the community to be self-sufficient. In addition to the public space of the square itself, Atterbury designed a large building for community gatherings. The company set aside nearby lots for schools and churches. The Sautucket Inn, described as an "exalted boarding house for bachelors embodying the features of a club," a similar institution for the "bachelor girls of the office force," and a communal dining hall would incorporate single workers into the community.[37] Designated for office workers, the boarding facilities emphasized the community's middle-class aspirations by providing institutional alternatives to what housing reformers and welfare workers usually referred to as "the boarding evil." Taking in boarders was a common practice in many working-class households and the large size of Indian Hill houses invited boarding. Considering "promiscuous mixing" between boarders and the family to be dangerous to wholesome family life, Norton had already taken advantage of the YMCA industrial welfare department's supervised living arrangements for single workers by funding a YMCA dormitory for male members of their staff.[38] The Indian Hill facilities would ensure that boarding would not tarnish the community's model character.

Although many of Indian Hill's residents were already active in Norton recreational and educational programs, the company planned new leisure and athletic facilities that would equip the new community at Indian Hill at a level previously unknown in company towns. They cleared a wooded area at the top of the hill to serve as a picnic area and planned to build a sports arena containing a baseball diamond, running track, and other athletic facilities into a natural amphitheater on the side of the hill. At the bottom of the hill a winding drive would follow the lake shore leading to a boating and swimming beach. The parks within Indian Hill's blocks would become supervised playgrounds for neighborhood children, and natural springs on the hill would be diverted to form small bathing pools.[39] To encourage gardening, the Norton Agricultural Society assigned residents large garden plots on the hill. The community hall in the town square would present regular programs of lectures and entertainment, and serve as the headquarters for branches of company social and recreational clubs.

"THE CHANCE OF A LIFETIME"

Atterbury visited the Norton plant in April 1915 to present Indian Hill's preliminary plan and housing designs to company officials and employees. Although Norton had set up a subsidiary building operation several months earlier, this was the company's first official glimpse of the project. Atterbury described his ideas for the village in great detail, outlining the financial arrangements and illustrating the town's layout and housing with plans, drawings, and models. To emphasize the "ideal nature of the village," he played the role of educator, explaining the benefits of comprehensive planning and regulation. To make his point, Atterbury showed slides of "neighborhoods where the American workman was living in squalor and filth," contrasting these with planned settlements such as Forest Hills Gardens. According to the *Norton Spirit,* "the contrast spoke volumes for the community settlement idea."[40]

Since Norton intended to sell the Indian Hill houses, they had to appeal to their workers as consumers. As a result, the company began the new project cautiously to ensure that they could provide "what the employees want and will pay for." The company planned to build thirty houses each year for at least five years – a small beginning compared to Goodyear Heights or Fairfield.[41] By the summer of 1915, the first thirty houses were completed. The company set prices from 2,800 to 3,200 dollars, amounts adjusted to the wages of skilled workers and foremen earning from 22 to 35 dollars a week. According to the company's calculations, workers could afford to pay the equivalent of a week's pay as a monthly payment. Since banks would lend only 40–50 percent of the value of a house and demanded repayment in three to five years, Norton had to set up its own financing program. Atterbury provided the company with a purchasing plan covering a much larger percentage of the cost over a longer term. Based on similar plans such as that used at Goodyear Heights, the complexity of the arrangements struck an uneasy balance between the company's and the workers' mutual suspicion.

The worker first paid a downpayment of 10 percent. He then took out two mortgages from the company; one for 1,000 dollars, the other for the balance. In addition, the company stipulated that the buyer must purchase enough shares in a cooperative bank to cover the 1,000-dollar mortgage. In spite of their interest in the workers' preferences, this requirement, intended to familiarize the worker with cooperative banking, to encourage the habit of saving, and to establish that the company was not making any profit on the transaction, reflects the company's continuing desire to "improve" the worker. At the end of twelve years, these savings would pay off the first note, and the worker could then go to a bank and arrange a conventional mortgage for the balance. At the same time, the worker would pay the interest on the second mortgage to the company. The company did not take payments from the workers' wages, but required workers to pay directly to the company cashier. The owners took care of taxes, insurance, and all other additional costs. After prospective purchasers indicated concern about the possible loss of the house after their death, the company added an insurance clause, providing that the company would give their heirs full credit for the amount of investment in the house, to the contract.[42] The contracts specified that ownership did not depend on continued employment with the company and that the houses could be sold at any time, as long as they were first offered to the company.[43]

To the company's surprise, the workers were in no immediate hurry to buy the houses. Reluctant to commit themselves to a long-term and expensive purchase when other housing was available, they had to be convinced. From May until the final house was sold in December, the *Norton Spirit* promoted Indian Hill with increasing vigor. An article entitled "Chance of a Lifetime" celebrated the advantages of homeownership:

This article would not be complete without some mention of what it means to a man and his family when he buys a home of his own. None will deny that the most respected citizens of a community are those who own property. It gives one a standing in the community which the rent payer has not. You are rated as a solid, substantial citizen whose acquaintance is worth cultivating. You are relieved of the worry, uncertainty, and continual shifting around which the rent payer goes through. The man who has acquired a home of his own has attained a certain degree of success. He knows it and his neighbors know it. This knowledge gives him a confidence in himself which is a long step toward the goal he has set out to attain.[44]

One barrier to immediate sales was the company's insistence that only "model" workers and citizens could settle in Indian Hill. Publicity constantly reiterated the elite character of the development, emphasizing the high status that residence would confer within the Norton hierarchy. Although meeting the downpayment and monthly payments required both an adequate salary and the ability to save, Norton also demanded that residents be exemplary workers and citizens. The plant newspaper assured prospective buyers that:

The man who buys on Indian Hill will have good neighbors, there is no doubt about that. When you buy a house in a certain locality you want to know who is going to live near you. There are a number of questions about them that you will ask. Who are they? Are they respectable, companionable and worth cultivating or will they be somebody I wouldn't care to recognize in public, slovenly in appearance and altogether "good for nothings"? Will I derive mental and moral benefit from associating with them, will their nearness and example set a precedent for me to live up to, or will I be apt to lose my own standing amongst my friends by mixing with such people or living near them? Will they keep their house and grounds as attractive as my own, or must I feel ashamed to invite my friends to visit me because of the unsightly appearance of my neighbor's backyard? The man who buys a house on Indian Hill will be assured of good neighbors. He cannot have otherwise for the restrictions in this respect are rigid. The Indian Hill Company does not intend to sell houses to anyone who would not be a credit to the settlement and every prospective purchaser is carefully considered in this respect before a sale is finally closed.

As the company accelerated its efforts to sell Indian Hill, every Monday night general manager George Jeppson sat at the information desk in the Administration building to answer questions and provide information about the project. When this failed to attract enough buyers, he personally sought out employees whom he considered suitable. Not surprisingly, most of the early buyers were, like Jeppson, of Swedish origin and a high proportion came from Hoganus, the town where Jeppson's father had grown up.[45] Twenty-four of the first thirty homeowners at Indian Hill were Swedish. This reflects not only Norton's traditional favoritism toward Swedish workers but also the Swedes' high status among Worcester's working population. A 1916 survey of wages and ethnicity listed Swedes as the best-paid workers in the city, followed by English and native-born Americans.[46]

Norton used Indian Hill to transform its Swedish employees into honorary Americans, the colonial theme reinforcing their identification with Anglo-Saxon and New England values. Most of the buyers were active in Norton Company activities, serving as officers of groups such as the Mutual Benefit Association, the Norton Agricultural Society, and the Safety First Association.[47] Thanks to Jeppson's efforts, Indian Hill's first residents, as the company intended, were "model" employees who held responsible jobs, led respectable lives, and had demonstrated their loyalty to the firm.

Recognizing the high quality of Atterbury's designs, the company wanted to ensure that the occupants would maintain the same standards inside their homes. To upgrade and standardize the workers' taste, the company furnished a "model house." Introduced by tenement house social workers, the use of tastefully furnished model interiors as "object lessons" in middle-class mores was already part of welfare capitalism's campaign to shape and improve the working-class way of life. Norton arranged for a Worcester furniture store to decorate and furnish several of the first houses at Indian Hill as what they called "friendly counsel" to the new owners. Already upwardly mobile, workers quickly absorbed these lessons. According to company spokesman Clifford Anderson, the "remarkably high average taste displayed in [Indian Hill] homes" would give a sharp mental jolt to visitors who approached them with condescension. Anderson found "very little overcrowding; the mass of gimcrackery is conspicuously lacking; there is discrimination, selective choice, and restraint everywhere."[48]

The first year's promotional efforts finally succeeded: employees quickly bought up the second group of houses, finished in the summer of 1916. The company judged Indian Hill, although still incomplete, a major success. Beginning in 1916, the *Norton Spirit* featured a new column, "Indian Hill Notes," devoted to the residents' social activities. This format presented the residents as an elite group among the employees, similar to Worcester's local elite, a group whose members included the firm's directors, and whose activities were reported in the social columns of the Worcester daily newspapers. Norton published a laudatory account of the project in an extensively illustrated booklet, "Indian Hill – An Ideal Village," which served as publicity and as a prospectus. The firm's public relations director actively publicized the project's achievements. Trade publications such as *Iron Age* and local newspapers based approving articles on his effusive press releases. In 1916, when Theodore Roosevelt visited Worcester, Norton organized a festive tour of Indian Hill complete with brass band and dancing children. Roosevelt, a long-time supporter of Progressive housing reform and welfare work, expressed great enthusiasm for the project.[49]

After this the building program ended. In 1917, the *Norton Spirit* announced "with regret . . . and general disappointment" that the high cost of building material and labor had forced the company to suspend building activities temporarily on Indian Hill that year. The entry of the United States into World War I created a shortage of building materials and this produced an immediate and massive increase in already escalating building costs. In 1916 the range of housing prices had risen from 2,800–4,000 dollars to 3,600–5,200 dollars, and further wartime increases would put this far beyond the budget of even foremen and skilled workers.[50] In the interim, Atterbury continued to monitor Indian Hill's development. To maintain the settlement's model character, he drafted a series of protective regulations and organized an improvement association, made up of company officers and residents, to supervise the community as it continued to grow.[51]

NEW WORKERS AND NEW PROBLEMS

In the meantime, the Norton Company faced new labor problems. Previously, like most manufactures, Norton's "hiring and holding" efforts had focused on skilled workers. As the European war dried up sources of once-plentiful unskilled labor, employers struggled to recruit new groups of workers. They expanded existing welfare programs to attract unskilled workers and created new programs aimed at integrating immigrant workers into industrial life. As one industrial engineer noted, "heretofore industrial management has been satisfied to treat the alien somewhat cavalierly," until the war forced them to "study the alien residential and employment problem with more intelligence."[52] The war brought other problems. With the threat of unemployment disappearing, workers became more independent. Turnover rates rose alarmingly and labor unrest dramatically increased. Both 1916 and 1917 set new records for work stoppages. The Bolshevik revolution in Russia fueled employers' fears that foreign workers would become radicalized.

Employers responded by raising wages and by recruiting underemployed groups of workers. By 1917, worsening labor shortages forced the Norton Company with reluctance to recruit women for factory work. Although Norton had employed women in its offices since the 1890s, in the factory George Jeppson hired only women who had previous work experience in order to avoid recruiting women directly from their homes into the labor force. Like most welfare employers, Norton insisted that women workers required special conditions and services to maintain "modesty" and morality in the workplace. To protect "the moral atmosphere surrounding our girls," Mrs Emil Styffe, the wife of a foreman and an Indian Hill resident, became the company matron. The company segregated its 260 female workers from male employees and assigned them light manufacturing tasks in keeping with their "delicacy." For other jobs, Norton's Employment Department relaxed its normally high standards and began to hire almost anyone. The company doctor now asked only one question: "Is he breathing? Well, then let him work!"[53] The proportion of Swedish employees dropped to 24 percent as Norton began to hire Irish and Italian workers.

The company increased its pay rates but unrest and general malaise in the factory alarmed Jeppson, who attributed the problems to "the class of men that we hire now and the temper they are in when they come to work."[54] Jeppson was particularly concerned about the social and political dangers posed by Norton's increasing number of Southern and East European workers, whom he considered dangerous and radical. In response, he began to "Americanize" Norton's welfare programs. The Education Department expanded to include courses in citizenship and English, while the Recreation Department made special efforts to incorporate recent immigrants into their athletic programs. Jeppson saw recreation as an ideal venue for inculcating American values, particularly to "the young men who come here as immigrants and are away from a home or church influence, and who are ready material for the radical." Jeppson urged:

> Let their American-born fellow employees assist them in their recreation. . . . In these days our greatest danger is from the young men who are not seasoned by experience and ignorant Europeans who have nothing to base their ideas of government on . . . get all the young men into some healthy recreation where they come in personal contact, outside of work, with their superintendents, foremen and other steadying influence they will gain the friendship of these men. They will understand them better.[55]

Company housing offered an even more promising method of integrating these workers into the firm, making them part of the Norton "family." Norton began to tackle the problem of housing unskilled workers. In 1916, the company built a housing tract, "Nortonville" as a way of attracting workers to its plant in Chippewa, Ontario. Rapidly constructed without the services of an architect, the settlement was a hodgepodge of different types of rental housing. Single houses, double houses, tenements and boarding houses for male workers were tightly packed together without amenities such as landscaping, site planning, or recreational facilities.[56] Hoping to avoid similar problems at Worcester, Norton asked Atterbury to prepare a new housing plan to accommodate three grades of employees: providing houses in the 5,000–7,000 dollar range to sell to foremen and office employees; houses at the 1915 Indian Hill prices (from 2,800 to 3,500 dollars) for skilled laborers, now priced out of Indian Hill; and rental housing for unskilled laborers, primarily "Italian and Polanders," with salaries of 20 dollars per week. Since the company insisted that employees should spend no more than 25 percent of their earnings for housing, this group could not afford to purchase houses.[57]

In 1917, after conferring with Norton's directors, Atterbury proposed expanding the

Indian Hill settlement to include these new categories of housing. His plan allocated housing by job, ethnicity, and income, establishing a hierarchy based on elevation. At the top of the hill, above the proposed community center, Atterbury planned to continue building the Indian Hill designs, now more expensive, to sell to foremen and white-collar workers. Just below the existing settlement, on the hill's lower slopes, he planned modest cottages for skilled workmen. At the bottom of the hill, near the factory, concrete double- and triple-decker apartment houses would be rented to Italians, Poles, and other unskilled laborers. Although the directors pronounced this layout ideal, they expressed their concern about the segregation implicit in the plan. Hoping that the "Norton Spirit" would integrate the different groups, they suggested that the Norton athletic fields, situated between the apartment settlement and the Indian Hill development, could "serve as a mixing ground for the two classes" and expressed their hope that the Italian residents would create terraced gardens on the side of the hill "as they do in their native land."[58]

Atterbury welcomed the challenge of building extremely low-cost housing. Since 1904, he had been experimenting with concrete panel construction in an attempt to lower building costs. Funded by the Russell Sage Foundation, he perfected a new system of standardized mass-produced housing components that were not only durable, fireproof, and low-maintenance, but could be designed in a variety of styles. At Forest Hills Gardens, he built houses using hollow-core concrete panels, produced at a factory on site then lifted into place with a crane. A typical two-story house consisted of fewer than one hundred panels for walls and roof. Plumbing and electricity could be installed through precast conduits

Atterbury's precast concrete panel system used at Forest Hills Gardens, 1918. Atterbury called the system "a child's blocks raised to the *n*th power, assembled by giant fingers." Although prefabricated, the system produced picturesque rather than industrial results.

and holes in the hollow cores. Encountering problems with the quality of the concrete, Atterbury invented "nailcrete," a concrete mixture with the nailability of white pine. This made it possible to attach wood easily to concrete surfaces. Unlike most concrete housing, the Forest Hills houses were aesthetically interesting. Brushed to expose the gravel aggregate, the smooth concrete surfaces left by the steel forms revealed rich textures that lent themselves to the picturesque detailing Atterbury favored. Once wooden door and window frames, dormers, porches, and landscaping were added, the houses bore no resemblance to the stark concrete industrial housing found in many company towns.[59]

In early discussions about the Indian Hill project, Atterbury had proposed his concrete panel system, but the company, unwilling to take risks, had opted for conventional construction. In 1916, the journalist Ida Tarbell, while praising Indian Hill's "utility, economy and beauty," objected that it only met the needs of highly paid workmen. Atterbury responded:

> As a result of a good many years' study of the housing problem from various points of view, I am fully convinced that the crux of the problem is not in a subdivision of the land or in the field of economic administration and taxation, but in the cost of construction . . . . It is a curious fact that scientific and co-operative principles have been practically applied to the production of almost every other item in the poor man's living account, but the second largest single one – that of his housing.
>
> We have been working for the past six or eight years on the idea of standardized dwellings . . . . The scheme, of course, is to do for the laboring man's house what Ford has done for the automobile, with certain additional conceptions relative to educational, hygienic and aesthetic purposes.
>
> To be successful, it must be commercial, and I believe that it can be made to pay . . . . This is seen, not only as a benefit to the laboring man, but equally to the employers of labor who must from now on take serious consideration of the housing problem.[60]

The new Norton project offered Atterbury an opportunity to experiment with concrete as a method of producing extremely low-cost dwellings. For the double- and triple-decker houses, the company could cut the cost of concrete by using gravel from its own gravel pits, pouring the panels on the site and then lifting them into place with a traveling crane. Since the price per unit could be dramatically reduced by using the system on a large scale, the company proposed building 250 four-room apartments. Atterbury projected a total cost of 500,000 dollars for the project – 2,000 dollars per apartment. This meant each flat would rent for 16 dollars a month, an amount that unskilled workers could easily afford and that would leave Norton with a 5 percent profit after expenses and maintenance. For skilled employees, Atterbury suggested building five-unit terraced houses of concrete blocks with decorative surfaces, similar to those he had designed for Forest Hills Gardens. By using templates to guide unskilled laborers, Atterbury hoped to build these houses for 11 cents a cubic foot, comparable to Indian Hill's 1915 prices.[61]

Although Norton planned to continue its ambitious housing scheme and complete

Atterbury's plans for Indian Hill, inflation and unexpected costs continued to delay the project. In 1919, instead of reactivating the Indian Hill project, the Norton Company quickly constructed Norton Village, ninety-four houses in a grid tract on the opposite slope of the hill from the area platted by Atterbury. In a hurry to build, the company dynamited the basement holes to save time. These houses, although initially less complicated to construct than Atterbury's industrialized system would have been, were smaller than those in Indian Hill Village and cost more because of the inflated cost of war-time building. Norton workers, comparing them with the Indian Hill houses, showed no interest in purchasing them. Unable to find buyers, the company rented out the houses, then later sold them at a loss.[62] Discouraged and uncertain of the employees' housing preferences, the directors terminated the company's building activities on Indian Hill.

After 1921, whatever their intentions, Norton was no longer able to pursue innovations in housing and welfare work. The 1921 depression, particularly severe in the machine tool and metalworking industries, devastated the firm. Production and sales plummeted by nearly 70 percent. Norton survived only by severely contracting its operations. The firm closed its plants in Canada and Arkansas and reduced the workforce by 80 percent – a drop from more than four thousand to fewer than eight hundred employees. Management used the wholesale lay-offs as an opportunity to reduce the number of Southern and East European workers, while retaining Swedish and native-born employees. The crisis forced the company to eliminate many of its educational, athletics, and recreation programs, but, with a newly consolidated group of workers, there was less need for welfare programs.[63]

The fifty-eight-house settlement on Indian Hill survived in its unfinished state. None of the community buildings was built, although a public elementary school was later added. In 1936, the company was still considering building the Holden Street bridge, but it was not completed. Without these critical connections, and lacking public spaces and services, the area remained extremely isolated, an attractive housing development without any particular focus or physical identity as a community. Ownership, however, remained remarkably stable. In 1953, nearly forty years after Indian Hill was built, the majority of the original owners were either still employed by Norton or had retired after twenty-five or more years with the company. The initially very narrow range of income and occupation widened considerably over the years, as employees who advanced to better jobs continued to live in the community.[64] The Norton Company continued to portray the project as a success. Responding to a 1936 survey, Clifford Anderson, author of the Indian Hill brochure, stated emphatically that the original objectives of the company had been fully realized in "providing better living and working conditions; that the development had been a good influence in lowering labor turnover" and concluded that "the physical arrangement of the plan could not be improved upon."[65]

FROM MODEL TOWNS TO MANUFACTURED HOUSING

Indian Hill's inconclusive outcome confirmed Atterbury's doubts about the usefulness of "model" approaches in providing individual small houses for the working class. Although he continued to design architecturally distinguished housing for planned communities and to participate in housing reform activities, he spent the rest of his life trying to solve the technical and economic problems of manufacturing reinforced concrete housing. Atterbury's interest in concrete fabrication was not new, but his insistence on a solely technical solution to the housing problem was. In 1920, in spite of his success in producing concrete houses at Forest Hills Gardens, he was unable to expand the system from the philanthropic arena into a profitable industry. The Forest Hills houses, although attractive, strong, maintenance-free, and exceptionally durable, required an enormous investment in plant and equipment to produce relatively few panels, and the fact that each panel had to remain in an expensive mold for twenty-four hours made them more expensive than brick.[66]

In 1912, Atterbury, speaking to the National Conference on Housing, had focused specifically on economic issues. Analyzing the obstacles to providing affordable suburban houses for workers, he identified the fundamental problem as the high cost of construction.[67] In 1916, in answer to the National Conference on Housing's question, "How to Get Low Cost Houses?" Atterbury, citing his fifteen years of experience with model tenements and model towns, was more specific. Honest and efficient government and a uniform national building code based on scientific principles were needed, to lay the groundwork for organized research work in economic construction to develop standardized, factory-made housing components.[68] Since lack of interest suggested that "no commercial concern could be expected to solve these problems scientifically, economically and rapidly with the sole object of creating a new basic industry devoted to the production of minimum cost housing," Atterbury concluded that "such work could only be done satisfactorily by a non-profit agency." He founded an independent research institute, the Research Institute of Economic Housing, but was never able to raise the 3,000,000-dollar endowment he considered essential to conduct adequate research.[69] The depression quickly eliminated the possibility of even minimal private financing and Atterbury, still an advocate of market solutions, adamantly refused to consider the possibility of government sponsorship.

Atterbury persevered in his search for industrialized methods. According to his wife, he devoted his own assets and accepted other architectural commissions only to support his research in prefabrication.[70] In 1949, Atterbury used his system to construct Amsterdam Houses, a large public housing project in Manhattan. Although these high-rise projects were far from Atterbury's dream of small-scale group housing for workers, they made it possible to test his system on a large scale. Atterbury also continued to improve production techniques, introducing cheaper forms and a system of "cooking" the concrete so that the panels set within a half an hour, removing the last technical obstacles to the system's profitable production. In 1951, when he was eighty-two, Atterbury finally found sponsorship to mass produce his system. He set up an assembly line in a factory on Long Island which could turn out 4,000 square feet of panel a day. *Fortune* reported enthusiastically on the project, noting that Atterbury's system had required a lot of capital to develop, but that "today's scarce, sky-high labor may pay it back fast."[71] The system was used successfully on a large scale in Queensview, a non-profit, high-rise development for white-collar workers, but when Atterbury died five years later, without his personal commitment, production ceased.

In spite of the advantages of the system and Atterbury's continued efforts in promoting it, it is not clear that Atterbury could have succeeded in a field often characterized as one of the great failures of American technology.[72] Lewis Mumford, with Atterbury specifically in mind, accused proponents of prefabrication of taking an "easy way out from all the thorny problems of co-operative planning and distributive justice."[73] Although Atterbury undoubtedly erred in identifying the difficulties in producing low-cost housing as being solely technical, the issue was more complex than Mumford suggests. The organization of labor, the structure of the residential construction industry, housing finance, as well as a lack of interest among both entrepreneurs and architects all played a role in the failure to rationalize housing construction.[74]

THE WORKINGMAN'S HOUSE

In spite of its incomplete state, Indian Hill had an immediate impact on industrial housing and company town design. Widely praised in the architectural and industrial press, the project was consistently described as "one of the most noteworthy industrial communities in the country." Ida Tarbell regarded it as the "most attractive town of its kind in the United States, if it is carried out as begun." The National Housing Association sponsored a publication describing Indian Hill's planning and financial organization. The rapidly growing number of textbooks on industrial town planning and housing featured the town prominently. In 1936, with the project still unfinished, the Urbanism Committee, conducting a national survey of housing and urban life sponsored by the Roosevelt administration, judged it to be one of the best designed industrial communities in the nation.[75]

Indian Hill's immediate effect was significantly to raise the level of planning, urban design, and architecture in company towns. Although his plan was never fully realized, Atterbury's ambitious and sophisticated design set a standard to which subsequent industrial towns aspired. For the first time, architecture and planning successfully overcame the industrial limitations of the company town to produce a comprehensive living environment with a unified aesthetic. In contrast with earlier company towns, that had reproduced existing styles rather than expressing new meanings, Indian Hill possessed a unique identity. Using the Norton Company's location and intentions as a starting point, Atterbury invented an eclectic design vocabulary that superimposed American images on garden city planning techniques. Once other architects adopted this approach, other places and situations generated new interpretations.

Company town designers quickly adapted the techniques used at Indian Hill to their own needs. Pedestrian circulation, cul-de-sacs, and well-designed town squares began to appear in company towns across the country. Although Kohler, Wisconsin, planned by Werner Hegemann and Elbert Peets, reflected garden city prototypes more literally than Atterbury's design, Lincoln Circle, a landscaped cul-de-sac surrounded by colonial cottages, virtually duplicated Nashoba Place at Indian Hill.[76] George Post's 1917 design for Eclipse

George Post's drawing for the central square at Eclipse Park bears a striking resemblance to Atterbury's concept for Indian Hill's village center.

Park, a company town sponsored by the Fairbanks, Morse Company of Beloit, Wisconsin, followed Indian Hill even more closely. A Beaux Arts town square leads into park-like residential areas, with tree-lined streets furnished with colonial cottages. Indian Hill's housing proved to be equally influential. Over the next five years, as industrial housing became a prominent architectural concern, Indian Hill's houses served as a model for numerous housing projects. Encouraged by the growing anti-German feeling in the early years of the war, architects widely adopted colonial revival styles to "Americanize" company towns. Atterbury's updated colonial cottage design replaced what architects had previously considered the most up-to-date industrial housing prototype – group houses and cottages based on the vernacular styles used in German and English garden cities. Only a few years earlier, Albert Spahr, for example, had borrowed the picturesque Germanic half-timbered style he used for Midland Steel Company houses in Pennsylvania directly from the Krupp colonies in Essen.[77]

The extent of the Indian Hill house's influence and popularity was immediately visible in the Immigrant Housing Competition, held in early 1917. Sponsored by the National Americanization Committee, the national Chamber of Commerce, and advised by a committee of welfare housing and architecture experts, including Atterbury, the competition addressed the issue of providing adequate housing for immigrant workers. The program specified a site in an industrial town and asked for designs for both single family and group houses of four and five rooms. Although the competition mentioned only sanitation, comfort, and economy as the basis for judgment, many of the winning entries closely followed Atterbury's colonial cottage prototypes.[78] Over the next few years, the colonial cottage dominated American industrial housing, appearing across the East and Midwest in a variety of different forms.[79] Following Atterbury's lead, other firms established themselves as specialists in company town design. Firms such as Murphy and Dana, Schenk and Mead, Mann and MacNeille, and Clinton MacKenzie produced designs based on Atterbury's plans for Indian Hill. These included projects at Kistler, Pennsylvania, Perryville, Maryland, the Massachusetts Homestead Commission houses at Lowell, and the Connecticut mills town at Danielson.[80] Thus, although none of the public buildings and fewer than one hundred houses were actually constructed at Indian Hill, Atterbury's designs transformed the possibilities of company town design and had an important effect on subsequent architects and planners.

7

REDESIGNING
THE MINING TOWN:
BERTRAM GOODHUE AND
TYRONE, NEW MEXICO

Like Indian Hill, Tyrone, New Mexico, the mining town that Bertram Goodhue designed for the Phelps-Dodge Copper Company in 1915, received glowing praise from architects, reformers, and businessmen. However, unlike Indian Hill, located in a region of model company towns, Tyrone's romantic design made a striking contrast with the dirt streets, open drains, and shacks found in other western mining camps. After 1910, conditions in resource extraction settlements had become a new focus for reformers and labor unions. As large national corporations increasingly replaced local mine owners, they began to introduce standardized management policies, including welfare work, into settlements once notorious for primitive living conditions. A 1915 article proclaimed a "new era for mining towns" in which their "scientific treatment" had led to "greater self-respect and increased efficiency" of their residents.[1] Launching an effort to restructure copper mining and defeat unions, Phelps-Dodge commissioned Bertram Goodhue to design a "million dollar" mining town. Goodhue's plan for Tyrone took Atterbury's picturesque approach in a new direction by adopting "Latinization" as a design strategy. Creating the illusion of an idyllic Mexican colonial town on the mining frontier, Goodhue, like Atterbury, reached back in history for the image of a pre-industrial community. Unlike the democratic values conveyed by the New England village, however, Tyrone's Spanish urbanity evoked a hierarchical social order, suggesting an almost feudal relationship between Mexican miners and their American bosses.

WALTER DOUGLAS AND THE PHELPS-DODGE COMPANY

The Phelps-Dodge Company had entered western copper mining in 1885 with the lucky purchase of the Copper Queen mine near Bisbee, Arizona. This legendary mine turned out to be the purest and richest copper vein in American mining history. By 1900, the New York-based company dominated copper production in Arizona and, by 1909, Arizona led the world in copper production. Phelps-Dodge also operated mines at Douglas, Morenci, and Globe, as well as owning thousands of acres of undeveloped mineral deposits. Dr James Douglas oversaw the company's expansion from a family mercantile firm to one of the world's largest mining corporations. Douglas, a devout Presbyterian who had studied for the ministry, brought Phelps-Dodge's traditional paternalism west with him. He abolished Sunday labor in the mines and furnished mining camps with schools, churches, and hospitals. Although some observers derided Douglas's moralism, and called the company "Presbyterian Dodge," others praised it as "uncommonly altruistic in its methods."[2]

The company's western headquarters were at Bisbee. Incorporated in 1903, by 1915 the town had a population of 8,000. Although Phelps-Dodge was its most powerful economic presence, the firm shared the town with other mining companies and a diverse group of inhabitants, including independent merchants and professionals. Still, Phelps-Dodge dominated many of the town's activities. It financed an extensive welfare program for miners, including a large hospital, a library, and a YMCA sponsored by Grace Dodge, the daughter of a Phelps-Dodge partner. The company also owned the town's largest hotel (the Copper Queen), its newspaper, and the main department store, the Phelps-Dodge Mercantile Company.[3]

Bisbee's downtown boasted several buildings designed by the noted southwestern designer Henry Trost, and even had a resident architect, F.C. Hurst, but otherwise the town was not physically prepossessing. A jumble of frame buildings lined its steep canyons, which were accessible only by long flights of wooden steps. Fires regularly swept through its densely developed hills. Bisbee was notorious throughout the West for its main street, Brewery Gulch, a precursor of Las Vegas, with saloons, dance halls, and brothels open twenty-four hours a day. The only urban planning in the area was in Warren, a formally laid out suburb for mining executives, connected to Bisbee, 8 miles away, by a streetcar line. Unlike Bisbee's chaotic urbanism, Warren's planning followed City Beautiful principles with level lots laid out along a central axis, aligned with a distant cluster of mountain peaks. At the upper end of Vista Park, a linear park landscaped with grass and flowers, the forty-one-room mansion belonging to Walter Douglas commanded the town.[4]

In 1911, Walter Douglas, a mining engineer trained at Columbia University, took over from his father James Douglas as general manager of Phelps-Dodge mining operations.

Bisbee, Arizona in 1915. Although Phelps-Dodge dominated the local economy with the Copper Queen mine and built most of its major buildings, it did not control the town, a wide-open western mining camp famous for its saloons and brothels. Without any planning or control, the town expanded up the steep hillsides. Courtesy of the Bisbee Mining and Historical Museum, Crockett Collection.

Commuting between New York and Arizona in his private railway car, the "Cloudcroft," he dramatically changed the focus of Phelps-Dodge management policies and introduced a new set of corporate values. Instead of focusing on the technical problems of mining and metallurgy that had primarily occupied his father, he introduced new organizational and managerial policies. Like the directors of the Norton Company, Douglas advocated modern corporate methods and was vehemently opposed to unionization – he vowed to close down the Copper Queen rather than allow workers to organize there. Equally aware of the growing importance of public relations, he became a national spokesman for anti-union mine owners, taking the offensive against labor's growing power. Elected president of the American Mining Congress, Douglas redirected the organization's emphasis away from mining and geological problems to labor relations, politics, employer organization, and taxation.[5]

On the local level, one of Douglas's major concerns was the changing balance of political power between labor and capital in Arizona, which was then on the verge of statehood. Arizona miners and their middle- and working-class sympathizers had created a powerful political coalition that threatened Phelps-Dodge's heavy economic stake in the area. Proposed legislation would tax corporate earnings, introduce extensive workmen's compensation laws, increase corporate liability, and otherwise favor the workers' interests. In 1912, Arizona became the forty-eighth state with the most pro-labor constitution in the nation.[6] At this point, Douglas became concerned and Phelps-Dodge started buying up mining claims and large tracts of land in neighboring New Mexico. In 1915, for the first time, Governor George Hunt, a liberal Democrat who was pro-miner, intervened in a strike against Phelps-Dodge at Clifton-Morenci, directing the state militia to protect the strikers and arrest several mine owners. Furious over Hunt's actions, Walter Douglas debated the governor in the pages of the *New Republic*, angrily defending Phelps-Dodge's labor policies.[7]

Even worse from the mine owners' point of view was the growing strength of labor organization in the West. During the nineteenth century, miners, like other resource extraction workers, were generally hardworking and independent men, who pursued a rootless and nomadic lifestyle. If they disagreed with the boss, they simply turned in their pay card and moved on. After 1900 changes in the nature of mining operations resulted in increasing labor organization among copper miners. Traditionally, hard rock copper mining had been done by hand by skilled miners. These were a succession of immigrant groups who had learned their craft in their homelands; first Cornishmen, followed by Serbians, Hungarians, Finns, and Italians. The introduction of newly mechanized extraction methods, in which machines and unskilled workers took over a large part of mining operations, undermined the wages and dominance of skilled workers.[8]

In response, miners organized for better and more consistent wages and improved working conditions. After its defeat in the 1913 Calumet and Hecla strike, the once radical Western Federation of Miners (WFM) became more cautious, and, in 1915, finally rejoined the conservative AFL. Increasingly dissatisfied miners turned to the Industrial Workers of the World, now actively organizing on the western resource frontier. In 1908, the WFM had been unable to organize Bisbee, but after this union membership started to grow, leading to a series of bitter confrontations between labor and management. Beginning in 1914, a wave of strikes swept across Arizona. Miners struck in the Clifton-Morenci and Ray districts in 1915, and in Jerome the following year. After the Clifton-Morenci strike, Walter Douglas swore that Phelps-Dodge would never again negotiate with strikers.[9] Douglas, like many mine owners, feared losing control over the conditions of production.

BERTRAM GOODHUE, "ARCHITECT AND MASTER OF MANY ARTS"

In early 1915, Walter Douglas approached Bertram Goodhue with the possibility of designing an entire copper mining town in the remote mountains of southwest New Mexico. Although Douglas, a New Yorker, was probably already familiar with Goodhue's ecclesiastical work in the East, the triumphant and well-publicized opening of the Panama–California Exhibition in San Diego confirmed the architect's mastery of urban design and his romantic vision of the Hispanic southwest. Goodhue responded with enthusiasm to both the client and the commission. Goodhue and Walter Douglas struck up an immediate friendship. In the summer of 1915, both men and their wives spent what Goodhue called "a delightful week" traveling through the southwest in Douglas's private railway car, stopping at Tyrone's site along the way. Goodhue went to considerable trouble to propose Douglas for membership in his New York clubs, the Grolier and the prestigious Century Association. In 1918, he designed a large house in Westchester County for Douglas and his family. Equally impressed with Phelps-Dodge, Goodhue, on Douglas's advice, invested considerable sums of money in copper shares.[10]

Tyrone was one of Goodhue's first independent commissions after severing his twenty-five-year partnership with the firm of Cram Goodhue and Ferguson. Goodhue was at a critical stage in his career, having left one of the most successful firms in the country for a less certain future. With little formal education, Goodhue had begun his architectural career at fifteen as an apprentice in the office of James Renwick. At the age of twenty-two, already notable for his winning entry in the Dallas cathedral competition, he joined the firm of Cram and Wentworth as a full partner. Ralph Adams Cram later described Goodhue as a genius whose creative imagination and vivid sense of fantasy "actually left one breathless." During his years with the firm, Goodhue developed his already formidable skills in rendering and decoration into a solid command of three-dimensional design.[11]

Intensely romantic, Goodhue admired the aesthetic coherence of pre-industrial cultures. During the 1890s this found various outlets. He and Cram joined forces to produce the journal *Knight Errant*, a nostalgic exercise in pre-Raphaelite medievalism. Goodhue also traveled to investigate other architectural cultures. He first visited Mexico in 1892, returning in 1899 with Sylvester Baxter to measure and draw Spanish colonial buildings for Baxter's ten-volume work, *Spanish Colonial Architecture in Mexico*. The Mexican villages Goodhue visited, with their apparently docile peasants and life focused around the church, captured his imagination, suggesting an organic unity of craft, structure, function, and cultural purpose. Even before his journey to Persia and India in 1902, Goodhue had pursued his interest in exotic images by inventing descriptions for imaginary locales such as "Monteventosa," a picturesque Italian hill town, "Traumberg," an ancient Bohemian settlement, and the "Villa Fosca," set on a forgotten island in the Adriatic. He illustrated these romantic travelogues with drawings that convincingly evoked architectural settings that had evolved over time.[12]

Architecturally, Goodhue made free use of historical styles as a framework for expanding his design capabilities and his romantic sensibility. In the first decade of the twentieth century, as Goodhue, Cram, and Ferguson moved beyond ecclesiastical specialization to larger institutional projects,[13] Goodhue's work moved away from the Gothic, the firm's trademark. According to Cram, after proving himself in the Gothic, Spanish Renaissance, Byzantine,

Goodhue's drawing of the Piazza Re Umberto, the central square of his imaginary Italian town, Monteventoso. Without "buildings of architectural distinction," the town demonstrated Goodhue's admiration of urban life on a small scale and the charm of vernacular architecture as it accumulated over the centuries. Goodhue described the piazza: "its musical and unmusical sound, its clamouring people, its miserable bronze Umberto, and rickety iron café tables."

Romanesque, and colonial, Goodhue finally lost interest in historical styles altogether and became a modern architect.[14] The Spanish colonial style was a particularly important stage in this development. Even clothed in ornament, its architectural vocabulary lent itself to the expressive mode of design Goodhue was seeking, allowing him to manipulate cubic forms, planar surfaces, and abstract massing. After hearing about plans for the Panama–California Exhibition from the Olmsted brothers, who had been commissioned to lay out the site of the Exhibition, Goodhue immediately recognized the commission as ideal for his talents. Employing his considerable charm, he got the job, beating Californian architects Irving Gill and John Galen Howard.[15]

The Exhibition marked the peak of Goodhue's involvement with the Spanish colonial style. Exploiting the possibilities for architectural theater offered by a temporary exhibition, Goodhue invented a mythical past for California. He constructed a Spanish city that, he felt, "would have fulfilled the visions of Fray Junipero Serra as he toiled and dreamed while he planted missions from San Diego to Monterey." The Exhibition's dramatic urban design and cohesive architecture expressed Goodhue's romanticized vision of the Hispanic south-west, a region settled long before the East Coast, where, he rhapsodized, "the tenderest of skies, the bluest of seas, mountains of perfect outline, and the richest of sub-tropical foliage" combined with the "soft speech and unfailing courtesy of the half-Spanish, half-Indian peasantry."[16]

Set on top of a mesa and approached across an arched concrete bridge spanning the deep arroyos of Balboa Park, the Exhibition's pile of glistening white buildings appeared to be a city in miniature. The elaborate Churrigueresque dome and tower of the California Building, modelled on the Mexican churches Goodhue had drawn for Baxter's book, crowned the Exhibition. Although organized around the east–west axis of El Prado, the plan avoided the broad vistas and open space of Beaux Arts planning. Instead, following the continuous arcade that lined the street, the visitor passed through a succession of spaces defined by sunlight and shadow and crossed by a sequence of courtyards that led to secondary plazas or framed views of the landscape. As much as the drama of the architecture, this "Latin" urban experience defined the nature of the Exhibition, where, according to Goodhue, "everything that met the eye and ear" was meant to "recall the glamour and mystery and poetry of old Spanish days."[17] Local observers immediately seized on the imagery as a new source of regional identity. Christian Brinton called it "a visible expression of the collective soul of the southwest."[18]

This view of one of the enclosed courtyards at the Panama–California Exhibition in San Diego captures Goodhue's mastery of the romantic Spanish colonial architecture. Note the arcade with tile roof and the elaborate Churrigueresque ornament, trademarks of the Exhibition.

Coming just after the Exhibition, Goodhue's first independent projects, Tyrone and the new campus of the California Institute of Technology, offered similar architectural opportunities. The architectural variety of an entire town encouraged Goodhue to pursue his interest in large-scale planning, while Tyrone's remote setting served as an ideal vehicle for his continuing exploration of historical and regional imagery. Goodhue's talents and interests made it almost inevitable that his primary focus would be architectural design rather than, like Grosvenor Atterbury, building technology or social programming. However, in spite of his primarily formalist approach to architecture, Goodhue, a close friend of Frederick Law Olmsted, Jr and a friend and correspondent of Herbert Croly, was undoubtedly familiar with the social and economic issues of industrial housing and company town design.[19]

RESTRUCTURING THE COPPER MINING TOWN

It seems unlikely, however, that Goodhue recognized that, from Walter Douglas's viewpoint, the new town of Tyrone was merely the visible and physical embodiment of a new model of copper mining. In response to the changing political and labor situation in Arizona, Douglas was in the process of restructuring both the productive and social bases of copper extraction. This strategy involved reorganizing the political, economic, and technical conditions under which production took place. This suggested that the mine owners' control over the political conditions in the state had seriously eroded.

To begin with, the selection of New Mexico as a site avoided many of the problems Phelps-Dodge had faced in Arizona. Sparsely populated, with an economy dominated by cattle ranching, labor issues rarely appeared on the political agenda in Santa Fe. Copper had been discovered in the state three centuries before, but profitable extraction had to wait for the development of new technology to recover and smelt low-grade ores. The ore body at Tyrone consisted of only 2 percent copper, in contrast to 12 percent at the Copper Queen. The introduction of mechanized techniques such as block caving made extraction of low-grade ores profitable. With the beginning of World War I in Europe, the phenomenal rise in copper prices – both prices and production doubled between 1914 and 1916 – justified the expense of new technology. Such newly mechanized extraction methods also allowed the replacement of skilled hard-rock miners by unskilled laborers.[20]

These were generally Mexicans. Between 1910 and 1920 five times as many Mexican immigrants entered the United States as during the previous decade. Most were young men, single or with wives at home, who planned to return to Mexico with the money they earned. Mexican miners encountered a double standard in southwest mines; operators paid them a lower "Mexican wage" – often less than half an American's pay – and allowed them to work only at menial tasks. Mine operators often imposed a "half-pay, half-goods" system on their Mexican workers, paying part of their wages with credit at the company store. Segregated in Mexican camps with poor living conditions, they received few of the benefits that companies like Phelps-Dodge offered their American workers.[21]

In Arizona, the growing number of Mexican workers heightened racial tensions among the miners. Many American workers regarded Mexican miners either as cheap labor that threatened their wage rates or as potential strikebreakers. The exclusion of Mexicans from the mines became a pressing demand of miners' organizations. In 1907, the Western Federation of Miners struck in Bisbee in protest at the use of Mexican workers. As a result, Bisbee remained a so-called "white man's camp," where Mexicans were prohibited from working underground. One of the first labor-sponsored referendums passed after Arizona statehood was an 80 percent hiring law, which limited the percentage of non-citizen workers in an establishment to 20 percent.[22]

Mine owners, on the other hand, often preferred to hire Mexican workers because they would work for less money, could not vote, and were considered less likely to join a labor union. Operators extolled the Mexican worker as "obedient and cheap" and asserted that "his strongest point is his willingness to work for low wages." Walter Douglas claimed that Mexican workmen were "easily led and just as easily intimidated." In spite of their reputation for docility, in 1915 in the Clifton-Morenci district, Mexican miners had led Indians and sympathetic American workers in a successful strike against unfair treatment and the double wage standard.[23] Moreover, the IWW, now active in the region, made organizing immigrants one of its highest priorities.

Douglas was determined to avoid these problems in Tyrone. There, with the exception of a few white foremen and supervisors, Phelps-Dodge planned to hire unskilled workers from the large labor pool available just over the border, less than 60 miles away. Unlike Bisbee and other towns where Phelps-Dodge operated, from the beginning the company completely controlled Tyrone's planning and development and the town was completely owned by the company. The main transportation link from the remote town to Silver City and El Paso across the Burro Mountains was a railway line owned and operated by Phelps-Dodge. No houses or businesses could be privately owned, but had to be built on land leased from the company.[24]

TYRONE: "A MODERN MINING TOWN"

During his 1915 visit to Tyrone, Goodhue selected a site for the new town, the only flat area in an arroyo surrounded by smaller canyons. Located in the remote southwest corner of New Mexico, Tyrone was set in a rugged landscape of hills and canyons dotted with piñons, juniper, and live oaks. The new site, a mile from the mouth of the mine, was just over the east side of the Continental Divide at an elevation of 6,000 feet. With the exception of a few trees, which Goodhue carefully preserved, the only existing features were a road across the valley and the terminus of the newly built Phelps-Dodge railroad line. Unlike the restricted budget the Norton Company had allocated for Indian Hill, Phelps-Dodge was prepared to spend more than 1,000,000 dollars to develop the new town, a small part of the far larger investment required to begin extracting copper.[25] Anticipating an expanding copper market, Phelps Dodge hoped that Tyrone would become the center of a new mining district in the Burro Mountains, attracting other mining companies and serving as a trading center for the ranchers in western Grant County.[26]

Goodhue's design for an idealized Mexican town fit Phelps-Dodge's intentions perfectly. A scaled-down and more realistic version of the San Diego buildings, Tyrone's plan still conveyed considerable monumentality and urbanity. In spite of the town's Hispanic vocabulary, Goodhue introduced many of the same garden city principles that Atterbury had used at Indian Hill.[27] Faced with an equally unpromising site, Goodhue exploited the difficult terrain for dramatic effect, carefully fitting a formal town center into a narrow arroyo and scattering informal housing areas on the hills above. The town center was symmetrically organized around two axes that crossed in a large central plaza. The main axis, Mangas Street, was a formal avenue 60 feet wide that terminated in two symmetrical, balanced circular plazas. Although Tyrone's plan reads as pure Beaux Arts geometry, Goodhue's perspective drawing suggests a more picturesque effect. A flat skyline broken by towers recalls the Mexican colonial towns Goodhue had drawn for Sylvester Baxter more than fifteen years earlier. These towers symbolically marked the town's two most important

The plan of Tyrone. A combination of a formal Beaux Arts center with informal garden city housing areas on the hills above, Tyrone sits in a narrow arroyo.

buildings – the massive church, whose tower and dome lent authority to the buildings below, and the Phelps-Dodge Mercantile Company, which dominated the central square.

Even more than Atterbury's colonial village, Goodhue's plan for Tyrone alluded to a specific type of pre-industrial community – the Mexican colonial town – in which a stable and hierarchical social order prevailed. Far from the egalitarian ideal that the New England village signified, the use of this style suggested an almost feudal relationship between Mexican miners and their American superiors, in which the miners played the role of the peasants Goodhue idealized. Set down on the mining frontier, historical and vernacular styles simulated growth over time, providing a history that the town lacked in fact and promising a permanence that its founders did not actually intend. Unlike the raw and chaotic mining towns which visibly expressed their newness and provisional social order, Tyrone's unified design smoothed over the multiple social and economic contradictions on which it was based. In a wild and unsettled region, the charming colonial town performed the same utopian function as the picturesque rural village, offering a benign myth of refuge counterposed to the dangers of the surrounding environment.

A continuous arcade lined the central plaza, a feature that Goodhue considered symbolically and functionally essential: "arcades . . . [give] more Spanish character than any other single architectural detail. Not only do they lend picturesqueness and interest but they [are] a haven of refuge from the heat of the midsummer's sun and the coolness of the winter."[28] The arcades connected the main buildings and structured a sequential passage through the town. Following a functional hierarchy, the town moved in a legible progression from west to east. Visitors entered either from the garage at the west end of town or

Goodhue's perspective drawing of Tyrone shows the idyllic town as it was meant to be – a bustling but serenely urban place, where residents strolled along tree-lined streets and found shelter from the sun in shadowed arcades.

from the railway station, where an arcade began at the outdoor waiting room. The arcade continued around the generously landscaped plaza, the town's commercial center, with bank, post office, shops, and offices, to the eastern end of town, passing the Phelps-Dodge club, movie theater, and, finally, ending at the high school. A monumental Catholic church, modeled after the California Building at the Panama–California Exhibition, sat on a small hill overlooking the square. Rows of shade trees maintained the experience of enclosed passage through sunlight and shade that had enchanted visitors to the fair.

Tyrone's architecture represents a new stage in Goodhue's development. Goodhue ornamented the church with an elaborate dome and tower and detailed the store and office building in the square with heavy cornices and moldings, but otherwise abandoned the Churrigueresque ornament he had used profusely at San Diego. Instead, he designed a series of stripped-down classical buildings that he described as "without an ounce of ornament anywhere, nothing but plaster walls with tile or flat parapeted roofs."[29] In the absence of ornament, textured stucco and subtle coloristic effects enhanced their cubic volumes. Each building was stuccoed in a slightly different shade: the store was pearl white, the clubhouse silver grey, the movie theater a pale blue; the bank and shops were soft purple, the warehouse yellowish buff, and the post office and railroad station pinkish buff. Goodhue felt color was particularly appropriate in the West, where "the atmosphere adds nuances of light and where color is seen through delicate shadows."[30]

The absence of ornament reveals the increasing importance of modernist and vernacular influences in Goodhue's architecture as he sought alternative images less tied to strict historicism. Writing to a friend in 1915, he described the Spanish style as "without artistic pretentiousness – [it] is in fact a bad style. My work in it is at the best scarcely serious."[31] While in San Diego he had admired Irving Gill's abstract distillation of the Mission style, which he considered "the most thoughtful work being done in the West."[32] Like Atterbury, Goodhue also sought out local vernacular prototypes. Doing research for Tyrone, he traveled through New Mexico, photographing Indian pueblos and early colonial adobe houses.[33]

HOUSING THE WORKERS

To attract workers to Tyrone, Phelps-Dodge needed to guarantee low living costs – particularly low rents. Thus, in contrast to Tyrone's large and elaborate town center, its housing was more modest, similar in size and plan to other industrial housing built at the same time. In spite of the town's Mexican imagery and the fact that the majority of its inhabitants were Mexicans, Goodhue designed the housing primarily with the American employees – technical and office workers and foremen – in mind. Initially, the company planned to rent

Mexican miners a piece of company land on which they could build a shack or pitch a tent, the usual practice in mining towns. In 1916, as an experiment, Goodhue designed several small houses for the Mexicans. These proved to be unexpectedly popular, so the company continued to build them. As at Indian Hill, housing was carefully segregated by price and ethnicity, with elevation denoting status. Like Atterbury, Goodhue juxtaposed picturesque housing areas with a formal town center. The American houses were set along narrow roads that wound along the crest of the ridges above the town and sited for advantageous views.

To provide variety, Goodhue designed six types of single family houses and three types of duplexes. The first group of American houses, built in 1916, ranged from three to five rooms; they cost the company from 1,500 to 2,800 dollars and rented from 25 to 30 dollars a month. The small houses were not successful, and the next year only more expensive four- and five-room houses were built, with costs rising to 3,200 dollars.[34] In spite of such low prices, the houses were well-planned and equipped with complete bathrooms, kitchens, wooden floors, and often a fireplace or sleeping porch.

The austere forms of the simple cubic houses, relieved only by arched openings, were unprecedented for Goodhue. Architect Marcia Mead featured the houses in an article on industrial housing, praising their responsiveness to their southwestern setting.[35] Although they resembled adobe, they were actually built of 8-inch-thick hollow tile, covered with tinted stucco in pale shades of salmon, green, brown, and cream. For climatic reasons,

American houses in Tyrone. The distinctive designs, derived from both local vernacular prototypes and Irving Gill's stripped-down Mission style, attracted a great deal of attention. The plans, however, resemble those in other industrial housing of the period. The flat-roofed houses, built in 1916, were replaced by houses with pitched roofs the next year.

windows were small and positioned for cross-ventilation. After residents complained that the flat roofs leaked, Goodhue replaced them with red tile roofs with a slight pitch.

The Mexican houses lined Pinal Street, a narrow canyon that angled off the central plaza, directly behind the railroad tracks. Much cheaper to construct than the American houses, they cost from 525 to 1,000 dollars to build and rented at 6–12 dollars a month. They also provided fewer comforts. Grouped into duplexes or row houses, the flat-roofed minimal dwellings provided only running water, electricity, and outdoor privies. Like the American houses, they were constructed of hollow tile or wood frame, but their stucco covering was left in its original grey color.[36] In spite of this, the Mexican workers were eager to rent the houses, since they represented a vast improvement over the tents and shanties they were forced to inhabit when left to fend for themselves. The company established a waiting list, noting that the houses "cannot be built fast enough" and reported a growing demand for larger houses with indoor bathrooms.[37]

A row of Mexican duplexes. Segregated in a single canyon behind the railroad tracks, the two-room Mexican houses, equipped with outhouses, were extremely popular. If in comparison to the American houses they were cramped and lacked basic services, they were far superior to the tents and wooden shacks that Mexican workers and their families usually occupied in mining towns.

When construction was halted in 1917, due to wartime restrictions on building materials, 67 American houses and 124 Mexican houses were complete. This housed only 25 percent of Tyrone's population; the remainder, both Mexicans and Americans, leased lots from the company, for 50 cents a month, and erected either frame houses or tents. These less desirable areas were also segregated; Mexicans were restricted to the upper end of Pinal Street while the company designated other canyons for American houses costing at least 1,000 dollars.[38]

After completing his design, Goodhue dispatched his chief draftsman, Clarence Stein, to supervise construction at Tyrone and, from 1915 to 1917, visited the town twice a year.[39] He provided detailed drawings for the large two-story buildings on the plaza and took particular care with the construction of the arcades, built of hollow tile to his exacting specifications. When, in late 1917, Stein left to serve in the Army, Goodhue anticipated resuming construction as soon as the war was over. Given Phelps-Dodge's ample budget and Douglas's personal sponsorship, he had every reason to expect that Tyrone would rank as one of his major works. Although only half of his plan had been executed, enough had been built to create a booming town of four thousand people.[40]

Tyrone did not exhaust Goodhue's interest in mining towns. In 1916, after meeting Colonel Jack Greenway, a friend of Walter Douglas who was planning to develop a new mining town in southern Arizona, he envisioned a succession of mining town commissions. Writing to a friend for sketches of North Africa, he outlined his plans for a mining town in the desert, complete with palm trees, based on Moorish imagery.[41] The same year, invited to set the program for the LeBrun Fellowship, a prestigious competition for young American architects, Goodhue proposed a gold and silver mining town in the southwest. His brief posited "directors who hold that the miners' surroundings, to be tolerable, must be beautiful" and a site "very near the borderline of Mexico." Goodhue's discussion of the project's style suggests both a certain amount of dissatisfaction with Tyrone's design and a continuing search for exotic imagery. Since "the architecture of the Pueblo Indians, when modified to suit modern requirements, must of necessity lose its character . . . and Spanish work is less adapted to desert conditions than the work done by the Moors in North Africa," he directed that "the walls should be thick, the openings small, courtyards are desirable and what little architectural ornament should be produced by means of glazed and colored tile, instead of carved stone, terracotta or cast concrete." The winning entry, a romantic rendering of a walled city topped with a dome and a tower, closely resembled Goodhue's own work.[42]

LIFE IN A MODEL MINING TOWN

In Tyrone, Phelps-Dodge maintained its unusually high level of welfare work while taking care to avoid the problems that had afflicted Bisbee. The company established a complete set of social institutions but avoided any possibility of self-government. Since the only governmental unit was the distant county seat, the company ruled its own domain, maintaining police and fire departments as well as a city jail in a park. The company physically maintained the town's model character with a "sanitary squad" that cleaned the streets, collected garbage, and kept the town tidy. A well-equipped modern hospital, staffed with two doctors and five nurses, the first building constructed in the community, provided medical care to employees at a fee of 1 dollar a month.[43] Goodhue designed a large school, accommodating six hundred students, leased to the county school system for a nominal fee.[44]

Commerce was dominated by the Phelps-Dodge Mercantile Store, whose elaborate two-story structure framed the south side of the town plaza. One of the largest department stores in New Mexico, it offered all the necessities of life – groceries, clothing, furniture, and even an undertaker. To avoid monopoly, however, Phelps-Dodge encouraged a competing, independently owned store to locate across the plaza by offering a very low rent. Other local merchants and professionals included a large restaurant, a confectionery, a barber shop, a doctor, a dentist, a lawyer, and a photographer. The company kept strict control of leisure time; they forbade the sale of alcohol and eliminated the unwholesome influences of saloon and dance hall in favor of company-sponsored movies and town dances. The company organized baseball teams, and residents formed a band and an orchestra to play at weekly dances. Photographs show Tyrone's residents dancing in the plaza, gaily decorated with Chinese lanterns.[45]

Although Phelps-Dodge extended its welfare programs to Mexican workers, they segregated many of the facilities. The company built a small club with tennis courts for white-collar workers and planned to build two separate recreational clubhouses for the other workers – one for Mexicans and one for Americans. With Goodhue's monumental church still unbuilt, the community split into two separate congregations, the Catholic church, attended by Mexican workers and the Union church, which provided Protestant services for the Americans. Like many firms dealing with unskilled immigrant workers, Phelps-Dodge felt the need to educate and "Americanize" Tyrone's Mexican residents. The company considered its programs, including company housing, as an effective way of "[educating] the Mexican laborer to better methods of living."[46]

Descriptions of Tyrone's size, amenities, and beauty figured prominently in Phelps-Dodge publicity of the period. Goodhue's growing fame, the project's large budget and the company's efficient public relations department guaranteed that the town would attract interest from both architectural and business publications. By 1918, the town had become a landmark of company town design. *The Architectural Forum* and *Architectural Review* devoted extensive and well-illustrated articles to Tyrone's architecture, while *Architecture* and the *Architectural Record* prominently featured its housing in survey articles documenting outstanding examples of industrial housing. They described the town in glowing terms, praising its unified urban design and the distinctive regional quality of the architecture. In their 1922 urban design compendium, *The American Vitruvius*, Werner Hegemann and Elbert Peets used Tyrone to illustrate the value of architecture and planning that expressed a single coherent image.[47]

Other observers, more interested in industrial welfare and housing, were equally impressed by Tyrone's high standard of housing, services, and community facilities. After visiting Tyrone, Leifur Magnussen, the Bureau of Labor Statistics' expert on industrial housing, examined it in a lengthy article. In comparison to poor conditions in many mining towns, he found its physical amenities admirable, but the town, completely controlled by the company, too paternalistic.[48] Phelps-Dodge in turn defended its paternalism as a successful method of reducing turnover and improving labor relations. Charles Willis, supervisor of the company's industrial relations department, wrote a series of articles and publicity handouts in trade and technical journals claiming that Tyrone represented good value for Phelps-Dodge expenditures. According to Willis, simultaneously developing the town and the mine allowed the company to demonstrate its concern for the workers and avoid the hostility Phelps-Dodge had encountered in Bisbee and Morenci.[49]

THE NEXT GENERATION OF MINING TOWNS: CLARKDALE AND AJO

Tyrone was the first, but not the only example of the restructured copper mining town. Other mine operators experiencing labor problems were impressed by Phelps-Dodge's apparent success at Tyrone. Williams Andrews Clark and Colonel Jack Greenway, for example, both friends of Walter Douglas, shared his hard-line anti-unionism. Their extreme position, however, did not completely dominate the mining industry. S.R. Guggenheim of the Kennecott and Tye Company and Sam Lewisohn of the Miami Copper Company held more moderate views. Lewisohn initiated the "Miami Scale" which significantly raised wages. In 1914, Guggenheim, testifying before a Federal Commission, blamed the high cost of living for industrial unrest and acknowledged that "employees are fully justified in organizing outside the plant." Clark and Greenway instead followed Douglas's example and brought in architects to redesign and improve their company towns.[50]

At Ajo, Arizona, Greenway attempted to emulate Tyrone. In Ajo, as in Tyrone, new technology and labor relations formed the basis for the new town. In January 1917, more than a thousand Mexican, Indian, and Anglo workers went on strike at the New Cornelia desert mining camp at Ajo. After their own efforts in seeking higher wages than Greenway was willing to pay at the isolated camp proved futile, they asked for help from the AFL Union of Mine Mill and Smelter workers (formerly the Western Federation of Miners), but in vain. After breaking the strike – and sending twenty-six miners to Tuscon for trial – the company brought in gunmen to ensure a continuing supply of low-wage labor.[51] Several months later, the company installed a new leaching process that removed oxidized ore and made mining in the area profitable.[52] With both technical and labor problems under control, Greenway decided to reconstitute the town on a new basis. Although Goodhue was keenly interested in the commission, Greenway hired the Minneapolis firm of Kenyon and Maine to prepare a town plan and design housing. Before coming to Bisbee, Greenway had worked in the

Lake Superior region and was familiar with several iron mining towns the firm had designed in the Mesabi range.[53]

On arrival in Arizona, William Kenyon found that Ajo, located in a harsh and desolate area close to the Mexican border, consisted of a mine and a "collection of shacks," occupied by indigenous Papago Indians and Mexican laborers.[54] He laid out a town that reflected the new realities of copper mining, separating the area into three distinct town sites. The largest zone contained the town center and housing for the American skilled workers, administrators, and office workers, who would control production. Two smaller areas, in an adjacent canyon, housed the Mexican miners and the Indians, who survived by scavenging around the mining camp. Kenyon platted the Mexican and Indian sites in grids, but, clearly influenced by Tyrone, laid out the American site as a formal plan focused around a central plaza.

Although clothed in more literal Spanish colonial ornament than Goodhue's buildings for Tyrone, the plan of Ajo included many of the same elements. It began with a sequential passage leading from the rail depot. Alighting from the train, a visitor would first pass through the commercial zone – a continuous arcade of shops, restaurants, and offices which surrounded the tree-lined central plaza. Less monumental than Tyrone's center, the low arcade was ornamented with colored tiles and heavy finials. The civic zone, a wide

The arcaded shops that surrounded the plaza at Ajo, designed by Kenyon and Maine, 1917. Although far less sophisticated than Tyrone, Ajo included many of the same elements – formal symmetry combined with picturesque areas, an arcaded town center, all unified by a simplified Spanish colonial revival style.

avenue lined with club houses and churches, led from the plaza and terminated in a monumental high school on axis with the depot. From here, two streets of hotels and boarding houses angled off into the American residential area, a grid of short blocks. Winding roads led into canyons above the American town, where the hospital and mine headquarters were located.

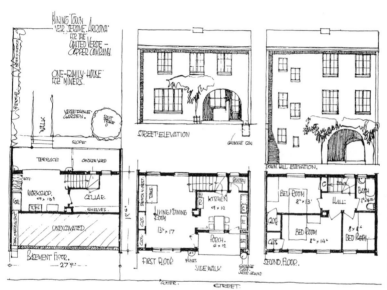

Herding and Boyd's design for an American house in "a mining town near Jerome, Arizona." Built with a concrete panel system similar to Atterbury's, the houses can be free-standing or combined in terraces. Taking advantage of the area's steep hills, the house presents an urban face to the street, then opens on to a garden on the downhill side. The plan indicates the architects' concern with the residents' lives. Provided with a minimum of three bedrooms on the upper floor and built-in furniture in the living room, the architects suggested that the garden plot be used for growing vegetables, raising chickens, and as a protected play space for children.

Different grades of housing underlined the company's labor policies. To encourage stability, the company encouraged American employees to purchase houses and building lots. Kenyon and Maine designed fifteen different types of four- and five-room houses. These were cruder versions of Goodhue's designs for Tyrone, with literal ornament derived from Spanish and Pueblo styles – wrought iron, mission gables, and wooden vegas – applied to simple cubic forms. As at Tyrone, pastel stucco covered hollow tile construction. The company offered Mexican workers no such incentives. Kenyon and Maine again followed Goodhue, providing them with a single simple type of housing, a small flat-roofed, hollow tile house with running water and an outdoor toilet, lined up in rows of repeated units.[55] To ensure their control over the unskilled miners, company policy prohibited Mexicans from buying land or houses. Instead, they could either lease lots or rent houses, from which they could be evicted at fifteen days' notice. The Indians were left to fend for themselves. When the first phase of building ended in 1917, the town center, a large hospital, and several blocks of American and Mexican houses had been completed. In 1920, the company began construction again, filling in Kenyon and Maine's plan with designs by other architects.[56]

In 1914, when the copper town of Jerome, Arizona threatened to spill over its steep site, the United Verde Copper Company established a new town 5 miles away, naming it Clarkdale, after the company's owner William Andrews Clark, the Montana "copper king." The company engineer laid out a street grid and, by 1917, American and Mexican miners had settled in haphazardly placed frame houses like those in Jerome. In early 1917, increasingly militant Jerome miners invited the IWW to start a chapter of the Metal Mine Workers Union, an act that outraged William Andrews Clark, who had threatened to flood his Montana mines rather than allow unionization. On 5 July, 1,500 American employees walked out of the mines, although Mexican miners remained at work. Five days later a group of company officials and local businessmen rounded up a group of sixty-seven "Wobblies" – members of the IWW – and deported them to Needles, California, so ending the first strike in Jerome's history. This dramatic act terminated all labor activity in Jerome, leaving wages and working conditions unchanged.[57]

Later the same year, United Verde began to upgrade housing and urban conditions in Clarkdale, hoping that improved living conditions would ease tensions and provide more control over their workers. First, they hired Arthur Kelly, a Los Angeles architect known for his bungalow designs. Kelly produced a row of Hispanic and Pueblo stucco bungalows similar to those at Ajo that residents immediately applauded as the best housing in town.[58] Encouraged, the next year the company hired the St Louis firm of Herding and Boyd to replan Clarkdale completely, with company housing for both Mexican and American workers.

Unlike Goodhue or Kenyon and Maine, who cooperated fully with the mining companies' requests, Herding and Boyd's final report to the company indicates a continuing struggle between the architects and their clients. Republished in 1920 in *The Architect and Engineer*, the report reveals the architects' evident dissatisfaction with the task of improving Clarkdale, a town one writer described as "purposeless, impractical, stupid." Instead, they submitted designs for a completely new town to be located nearby.[59] Shocked by the overcrowded and unsanitary living conditions they found in Jerome, they criticized the company's lack of "adequate provision for social welfare." They also took issue with United Verde's well-known labor policies and assigned the blame for labor unrest in Arizona not to the "spirit of radicalism," but to poor living and working conditions.[60]

Both designs were clearly influenced by Goodhue. Built on a far steeper site than Tyrone, the proposed new town was strung along the top of a ridge. The architects followed Goodhue in elaborating urbanism at a small scale, organizing the town as a single long axis with a series of plazas defined by arcades. As at Tyrone, the main public buildings – a high school and a hospital – were monumental classical two-story blocks with arched windows and minimal ornament. A massive Catholic church with dome and tower dominated the entrance to the town. In the residental areas, Herding and Boyd developed Tyrone's Spanish urbanism in a different direction, replacing the garden city synthesis of formal and informal areas with a densely built-up hill town. They designed a series of two-story hillside row houses that opened directly onto the street at the front, then stepped down to provide a garden at the rear. Even the smallest house had three bedrooms, the minimum possible, according to the architects, for families with children of both sexes. Instructed to rework the ground floor into two room and bath apartments to cut costs, they argued that the ideal home was a single family house and that anything else sacrificed the value of the community.[61]

Herding and Boyd expressed more concern with the town's social organization than had either Goodhue or Kenyon and Maine. Although they acknowledged – for economic reasons – the necessity of maintaining two separate housing areas for Mexicans and Americans, they connected them with a plaza and organized the Mexican town around a plaza with shops, dormitories, and a clubhouse – a community focus intended to "stimulate social life." When the company insisted on reducing the size and amenities of the Mexican houses, they again protested strongly, pointing out the importance of satisfactory living and social conditions to the town's continued existence.[62] After receiving their critical report, United Verde Copper abandoned plans for major improvements and allowed Clarkdale to develop on its own.

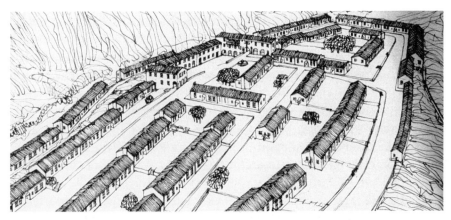

A bird's eye-view of "a mining town near Jerome, Arizona," designed for the United Verde Copper company by Herding and Boyd. The American town, across the crest of the ridge, is connected to the Mexican town below by a plaza, in the middle of which are the town's school buildings. Rows of houses are used to create an almost continuous wall around the town, creating the impression of a Spanish or Italian hill town.

ARIZONA DONS THE COPPER COLLAR

By the end of 1917, however, the existence of these impressive but controlled towns became far less critical to mine owners than they had been earlier. Walter Douglas's struggle against organized labor had climaxed in July 1917 at Bisbee, with Douglas winning a decisive victory. A peaceful strike, organized by the IWW and involving most of the town's miners, crippled Bisbee. Phelps-Dodge officials, following Walter Douglas's instructions, created a tense atmosphere in Bisbee by spreading rumors of pro-German sabotage by the anti-war IWW. On 2 July, they organized a mob of vigilantes, two thousand strong, who roamed the streets, arresting strikers and anyone who was suspected of supporting them, as traitors. The town was completely cut off while the vigilantes herded two thousand strikers and their sympathizers at gunpoint onto boxcars, then shipped them to a remote location in New Mexico. The army later rescued the deportees, then held them for two months to avoid further violence. Under threat of death, few ever returned to Bisbee. In the meantime, Phelps-Dodge brought in new miners and resumed operations.[63]

The Bisbee deportation became a national scandal and resulted in a Federal investigation, which fixed blame squarely on Phelps-Dodge and Walter Douglas, who had personally given orders for the deportations. Douglas was briefly arrested for "conspiracy to injure, oppress, threaten and intimidate United States citizens."[64] Arizona Governor Hunt warned: "a ruthless vested interest under the guise of patriotism is going to crush all organized labor." And, indeed, the outcome of the Bisbee deportations was to destroy labor's power in Arizona.[65] The extreme syndicalism of the IWW and the patriotic issues involved in wartime strikes polarized public opinion. Many patriotic citizens, like the virulently anti-German Goodhue, strongly supported Douglas's actions.[66] Goodhue also shared Douglas's dislike of labor unions. Only a year earlier, he had condemned unions as "extremely destructive" in lowering the quality of craftsmanship in building.[67] This changed political mood, both nationally and locally, allowed the mining companies to reassert their power. Arizona, as one writer put it, "donned the copper collar" once again.

Thus, by 1921, when the price of copper fell after its war-time high, and in spite of Tyrone's remarkable architecture and urban design, Walter Douglas did not hesitate to abandon the town only five years after its birth. In April 1921, Tyrone, still thriving, was the seventh largest city in New Mexico when Phelps-Dodge announced the mine's closure. In a meeting with company director Cleland Dodge in the plaza, the miners offered to take a 25 percent pay cut to keep working but Phelps-Dodge suspended operations and shut down the mines. The company ran special trains to El Paso for workers who wanted to return to Mexico. The Mexican government then provided free transportation from El Paso to agricultural areas in Chihuahua.[68] The rest of the miners drifted away. Within weeks, the population of the town shrank to seven hundred, and within a year to less than fifty.[69] Copper prices rose again the following year, but there was no longer any need to resume production in New Mexico. Arizona's changed political and labor climate allowed mining companies, led by Phelps-Dodge, to reassume the political and economic power that labor had challenged before the war. Over the next forty years, the abandoned town of Tyrone decayed romantically, regularly rediscovered by visiting architects. The town became a curiosity, as one writer called it, "a Beaux Arts ghost town."[70] During the 1960s, Phelps-Dodge introduced open pit mining on the site and the pit's expansion gradually swallowed the remaining buildings. By 1970, nothing was left of Tyrone.

What might have been a major achievement in Goodhue's career turned into a footnote. Architecture and planning, rather than being, as he assumed, the goal of the project, were simply by-products of Phelps-Dodge's need for control over the conditions of production. Like Indian Hill, Tyrone was an architectural success but an urban failure. This contradictory outcome highlights architects' continuing difficulties in designing company towns. Although their designs became more comprehensive, much of the increased power that architects had claimed was largely illusory, an ideological representation rather than real control over the towns' organization. Despite their fluency in the discourses of urban reform and industrial betterment, architects still operated, as they always had, completely at the behest of their corporate clients. Thus, in spite of the sophistication of their design and technical skills, Atterbury and Goodhue had difficulty in comprehending the social and economic premises of the "new" company town. This was due in part to the gap between the rhetoric the architectural profession employed to declare their independence from corporate clients and the actual conditions of practice. Similarly, adopting the progressive goals of social harmony, which downplayed class conflict, encouraged architects to accept the rhetoric of industrial betterment without comprehending the logic behind it – the elimination of unions and greater control over workers. Unable to identify the real rationale behind the company town, they could not understand the constraints clients placed on their activities. Moreover, socially sympathetic to their clients, neither designer was able to step outside their professional roles, as Herding and Boyd had done, to criticize the basic order of the company towns they designed. Instead, they continued to seek solutions that lay within their professional control: for Atterbury, this meant improved technology and for Goodhue, improved aesthetics.

8

PROFESSIONAL SOLUTIONS: JOHN NOLEN AND THE STANDARDIZATION OF COMPANY TOWN PLANNING

As a member of the new city planning profession, John Nolen proposed an alternative approach to the company town. Seeing the growing interest in company towns as an important professional opportunity, Nolen standardized company town planning. Unlike Grosvenor Atterbury and Bertram Goodhue, he had little interest in new architectural images or innovative building technology. Instead, he assembled a body of specialized knowledge and standard procedures intended to demonstrate the planner's organizational, social, and financial expertise. Attempting to circumvent the limitations of traditional client relationships, Nolen also sought a broader social base for company town planning. A prolific and persuasive writer, well aware of the value of publicity, Norton produced scores of articles and books advertising the value of planned company towns. These attracted new clients and Nolen's office produced more than twenty-five company town plans ranging from New England textile villages to Arizona copper camps. Although only a few of these were built, Nolen optimistically assessed his plans for company towns as an important step in the development of the planning profession.

THE PLANNING PROFESSIONAL

Nolen's education and professional background gave him a very different perspective from Atterbury or Goodhue. A graduate of Girard College, Philadelphia, a school for fatherless but academically promising boys, Nolen worked as a secretary for five years in order to finance his way through the Wharton School of Finance at the University of Pennsylvania.

He graduated in 1893 with a degree in economics and public administration.[1] A year-long sojourn in Europe sparked his interest in city planning, then called "civic" improvement. In 1903, at the age of thirty-three, already married and with children, he enrolled in the newly established Landscape Architecture program at Harvard, intending to specialize in "civic art." Even before graduating in 1905, he opened an office on Harvard Square. Although Nolen signed his projects "Landscape Architect," he considered "City Planning" to be his real field and his office quickly progressed from private landscaping to larger projects.[2] By 1909, when he attended the first National Conference on City Planning and the Problems of Congestion, Nolen had already identified himself thoroughly with the profession of city planning.

In spite of his Harvard training, which taught landscape architecture as a fine art, Nolen quickly became an ally of the "city functional" planners who dominated the meeting. Nolen agreed with New York landscape architect Robert Pope's pronouncement that "city planning for social and economic ends will logically result in . . . a genuinely and completely beautiful city,"[3] but was personally more concerned with establishing the planner's comprehensive responsibility for the city. In his address to the conference, he asked, "What is needed in American city planning?" and answered, "Everything."

> With few exceptions, our cities are lacking in almost all of the essentials of convenience, comfort, orderliness and appropriate beauty that characterizes the cities of other nations. . . . We should no longer be content with mere increase in population and wealth. We should insist upon asking, "how do the people live, where do they work, what do they play?"
>
> American towns and cities need (1) an open minded and skillful investigation of their problems (2) united and hearty cooperation on the part of various public authorities and private individuals (3) prompt and courteous execution of the plan found to be the best for all concerned.[4]

Nolen was active in many of the reform groups that later coalesced into the planning profession. Lacking Atterbury's entry to upper-class circles and without Goodhue's creative abilities, Nolen relied on these networks to establish himself professionally. In addition to joining the NCCP, he became a founding member of the National Housing Association, formed in 1910 for housing reformers excluded by the NCCP's focus on comprehensive planning. He belonged to the National Municipal League and served as vice-president of the American Civic Association. When the NCCP established the American Institute of City Planning as a separate organization for professional planners, Nolen was a charter member and subsequently became its president. Later, he succeeded Raymond Unwin as president of the International Federation of Housing and Town Planning.[5]

Nolen maintained his professional associations through a voluminous correspondence, regularly corresponding with most of the other members of the fledgling planning profession, including Charles Mulford Robinson, Frederick Law Olmsted, Jr, Charles Eliot II, Elbert Peets, and Harlan Bartholomew. Other correspondents were prominent housing reformers, such as Grosvenor Atterbury and Lawrence Veiller, European planners, such as Ebenezer Howard, Raymond Unwin, and Werner Hegemann, and important Progressives, such as Richard Ely, Simon Patten, and Charles A. Beard.[6] Nolen also wrote prolifically for professional journals such as *Landscape Architecture, American Architect, Engineering News-Record, City Planning*, and *Survey*. He wrote an article for the inaugural issue of the *American City*, the first journal specifically devoted to American urbanism, and served as planning editor of *National Municipal Review*. He edited a town planning textbook for the National Municipal League and regularly compiled his own articles and planning reports, publishing *Replanning Small Cities* in 1912, followed by *New Ideals in the Planning of Cities Towns and Villages* in 1919, and *New Towns for Old* in 1927.[7]

Nolen's practice supported and supplemented his public role. From 1915 to 1925, his Cambridge office was one of the largest planning firms in the country, producing anything from garden designs to city plans.[8] Nolen's particular talents were for organization and management. Unlike Atterbury or Goodhue, he took little interest in the aesthetic aspects of his plans. Hiring capable and talented designers such as Philip Foster, Nolen left the physical planning to them. According to a former employee, Earle Draper, the only question Nolen ever asked about a plan was, "Shall we make white or blue prints?"[9] Nolen worked tirelessly to publicize his work and maintain his contacts, travelling more than 30,000 miles a year and spending a least six months each year away from his office. Nolen was so busy that he interviewed job applicants while traveling, meeting them at the station and conducting the interview aboard the train.[10]

Fewer than a third of the plans Nolen's office prepared were even partially realized, but he did not regard this as a problem. As he wrote to Harlan Bartholomew:

> I look upon such plans as largely propaganda and publicity and do not share the opinions of others that because they did not get carried out or even followed up at the time, they are necessarily an indication of failure. To my mind they are stages in the development of public opinion.[11]

At this early stage in the profession's development, Nolen, like many other planners, such as Thomas Adams, considered the planner's role to be primarily educational. Constantly proselytizing for city planning, Nolen utilized public relations as an essential professional tool.

THE BUSINESS COMMUNITY AS CLIENT

Since no public planning agencies existed, planning efforts depended on private support. Recognizing that the business community could provide important financial and political backing for their activities, planners increasingly sought to involve them in planning. The 1917 American Institute of Architects' report, "City Planning Progress," advised architects and planners to follow these "steps in planning":

- Get a private backer – preferably a person with recognized standing and means.
- Collect a similar well-informed and influential small group around him.
- Begin an educational campaign simultaneously with the hiring of a planner, preferably a "first-class publicity man" with local newspaper connections.
- Keep planning continually in the public eye by publicizing each step.[12]

Nolen, always pragmatic, followed this strategy very closely, building another network of potential sponsors in the business community. He published articles in business publications such as *Chamber of Commerce News*, *American Industries*, the journal of the National Association of Manufacturers, *Manufacturers Record*, and *National Real Estate Journal*. Lecturing to local Chambers of Commerce, businessmen's groups, and organizations such as the National Association of Manufacturers, he exhorted them to "provide properly paved and properly ordered streets, decent housing for all the people, dignified and well-arranged public buildings, convenient and appropriate railroad approaches, ample and suitable schools, playgrounds, parks and public gardens, in fact, a convenient, healthful and beautiful city."[13] To make these expensive improvements more palatable, he presented them as business propositions, "opportunities to apply sound business methods to civic affairs" and "the legitimate reward . . . of getting more out of a city by putting more into it."[14]

While Nolen was touring the country urging businessmen to support planning, a new institution, the municipal planning commission, emerged. In 1909, the first independent planning commission was created by the mayor of Chicago to provide official support for the Plan of Chicago. Privately sponsored by the Chicago Commercial Club, the Plan represented the most ambitious attempt at large-scale urban planning in America. Operating independently of local government structures and politics, but with municipal backing, planning commissions usually included members of city government acting *ex officio* along with prominent citizens, who served as unpaid members.[15] Although devoid of real power, the commissions raised funds to commission and publicize comprehensive plans. Composed largely of business and real-estate interests, with a minority of lawyers and architects, the commissions reflected a more conservative bias than earlier progressive urban reform movements.[16] Planning commissions multiplied and, by 1923, they had sponsored comprehensive plans in eighty-three cities. Nolen's firm, well known in business circles across the country, produced twenty-nine of these.

Nolen's connections in the business world, consolidated between 1905 and 1915, provided him with planning commissions for the rest of his career. His supporters ranged from local businessmen in Reading, Pennsylvania, and Bridgeport, Connecticut, to the conservative New York financiers who founded Kingsport, Tennessee, to two progressive New England capitalists, Edward A. Filene, the Boston department store magnate, and Charles S. Bird, a paper manufacturer.[17] In 1910, Filene, an early practitioner of welfare work, met Nolen through his efforts to create, along with Louis D. Brandeis and other prominent Progressives, an ambitious metropolitan planning board for the Boston region. Although the plan was defeated, Filene became an ally of Nolen's and an advocate of comprehensive planning. In 1922, Filene and Nolen formed the Boston Liberal Club, an elite group devoted to civic reform.[18] Less well known than Filene, Bird, an unsuccessful Progressive Party candidate for Governor of Massachusetts, was equally devoted to scientific management, welfare work, and profit-sharing. The largest employer in Walpole, Massachusetts, Bird, an ardent lay practitioner of city planning, organized and controlled the Walpole Town Planning Committee. With Bird's financial support, the committee commissioned nearly fifty projects from Nolen between 1913 and 1935. Nolen produced everything from a playground to a comprehensive regional plan, and Walpole became a showcase for urban planning.[19]

NEPONSET GARDEN VILLAGE

In 1913 Bird commissioned Nolen to design an industrial village in East Walpole. Nolen and Bird named the settlement to reflect their affinity with garden city planning. Describing his plans for the town in the *Christian Science Monitor*, Nolen explained that the "garden village" was modeled directly on English and German garden city and garden suburb developments and would be financed as a co-partnership enterprise, "managed and conducted by the residents in the village for their own benefit." Nolen concluded by stating, "I have seen many of the best housing schemes in the United States but I know of nothing, either here or abroad, which seems to me on the whole so satisfactory and practical as this village plan for East Walpole."[20] Such hyperbole would become a trademark of Nolen's optimistic descriptions of his planning projects.

Despite its name and Nolen's rhetoric, Neponset Garden Village bore little resemblance to either the organization or design of English and German garden cities, but instead was informed by American sources. The plan, with the exception of a single cul-de-sac, clearly belongs to the American picturesque tradition. Like many of Frederick Law Olmsted, Sr's

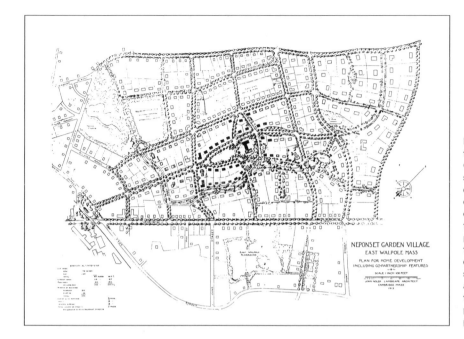

Nolen's 1913 plan for Neponset Garden Village. In spite of Nolen's claims of garden city planning and co-partnership financing, the proposed village in fact resembled older company towns, such as Whitinsville and Hopedale, and followed earlier picturesque planning styles.

plans, it features large areas of natural parkland, several ponds, a forest preserve, and enormous tracts of land set aside for recreation and gardening. Approached by a landscaped parkway that curves through the village, the plan's main focus is an oval town common with a community building at one end. In contrast to Unwin and Atterbury's tightly composed and controlled spaces, Nolen laid out a loosely knit, naturalistic landscape. The winding, tree-lined streets, large lots, and low-density housing recalled such earlier suburbs as Riverside.

Perspective drawings of Neponset, depicting an idyllic village with boxy colonial houses set among trees and an occasional church steeple, suggest another likely influence – the New England company towns. The textile towns of Whitinsville and Hopedale, less than 20 miles away, were greatly admired by both Bird and Nolen. The company town was an appropriate model since Bird's paper mill, adjacent to the village, would furnish most of Neponset's residents. The village's financial organization was also closer to the company town than to the English co-partnership suburb. Bird set up a separate corporation to buy land and develop it, with profits limited to 5 percent, but he owned all the shares and completely controlled the village. Nolen urged Bird to organize the town like Fairfield, Torrance, and Goodyear Heights, building several model houses, then selling lots to skilled workers with strict design reviews to maintain the village's character.[21]

In 1915, acknowledging Nolen's limits, Bird hired the New York architectural firm of Mann and MacNeille.[22] Although Bird hired them to design low-cost housing for unskilled workers, Mann and MacNeille, with far more practical experience working in company towns, questioned Bird and Nolen's plans for Neponset village. Thoroughly analyzing the economic and social needs of the industrial town, the architects rejected co-partnership financing as unrealistic. Based on their previous experiences in Goodyear Heights and the mining town of Hauto, Pennsylvania, they proposed a variety of ownership and rental arrangements. Skilled workers could buy houses with a special mortgage and insurance plans similar to those used at Goodyear Heights and Indian Hill, while unskilled workers had a variety of housing options, including rental houses and family "boarding houses," with separate bedrooms and bathrooms for boarders to avoid "the danger of lax morality."[23]

Mann and MacNeille also tackled social issues. While rhetorically deploring paternalism, they recommended highly controlling "social engineering" programs. This reflected the design profession's continuing absorption of welfare ideology. They proposed establishing a Social Department to oversee the village. A female social worker, employed by Bird, would live in a "model" house furnished as an example to workers. There, she would "befriend the villagers, aid them in sickness, instruct them in housekeeping and encourage unsophisticated enjoyment." Her job would include organizing company-subsidized entertainment such as "afternoon teas and little luncheon parties to bring the women of the community together." The social worker would collect rents and mortgage payments, allowing her to monitor the condition of the houses and, if necessary, take remedial action.[24] The architects also suggested encouraging "thrift and morality" by dispersing model families throughout the village to serve as a good influence on their neighbors. They structured the sports fields and allotment gardens Nolen planned, organizing company sports and a farmers' association to raise vegetables, chickens, pigs, and goats. These outdoor activities, they believed, improved the workers' health, and "better health makes for greater industry and efficiency."[25]

Mann and MacNeille designed Neponset's houses specifically for working-class tastes. Adapting the range of inexpensive standardized housing types they had developed with a New York construction firm, Standard Buildings, they provided twenty-one different house types priced from 1,500 to 5,000 dollars. Although they agreed with Atterbury that group houses were more "artistic," they designed the single family houses that workers overwhelmingly preferred. Altering the occupants' preferences was a matter for future education, they felt. Similarly, although they personally favored the "almost severe lines of the pure colonial type," they claimed that workers favored more variety and individuality, particularly picturesque details such as bay windows, porches, and trellises.[26] Heavily detailed dormered cottages in a vague colonial style, Mann and MacNeille's house designs resembled Atterbury's Indian Hill houses. However, in spite of his enthusiasm for planning, Charles Bird decided not to follow Nolen or Mann and MacNeille's recommendations, leaving Neponset Garden Village at the planning stage.

STANDARDIZING THE "NEW" COMPANY TOWN

Mann and MacNeille's systematic approach to Neponset Garden Village demonstrated the increasing organization and standardization of professional knowledge about company town design. From 1915 to 1917, as the war-time industrial boom dramatically increased the number of company town commissions, architects and planners began to collect and codify information and experience into a practical body of knowledge. In 1918 an advertisement titled "The Architect and Industrial Housing" appeared in *Architectural Forum*. Its message applied equally to other design professions: "No more attractive field opens before the architect, at the present time, than that of industrial housing. To provide livable homes for American working men has become a national problem which offers to the profession a rare opportunity for creative work."[27] Recognizing this, professional organizations and journals became clearinghouses for practical information and design proposals. Beginning in 1915, the National Housing Association devoted sessions at its annual conference to industrial housing and planning issues.[28] Articles on industrial housing appeared regularly in architectural, engineering, and planning journals. Textbooks proliferated, offering conceptual overviews and practical solutions to the problems of designing working-class housing and towns. *Homes for Workmen* compiled specialized articles, while engineer Morris Knowles used his professional experience as the basis for his book, *Industrial Housing*.[29] Government reports supplemented professional studies. Leifur Magnussen published detailed accounts of Tyrone, New Mexico and Morgan Park, Minnesota in the *Monthly Labor Review*, followed, in 1917, by his encyclopedic work, *Housing by Employers in the United States*, a detailed examination of company housing in industrial regions across the country.[30]

Architectural Review and *Architectural Forum* both published a series of special issues on industrial housing and towns. These combined detailed analyses of technical and design issues with discussions of the social and economic dimensions of workers' housing. The January 1917 issue of *Architectural Review*, for example, reprinted the complete results of the Immigrant Housing competition, along with an article by a social worker outlining the psychological and physical requirements of housing workers, an article by Frances Kellor discussing the "application of Americanization to housing," and a readers' forum asking, "Can the profession improve the architecture of the low-cost American house?" In April

1918, *Architectural Forum* reported on Tyrone and Goodyear Heights and published articles on industrial village planning, housing finance, housing for single male workers, and the cultural and social characteristics of immigrant workers.[31]

KISTLER, PENNSYLVANIA: "A VILLAGE FOR FACTORY WORKERS"

John Nolen, ever alert for professional opportunities, became part of this movement, expanding his comprehensive approach to include company town planning. Thus, in 1915, when the Mt Union Refactories Company asked Nolen to plan a small industrial village in Pennsylvania, he jumped at the opportunity to gain practical experience in the field. Impressed by Mann and MacNeille's expertise, he hired the firm to design the housing. Less socially and economically ambitious than Indian Hill, Tyrone, or Neponset Garden Village, Kistler was a pragmatic venture in attracting and housing unskilled labor. As war production rapidly expanded demand for silica brick, Mt Union brickmakers competed for increasingly scarce labor, recruiting workers in large eastern cities and in the South. Since brickmakers traditionally provided housing for workers, Mt Union Refractories hoped that building a model company town would give them a significant advantage in attracting and retaining workers.[32] Influenced by the industrial betterment movement, the company wanted to pursue welfare work but also needed to house low-paid workers cost-effectively.[33]

The low-paid residents, the company's limited budget, and a difficult site all posed problems for Nolen. The town site, across the bridge from the plant, was less than ideal. Much of the triangular area consisted of low land, annually flooded by the river. In order to save money, the company insisted on using the farm buildings left on the site.[34] Nolen adjusted his plan to meet these conditions, using the low-lying areas, unsuitable for building, as parks. Parkland occupied nearly 30 percent of the town's area, double the area Nolen usually recommended.[35] He crowded the housing into three dense areas around the edges. Rural landscaping softened the grid of rectangular blocks. Avenues of shade trees lined the streets, with a maple tree in every front yard. Several of the secondary streets were left unpaved and seeded with grass as play areas for children.[36] The village's public functions were housed in the old farm buildings around the edge of the site. The barn was remodeled into a colonial-style community center that also housed unmarried white-collar workers, the plant superintendent occupied a large brick farmhouse, and Nolen planned shops and a train station along the road. These dispersed structures left the town without a definite focus, a lack of unity that Nolen acknowledged "decentralizes community life."[37]

In spite of these problems, Kistler was the first "new" company town designed specifically for unskilled workers. Introducing welfare programs, Mt Union Refractories approached

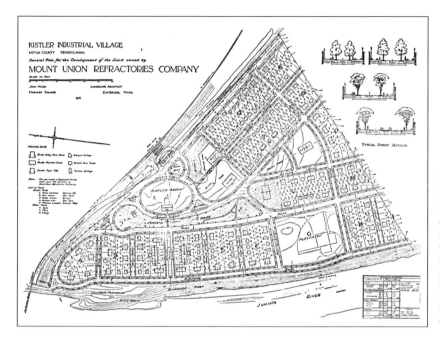

Nolen's plan for Kistler, Pennsylvania. This highly economical undertaking was one of the few towns explicitly designed for unskilled workers. Nolen balanced three dense zones of "small houses on small lots" with large areas of parkland and provided a dispersed town center.

their workers with a mixture of suspicion and benevolence. Although they maintained such features of old-style company towns as a high-priced company store and deducted rent payments, water, and the store bill from workers' pay envelopes, the company also introduced modern social programs and services, providing an elementary school, employing a playground worker trained in first aid to supervise the children's play and several visiting nurses, and offering sewing and knitting classes in the community building.[38] Nolen proposed agriculture as a means of supplementing the low-paid workers' diets and incomes, planning fruit orchards and vines, large allotment gardens, and chicken runs and animal pens in the park areas.[39]

Mann and MacNeille adapted their standard house plans to fit the incomes and needs of low-paid workers, providing decent accommodation at remarkably low prices. They developed houses that could be built for 1,000 to 1,600 dollars each. According to a survey made by the Harvard Social Museum in 1917, the Kistler houses were the cheapest industrial housing in the country, with the exception of unimproved mining camp houses without sanitation or electricity.[40] Although small – 20 × 28 feet – each had from five to eight rooms with a full bathroom, electricity, and a small furnace. Well-built, the wood-frame houses had full basements, and were finished with clapboard or shingles and a durable roof and porch. Rents ranged from 10 to 13 dollars a month, 20 to 25 percent of the brickworkers' monthly wages.

"Artistic" houses designed for Kistler by Mann and MacNeille. Although smaller than other houses, the Norman Cottage, Georgian Cottage, and Vermont Farmhouse styles proved unexpectedly popular with workers. Courtesy of Huntingdon County Historical Society.

Ethnicity raised other design issues. Kistler's new residents, recruited from eastern cities and rural areas in South Carolina and Virginia, were ethnically diverse. Eastern Europeans were the largest group, followed by Italians, Irish, and a sizeable number of southern blacks. Nolen saw the town itself as a form of Americanization: "The population being so largely foreign in its make-up, there is a distinct necessity for a lead to be given in the direction of Americanism – the provision of something tangible, in the form of good living conditions – more nearly express the ideals of this country." The architects, more familiar with the needs of immigrant families with low incomes, made specific adjustments. Kistler's houses, although much smaller than those at Indian Hill, had more rooms to accommodate larger families. The average Indian Hill family had three to four members while those at Kistler had more than five. One bedroom, accessible only from the kitchen, was intended for a boarder.[41] At the same time, the architects provided amenities usually reserved for the middle class, such as separate dining rooms.

Mann and MacNeille believed that each immigrant group had a distinct style of habitation. Although they had previously considered East Europeans to be poor tenants, compared to Scandinavians or Portuguese, at Kistler they discovered that they actively responded to architectural considerations.[42] Three of the six house types they designed were picturesque cottages with what the architects called an "artistic appearance." Similar to houses being designed for higher paid workers, the Vermont Farmhouse, the Norman and Georgian Cottage models, and the colonial revival and vernacular styles featured shingled surfaces, gambrel roofs, dormer windows, and elaborate porches.[43] These names and styles evoked, as they had in Indian Hill, the virtues of American rural communities. Although they were smaller than the plain houses, the "artistic" dwellings became the most popular and desirable houses in the village. The residents' preferences for "cozy and home-like" houses convinced Perry MacNeille that architectural imagery was essential for even the lowest-paid workers:

> Rest for the mind and soul, not just for the body should become the principle aim in designing work-ingmen's houses. . . . It is often claimed that these effects are produced only among educated and refined people but that the common workingman is insensible to them. . . . This has not been found to be the case. An artistic house in a picturesque village makes a pleasanter home to return to, is more restful, more inspiring and increases the family's pride.[44]

Construction at Kistler continued throughout 1915 and 1916, then was abandoned due to high war-time costs. The company developed only 40 of the 60 acres and built only half of the 220 projected houses. Black workers and their families, relegated to two blocks in the central housing area, were the only segregated group. Although they occupied the same style houses as other workers, without room to expand, these two streets became over-crowded and living conditions deteriorated. As black workers continued to arrive, they had to board with other black families, with as many as six boarders crowded into a single house. The lack of housing forced many blacks to leave their families behind in the South.[45]

Until 1941, when it decided to sell the houses, the company maintained the village. In twenty-five years, the company never raised the rents although wages were low and layoffs frequent during the 1920s and 1930s.[46] Most residents bought their houses and many of the original employees worked at the plant until retirement. Like Indian Hill, Kistler remained incomplete. The company never built the retail stores or station Nolen planned, so they converted one of the houses into a store. But in spite of this, Kistler fulfilled its goal, stated by Nolen as "insuring in some degree permanency of service on the part of the workmen and a better class of laborers."[47]

INDUSTRIAL TOWN PLANNING

In spite of its limitations, Nolen and Mann and MacNeille used Kistler to advertise their growing mastery of company town planning. Mann and MacNeille went on to design Jefferson Rouge, Michigan for the Solvay Process Corporation, Riverdale, New York for the Rome Copper and Brass Company, and Perryville, Maryland for the Atlas Powder Company. Their "artistic" Kistler house appeared over and over again in different guises.[48] Nolen also began to specialize in planning industrial villages, Using the same techniques he had used to publicize comprehensive planning, he compiled an enormous library of material on company towns and published numerous articles on industrial town planning, illustrating them with Kistler, Indian Hill, and Goodyear Heights.[49] Nolen drew on his existing professional and business networks as sources for company town commissions. The National Housing Association and other professional groups routinely referred inquiries from manufacturers interested in company towns to Nolen. His constantly expanding network of contacts provided other opportunities. After Nolen met architect Clinton Mackenzie at Kingsport, for example, Mackenzie hired him to prepare a plan for a mining town.[50]

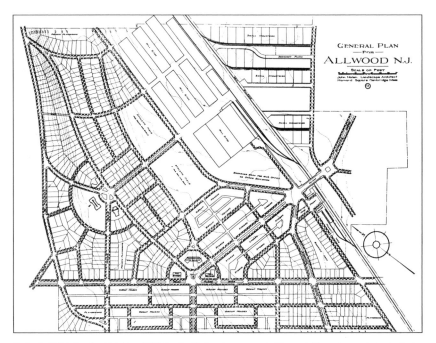

Nolen's 1917 plan for Brighton Mills' unbuilt development at Allwood, New Jersey is typical of his work after Kistler. He combined a formal town center with a grid of row houses for unskilled workers. Collaborating with architect George B. Post, designer of Eclipse Park, Murphy and Dana, and William Somerville, both winners of the Immigrant Housing Competition, as well as Pittsburgh engineer Morris Knowles, the town promised to be Nolen's biggest success. Nolen worked closely with the company's president, William Lyall, a prominent welfare advocate and director of the National Society for the Promotion of Industrial Education. Deeply concerned about the social basis of the town, Lyall supported Nolen's plans for an ideal workers' community which would house both skilled and unskilled workers and provide them with gardens, parks, athletic fields, a community house, and a full array of welfare services. However, in 1918, when the plan was complete, construction costs had risen so high that Lyall reluctantly abandoned the project after building only a few houses.

Nolen established a standard office procedure to respond to the hundreds of letters he received expressing interest in company towns. He provided potential clients with a brief bibliography listing "the best things in print," including copies of his own articles and planning reports. He listed examples of successful industrial towns, including Kistler, Indian Hill, and Hopedale, and urged clients to visit them. If a manufacturer responded positively, Nolen sent a list of detailed questions about the company, the local housing situation, and the workers' wages, ethnicity, and homeownership levels. Only then would Nolen send a member of his staff to survey the site, meet the client, and prepare a report with specific recommendations.[51] From 1914 to 1920, the Nolen office prepared more than twenty-five preliminary plans. These included every type of company town from New England textile mill villages (Nashua Mills, New Hampshire) to Appalachian coal mining settlements (International Coal Products, Clinchfield, Virginia) and western copper mining camps (Inspiration Copper Company, Miami, Arizona).[52] Nolen collaborated with architects specializing in industrial housing; working with Mann and MacNeille in a project for the American Brass Company in Waterbury, Connecticut, with Coffin and Coffin on Overlook Colony, a town near Claymont, Delaware, for the General Chemical Company, and with George B. Post and Murphy and Dana on Allwood, New Jersey, a textile town for Brighton Mills.[53] Of these, only seven were completely planned and none was built following Nolen's plans. In spite of this, the number of plans Nolen produced and published consolidated company town planning as a clearly defined professional task, rather than just a series of one-off projects.

KINGSPORT, TENNESSEE: "AN INDUSTRIAL CITY BUILT TO ORDER"

Late in 1915, a group of New York businessmen approached Nolen for advice about a new town they were promoting in a remote area of southern Appalachia. John B. Dennis and a local associate, J. Fred Johnson, had formed the Kingsport Improvement Company (KIC) to develop a multi-industry city in the northeastern corner of Tennessee, along the route of the Carolina, Clinchfield and Ohio Railroad. Ample supplies of waterpower, coal, and a local population of poor farmers and mountaineers made it ripe for industrial development. As factories began to locate in Kingsport, the settlement quickly turned into a crowded boom town. Anxious to impose physical order on the chaos, Dennis and Johnson turned to professional experts.[54] Always optimistic, Nolen announced, "the whole thing presents a very interesting situation that is full of possibilities for the application of the best planning principles." However, when his associate Philip Foster arrived in Kingsport in March 1916, he found other professionals already working on key tasks, including W.C.

Hattan, a civil engineer, F.S. Tainter, a New Yorker who specialized in water and sewer engineering, Lola Anderson, a landscape specialist, and Clinton Mackenzie, a New York architect and housing reformer. He also discovered that the downtown was already under construction following a plan made a decade earlier by William Dunlap, a railroad engineer.[55]

Nolen's office produced a preliminary plan in 1916, and in 1919 issued a far more comprehensive plan that included expansion for new areas, a larger scale plan of the downtown, and detailed plans outlining street sections, zoning, housing areas, landscaping and tree planting, and parks, playgrounds, and parkways.[56] Kingsport grew rapidly – by 1920 it had ten thousand residents – requiring Nolen's office, which continued to be officially associated with Kingsport until 1922, to prepare a succession of plans. The job served as a training ground for members of Nolen's staff. Earle Draper, Russell Van Ness Black, and Tracy Auger, all of whom later became well-known planners, began their careers at Kingsport.

Nolen's general plan for Kingsport acknowledged the centrality of industrial production, siting two linear industrial districts near rail lines on the south and west edges of town. He planned residential areas in proximity to workplaces – more expensive areas of single family houses occupied the hilly areas above the downtown while lower-priced dwellings provided easy access to the manufacturing districts. As in all his plans, Nolen reserved large green areas for parks. Just as at Kistler, Nolen provided a hierarchical street network, with wide boulevards in the central areas, then narrower curving streets and alley access in housing areas. Nolen worked closely with Clinton Mackenzie to lay out residential areas for different classes: Armstrong Village housed unskilled workers in group houses, the 'Fifties' and White City offered cottages for skilled workers in a garden city setting, while Orchard Court was modeled on upper-middle-class suburbs such as Forest Hills Gardens.[57] Mackenzie, who designed buildings that ranged from impressive Georgian residences for local notables to the Kingsport Inn, was only one of the prominent architects the KIC brought to Kingsport; others included Grosvenor Atterbury, Thomas Hastings of Carrere and Hastings, and Electus D. Litchfield.

Nolen, busy with other work, rarely visited the town himself, although, while passing through in 1919, he declared, "I am delighted with the growth and appearance of Kingsport. It is rapidly attaining every wish I had for it."[58] In spite of this claim, the KIC never officially accepted his plan and local engineers either ignored or rejected many of his recommendations. Both Nolen and his biographer John Hancock exaggerated the planner's role in Kingsport, claiming that Nolen supervised Kingsport's engineering and construction until the mid-1920s. Although both Nolen and the KIC publicly emphasized their association, which enhanced the planner's reputation and legitimized the town's

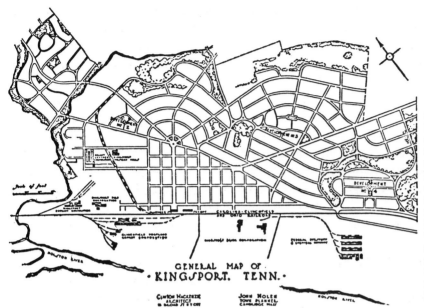

GENERAL MAP OF
· KINGSPORT. TENN. ·

Nolen's 1919 plan for Kingsport, Tennessee. Although Church Circle, the central design feature, was already present before Nolen arrived, he developed the residential areas to the east of the town center and planned the Beaux Arts Armstrong Village near the industrial sector. Note the large number of parks and woodland preserves across the city – a trademark of Nolen's planning.

"model" qualities, Nolen actually seems to have had remarkably little influence on the ultimate realization of Kingsport, which remained firmly in the hands of Dennis and Johnson.[59]

A telling example of the gap between the town's profit-minded developers and the socially concerned designers was Nolen and Mackenzie's plan for a "negro village." Nolen declared that "the colored population, being uncommonly high-class and industrious, is esteemed accordingly," and that Kingsport would "develop its colored section in marked contrast to the squalid 'Nigger-town' districts common in southern communities."[60] And Mackenzie announced "advanced plans" for laying out "a negro village of the first order providing the same grade of housing and general development as is furnished for the white population."[61] Somewhat later, Nolen's staff reported that the KIC had concluded that "it was too bad to give the colored people such a fine piece of land." Armstrong Village for blacks became the Borden Mill Village for whites working for the town's largest employers.[62] In spite of this, Nolen continued to praise Kingsport, particularly admiring its diversified industrial base, which he considered to be socially and economically superior to the single-industry company town. Nolen even maintained his support during the 1930s, when conservative businessmen used Kingsport – by then notorious for low wages, the absence of unions, and limited political participation – as an argument for the superiority of business control over government planning.[63]

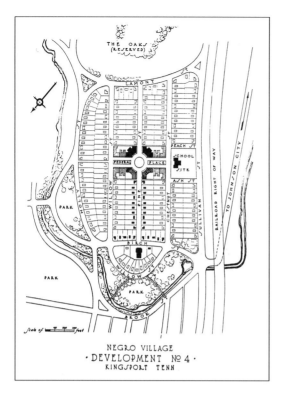

NEGRO VILLAGE
·DEVELOPMENT № 4·
KINGSPORT TENN

Nolen and Mackenzie's plan for the "Negro Village," indicated by no. 4 on the general plan, an excellent example of small-scale community planning designed to accommodate a population of one thousand and provide stores, a church, and a school. They proposed a symmetrical area of small but well-detailed single family houses surrounded on three sides by parks and organized around a village green leading to a school and a church.

THE GOVERNMENT TAKES OVER: WAR HOUSING PROGRAMS

By 1918, Nolen had become disheartened with the prospects for company town planning. Abandoning his characteristic optimism, he concluded that even the best planned new company towns were unsatisfactory as communities. For them to succeed, he argued, they needed more attention to human and social requirements, more services and public spaces, co-operative ownership, and "more art in planning and building" than private employers were willing to provide.[64] Almost in answer to these complaints, the government offered Nolen and other designers an unprecedented opportunity by sponsoring a new series of industrial communities. Even before the entry of the United States into World War I, the Federal Government had begun to assume a powerful role in governing all aspects of the nation's economic system. The war-time boom that had begun in 1915, although producing unprecedented profits, had exacerbated labor problems. In crowded boom towns, living and working conditions deteriorated dramatically. Housing, when available, was crowded and expensive, and rent profiteering was widespread. Near Philadelphia, an investigator discovered 140 workers living in a single garage. In new war plants in remote areas, where employers furnished lodging and food, living conditions became intolerable. Italian workers at DuPont's Carney's Point plant deserted their rent-free quarters en masse, declaring them to be uninhabitable.[65] Enormous increases in the cost of living made workers worse off in 1918 than they had been in 1914. Wages rose, but the cost of essentials escalated even higher; food costs increased 83 percent and clothing almost 139 percent. Food riots broke out in several cities.

Dissatisfied, workers changed jobs even more frequently than usual. Labor turnover rates were unprecedented, increasing from a prewar high of 300 percent to as high as 3,000 percent.[66] The unstable situation, raising the possibility of new strikes, threatened war production. To address these problems, the government intervened. Including moderate labor leaders such as AFL President Samuel Gompers in Federal planning efforts, President Woodrow Wilson negotiated a no-strike pledge in return for a guarantee of union hours and wages and the right to organize. Attacked by the IWW and the socialists as "class-collaboration," government-sponsored cooperation between labor and management prefigured later New Deal policies and alliances.[67] The government also encouraged new management practices. Prominent Taylorites introduced scientific management into war industries, many defense industries hired professional personnel managers, an occupation once limited to large progressive corporations, while others, urged on by the government, used war-time profits to subsidize extensive welfare programs.[68]

To address the desperate housing problem, the Federal Government chartered two new agencies to house workers in critical industries – the United States Housing Corporation, part of the Labor Department's Bureau of Industrial Housing (USHC), and the United States Shipping Board's Emergency Fleet Corporation (EFC). The USHC, directed by Otto Eidlitz, a New York civil engineer and housing reformer, built housing directly while the EFC lent money to shipbuilding companies, while retaining control over the design, rental, and management of their housing. After exhausting every other way of improving the housing situation, such as transportation and home registration services, the new agencies, began to build houses, apartment buildings, and boarding houses in industrial centers along the New England and mid-Atlantic coast.[69]

Just as welfare work advocates, personnel administrators, and efficiency experts dominated war industries, architects and planners attempted to shape the war housing programs. Professional groups urged the Wilson administration to construct permanent communities instead of providing only temporary shelter. Charles Harris Whitaker, editor of the *Journal of the American Institute of Architects*, sent architect Frederick L. Ackerman to England to report on war housing programs there. Heavily influenced by garden city ideas, the British built complete communities, designed to address the residents' aesthetic, physical, and social needs.[70] The *Journal* published detailed analyses of the English projects, praising their designs and outlining their legislative organization, technical specifications, and social implications.[71] Once Ackerman was appointed chief designer for the EFC, he adopted the British ideas, promoting complete communities equipped with shopping and recreation, collaboration between architects and planners, and group housing designed in regional styles. However, although Ackerman had first encountered these concepts in England, American company town designers had been advocating similar ideas for nearly a decade.

In fact, architects and planners who had designed and discussed American industrial settlements dominated Federal war housing programs. Lawrence Veiller wrote the USHC manual, *Standards Recommended for Permanent Industrial Housing Developments*.[72] Frederick Law Olmsted, Jr directed the USHC Town Planning Commission, where planners Arthur Comey and Arthur Shurtleff worked with architect Marcia Mead and the firm of Murphy and Dana on designs for USHC developments in Bridgeport and Waterbury, Connecticut. George B. Post served as architect and planner for the war town of Craddock, Virginia. Firms such as Kilham and Hopkins and Mann and MacNeille designed EFC communities at Atlantic Heights, New Hampshire and Bristol, Pennsylvania. Perry MacNeille, director of the housing branch of the Army Ordnance Department, commissioned Clinton Mackenzie to design the munitions town of Amatol, New Jersey.[73] John Nolen also became a supporter of Federal housing programs, organizing an NHA symposium on war housing and serving as an adviser to the Emergency Fleet Corporation. Nolen's high public profile won him a record number of government contracts – five USHC and one EFC projects. By 1919, he had laid out three housing sites in Niagara Falls and prepared plans for two settlements, Eddystone and Ridley Park, both near Philadelphia, when the Federal Government ordered all government-supported construction to halt.[74]

UNION PARK GARDENS

Since Nolen's project for Union Park Gardens, near Wilmington, Delaware, was already under construction, the EFC completed the project. Characteristically, Nolen had obtained the commission through his business network. The previous year, the Wilmington Chamber of Commerce, anticipating a housing shortage, hired Nolen to investigate Wilmington's housing situation and put forward some proposals. Once the United States entered the war, the Chamber of Commerce submitted Nolen's report to the EFC, and, after the agency accepted his plans, purchased the site Nolen recommended and donated it to the government.[75] The EFC then hired Nolen and the Philadelphia architectural firm of Ballinger and Perrot to prepare plans for a settlement of five hundred houses on the 58-acre site.[76] The occupants would be skilled workmen from the nearby Pursey and Jones shipyards and the Bethlehem Shipbuilding Corporation. Supported by the EFC's generous war-time budgets and their enthusiasm for community planning, group housing, and regional styles, Nolen's office produced one of his most successful plans.

Nolen designed the settlement to function as both a separate neighborhood and an extension of Wilmington's expanding urban grid. Nolen persuaded the EFC to purchase an area of shacks and hovels along Union Street to protect the site, while a cemetery and public park formed a partial greenbelt on the other side of the property.[77] One of the most sophisticated plans executed by Nolen, the scheme, clearly influenced by Forest Hills Gardens, balanced geometry and nature. A grid of rectangular blocks was broken by a landscaped parkway following a stream that flowed diagonally through the site. Like Forest Hills Gardens, the settlement moved sequentially from the urban square on the east of the site to terminate in a wooded park at the western boundary. A village green, surrounded by a community building, and a block of stores, apartments, and a large apartment house, was the social focus of the settlement, providing residents with shopping, recreation, and entertainment. Encouraged by the EFC's interest in welfare work, Nolen planned a large auditorium, games rooms, a gymnasium, a children's playroom, and sewing, reading, and writing rooms for women, to supplement playgrounds and recreational facilities along the parkway.[78]

Like Nolen's plan, Ballinger and Perrot's house designs maintained local traditions while bringing a new level of quality to industrial housing. The architect's previous project, a company town for the American Viscose Company at nearby Marcus Hook, Pennsylvania,

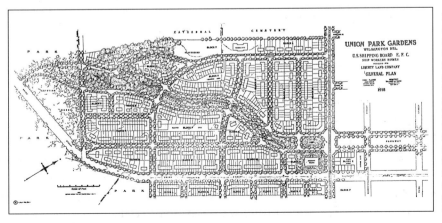

Union Park Gardens, one of Nolen's most coherent plans. The 50-acre site housed five hundred ship workers and their families. A landscaped parkway follows the creek through the settlement, providing a natural focus and terminating in a large park. The community center and shops were left unfinished.

171

introduced a series of variations that enlivened the local vernacular red-brick row houses. At Union Park Garens, they designed twenty different house types, mostly duplexes and row houses, with stylistic diversity that stretched local traditions. Highly detailed porches, chimneys, dormers, gable ends, and brick, textured stucco, clapboard, and shingle surfaces relieved monotony. Substantial and solidly built, the houses had slate roofs, full basements, warm-air furnaces, and yellow pine interiors stained a different color in each room.[79] The rents reflected the high quality of the design and construction, ranging from 27.50 to 50 dollars a month. This was high in comparison to Indian Hill or Kistler's prewar rents, but still within the budgets of skilled workmen earning high war-time wages.[80]

The undeniable excellence of NFC projects such as Union Park Gardens or Yorkship Village in nearby Camden, New Jersey, demonstrated the social and architectural possibilities of government-supported communities for workers.[81] Many observers agreed that the government programs, in spite of their short life-span – only a year – had produced outstanding results. Even before the war ended, architects, planners, and housing reformers began discussing the outcome of the war housing experience. Were these houses and communities the unique outcome of an extraordinary situation, or did they point to a wider government role? A number of different positions about where to go next emerged from the debate. Influenced by European examples, Whitaker, Ackerman, and housing experts Edith Elmer Wood and Carol Arnovici advocated legislation to allow Federal, state, and municipal governments to finance housing construction by private groups, housing associations, and building and loan societies. Others argued for cooperative ownership, asking the government to organize co-partnership schemes to avoid paternalism and land speculation. Nolen and Frederick Law Olmsted, Jr took a more moderate position, hoping for a Federal housing agency to support research and experimentation and collect information, "if the results of the war-time housing experience are to be salvaged and made the basis for further advances."[82]

In the midst of the "red scare" an increasingly conservative Congress was not receptive to any of these proposals. Anxious to distance itself from anything hinting of socialism, the House Committee on Public Buildings insisted that war housing had been strictly an emergency measure. Criticizing the USHC as wasteful and inefficient, the committee expressed particular disdain for the design professionals involved in the program, castigating them as "college professors and alleged experts in various lines [who] were called in and placed on the pay roll at large salaries and designated as 'town planners' 'town managers' etc. ad nauseam and ad absurdum."[83] Although the designers had hoped to keep the projects intact, Congress directed that all government housing be sold immediately at market value, preferably to individual home owners. In 1922 the government sold Union Park Gardens to a single buyer at a loss of nearly 1,000,000 dollars. The sale was made on the condition that the tenants could buy their units within thirty days, at an increase of 25 percent over the buyer's price, and many took advantage of the offer.[84] House values in the development rapidly appreciated. The quality of the project's housing and design attracted middle-class buyers and, by 1936, only 30 percent of the original working-class residents remained. A Community Improvement Association organized with the sale maintained the project's architectural character and real-estate values by deed restrictions that controlled building and landscaping and prohibited altering façades. In 1936, the Urbanism Committee, visiting Union Park Gardens, judged it to be "one of the most consistently successful of the suburban areas visited."[85]

After the war, Nolen continued to be an advocate for the planning profession, unlike other architects and planners such as Charles Whitaker, Frederick Ackerman, and Clarence Stein. Radicalized by their war-time housing experiences, they began to develop their ideas outside existing professional frameworks. In 1923, with Lewis Mumford and others, they formed the Regional Planning Association as a vehicle for exploring new ideas in housing and planning, and produced limited dividend, experimental housing projects such as Sunnyside, Chatham Village, and Radburn.[86] After 1920, Nolen's commissions for industrial communities dried up and, except for his limited involvement with Kingsport, he did not design any more company towns. During the 1920s Nolen worked on Mariemont, a limited profit model suburb outside Cincinnati, sponsored by Mary M. Emery. His office survived by preparing plans for towns such as Venice, Florida, a speculative venture that grew out of the Florida real-estate boom.[87] However, Nolen's company town plans, published in 1927, began to take on a life of their own, independent of the condition of the towns themselves.[88]

Nolen's professional aspirations culminated in the New Deal, as planning became part of a national endeavor. After years of struggling with city governments over implementing comprehensive plans, city planners found themselves sitting on Federal and state planning boards charged with large-scale and long-term decision-making. Nolen was an enthusiastic supporter of the Roosevelt administration, volunteering for various advisory positions. Selected as an adviser to the National Planning Board, he became a consultant to the state planning boards of New Hampshire and Vermont. He joined the Department of Agriculture's National Land Planning Committee and served as an adviser to the National Resource Planning Board. His office produced plans for Subsistence Homesteads projects at Penderlea Homesteads, North Carolina and Neptune Gardens, East Boston.[89] Always promoting planning, Nolen continued to travel around the country now lecturing on the new concept of regional planning. Shortly before his death in 1937 at the age of sixty-seven, Nolen declared, "I am favorable to the legislative ideals and administrative methods of the Roosevelt administration. They represent directly many of the causes to which my professional and personal efforts have long been directed."[90]

9

REGIONAL ALTERNATIVES:
EARLE S. DRAPER
AND THE SOUTHERN
TEXTILE MILL VILLAGE

Unlike Atterbury, Goodhue, or Nolen, who practiced at a national level and worked in a number of different geographical settings, Earle S. Draper worked within a limited regional and industrial context. A city planner trained as a landscape architect like Nolen, Draper settled in Charlotte, North Carolina, the heart of the Piedmont cotton mill region. As the economy of the New South boomed, the expanding textile industry provided Draper with commissions for mill villages in every southern textile state. As the only local expert in mill village design, Draper had to confront an already well-established settlement type. Unlike northeastern manufacturers who offered workers housing as a bonus, or mining corporations that built towns on a constantly shifting resource-extraction frontier, the southern textile industry depended on a physical setting – the mill village – for its economic survival. Like the New England textile towns a century earlier, the mill village embodied a social order directly reflecting the economic logic of the textile industry. However, as in the North, the growing pressure of public opinion and local reformers forced mill owners to find a more acceptable physical image for their mill villages. In more than a hundred plans, Draper completely redesigned the textile town, drawing inspiration from the Piedmont landscape and his knowledge of the lives of the mill workers. Towns like Chicopee, Georgia took garden city planning in a rural direction, providing a new image for the company town that ultimately would be adapted to the very different social and economic premises of New Deal regional community planning.

THE SOUTHERN TEXTILE INDUSTRY

In 1917, when Earle S. Draper opened his office in Charlotte, North Carolina, he became the South's first resident city planner. His arrival in the South coincided with a major expansion in the cotton textile industry. The war-time boom had spurred already rapidly developing production, and new mills were springing up all across the Piedmont region – the foothills stretching from southern Virginia through the Carolinas to Georgia and eastern Alabama. The southern industry, launched by the "cotton mill campaign" of the 1880s, was grounded in the region's strengths: local capital, fast-running streams, access to raw materials, good rail connections, and most important, a nearly inexhaustible supply of labor, drawn from nearby tenant farms and the Appalachian mountains that marked the western boundary of the region.[1]

Southern mills repeated the archetypal experience of modernization pioneered in the New England textile mills almost a century earlier: transforming a pre-industrial agricultural population into factory workers.[2] Small farmers, increasingly impoverished by crop-lien debt, tenancy, and sharecropping, left the land in search of wage labor.[3] Mill recruiters easily enticed a steady stream of rural and mountain families to what they called "public work," hoping to exchange a marginal existence for a secure hourly wage. A remarkably homogeneous group, these new workers were native-born Anglo-Saxon Protestants. If they lacked technical skills and formal education, they were eager to work.[4]

Unlike New England mills, the southern industry's late start allowed it to take advantage of new technology and increased automation that reduced the need for skilled labor. The southern industry's rapid growth – from 24 percent of the nation's spindles in 1900 to 72 percent in 1939 – was largely based on the low cost of labor, which kept production costs down. Regional wage differentials were significant. From 1894 to 1927, the average southern textile wage was 40 percent below that of other parts of the country.[5] Low production costs allowed southern manufacturers to undercut northern prices and dominate the textile market. As in early New England mills, such low wages depended on family employment. Mills purchased a family's labor as a package. Since a single mill income could not support an entire family, the family operated as an economic unit. This extended traditional working roles: in the mill, just as on the farm, men, women, and children worked together to sustain the family. Children too young to go on the payroll were used as "helpers," working alongside their mothers and sisters as unpaid apprentices.[6]

Since the industry's continuing expansion depended on adequate labor, manufacturers utilized every method at their disposal to maintain and discipline a restless workforce, possessed by what mill owners called a "moving habit." Turnover rates were extremely high and employers estimated a "floating element" of itinerant workers at 20–40 percent

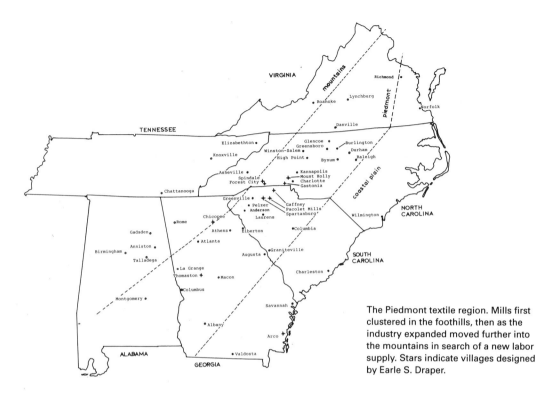

The Piedmont textile region. Mills first clustered in the foothills, then as the industry expanded moved further into the mountains in search of a new labor supply. Stars indicate villages designed by Earle S. Draper.

of the labor force.[7] A huge pool of impoverished black workers offered an alternative source of labor, which mill owners used as a threat – a reminder that whites could be replaced at lower wages – to enforce their terms of employment and silence complaints about wages and hours. In a heightened racial climate, white workers responded by declaring mill work to be a "white right," and defended it with strikes and riots. As a result, mills relegated the few blacks they hired to menial and low-wage jobs as loaders, drivers, or sweepers, always segregated from contact with white women workers.[8]

The economic logic of the southern mill village was similar to the Rhode Island textile towns. Since the mill owner had to furnish housing to attract workers, economic necessity formalized the industrial system into a way of life. To enable working families to survive on marginal wages with frequent layoffs, employers offered company houses at low rents, subsidizing housing in lieu of higher wages. The family system was built into the rental contract, with quotas specifying the number of workers provided by each house – usually at least one worker per room. Some mills offered rent-free accommodation, but 25 cents per room per week, or a dollar a week was a more standard rent for a four-room house. In case of layoffs, employers would often cancel or defer rent payments. New England textile workers usually paid a week's wages per month for housing in comparison to the one or two days' wages southern workers paid. The economic advantages of mill housing were clear to both owners and workers and, by the turn of the century, 92 percent of southern textile workers lived in mill villages.[9]

In addition to renting houses, every mill provided all the necessities of work, subsistence, and leisure through a characteristic set of institutions – a company store, at least two churches, and an elementary school. The mill employed preachers and teachers. Mill owners often described this as philanthropy, but the 1910 Federal *Report on Women and Child Wage Earners* dismissed this claim, pointing out that mills had to build complete communities to attract workers and these expenditures counted as normal costs of doing business.[10] In some cases mills merely fulfilled minimal obligations, but most structured an all-encompassing social order to manage their employees. In 1908, Federal investigators noted that "all the affairs of the village and the conditions of living of all the people are regulated entirely by the mill company . . . the company owns everything and controls everything and to a large extent controls everybody in the mill village."[11] Even after leaving the mill, workers lived, shopped, studied, played, and worshipped in an environment created by the employer.

Still, the owner's control was necessarily mediated by the workers' habits and customs. Life in the mill village was negotiated to accommodate the residents' daily activities and their social, religious, and medical preferences. Village institutions reflected this uneasy balance. The mill school, for example, not only taught the children of largely illiterate parents but also inculcated habits of industrial discipline with lessons that emphasized punctuality, reliability, and respect for authority. According to one mill official, "children who are educated become more valuable labor and are less destructive of property." Education ended at the seventh grade when children entered the mill's permanent workforce. The few village children who went on to high school rarely returned to work in the mill.[12]

Village churches continued the strong religious traditions workers brought with them, while preaching what sociologist Harriet Herring called "doctrines . . . acceptable . . . to a capitalistic employer – a gospel of work, of gratitude for present blessings, and of patience with economic and social maladjustment as temporal and outside the sphere of religious concern."[13] Mill owners, as sociologist Liston Pope demonstrated, openly acknowledged the useful role that religion played in releasing workers from the monotony of mill work and encouraging them to lead orderly and hard-working lives. Most supported conservative Protestant churches – Baptist and Methodist – in their villages, even if they were members of other denominations. Others took active roles as Sunday school teachers, deacons, and ushers. Church attendance was often used as the measure of a good worker and frequent pulpit exhortations against alcohol addressed a basic problem of industrial discipline.[14]

If company housing, schools, and churches addressed workplace issues of labor supply and discipline, the company store attempted to function as a brake on the mill workers' "moving habit." Originally established as a convenience in isolated villages, company stores also created an economic bond between mill and employee. Contrary to popular belief, they were rarely overpriced, but they still made money for the mill. More important, the practice of deducting store bills from earnings produced a state of chronic indebtedness. Without credit elsewhere, employees became dependent on the mill for daily necessities and, on payday, received either no wages at all or bills marked "balance due." This continuing cycle of debt created resentment but, by tying the worker to his employer, also helped stabilize the workforce.[15]

To justify such control, southern mill owners created a distinctive ideology of paternalism. By the beginning of the twentieth century they had adapted the feudal rhetoric of the Old South to the new industrial order, mixing it with claims of solidarity with fellow whites, Social Darwinist ideas about self-selection, and Christian notions of duty. They repeatedly invoked the image of the family to justify extending authoritarian and hierarchical discipline to workers "for their own good." A mill spokesman described the operatives: "They're all of one family. They're all of one community. They are all of the mill."[16] The fiction of "one big family" established a dialectic of benevolence and deference that created its own momentum. Paternalism's individual benevolence offered workers advantages while producing dependence that provided further justification for continuing the system. In the close community of the mill village, workers often actively collaborated with paternalistic claims, acquiescing in their own subordination.

Many owners and superintendents matched their control over workers' lives with a direct interest in their welfare, devoting considerable personal attention to them. Available for workplace complaints as well as for advice and help with family problems or financial difficulties, employers often performed sincere acts of kindness such as visiting the sick or distributing Christmas presents. Such generosity, however, usually also brought intrusiveness. As in early New England mills, owners enforced moral values of thrift, temperance, and strict standards of sexual behavior through regulation and punishment. They banned alcohol and cigarette smoking, and quickly evicted unmarried women who became pregnant. The owner of North Carolina's Bynum Mills walked around his village at nine o'clock every night, knocking on the doors of houses with lights on to tell the occupants to go to bed.[17]

Haphazardly applied according to the inclinations of individual mill owners, as in New England, paternalism never constituted a unified approach to industrial relations. Few owners tried to match the totalizing regime Captain Ellison A. Smyth imposed on his well-publicized "model town," Pelzer, South Carolina. A benevolent despot who provided workers with rent-free houses, a lyceum, savings bank, and recreational facilities, Smyth also indulged his own prejudices, restricting after-dark activities and banning dogs ("dogs are in ninety-nine cases out of a hundred worthless and troublesome").[18] In many towns, workers created their own close-knit communities based on networks of friendship and family. Economically marginal, they survived by mutual aid and cooperation. When sickness or injury struck, villagers collected "love gifts" of food and money for neighbors, a safety-net in the absence of workplace benefits. Since families migrated to mill villages where they already had relatives and their children usually married within the village, this strengthened family ties. By 1920, Bynum village, with three generations of mill workers, genuinely constituted "one big family." These connections gave workers a collective strength and security to offset the oppressively familial relationships mill owners claimed.[19]

Nearly self-sufficient, the mill village was set apart from the larger world outside. Mill workers inhabited a closed culture; poorly educated, economically insecure, and socially restricted, they were clearly differentiated from their Piedmont neighbors. Sociologist Herbert Lahne observed that, as the industry developed and mill families tended to marry within their own community, "cotton mill work [became] an almost hereditary occupation."[20] Identified as a separate caste, mill workers were treated with disdain by their urban and rural neighbors. Disparaging epithets, such as "lint head," "mill trash," and "cotton-tail," were common. Historian W.J. Cash wrote that a mill worker might wander the streets of a nearby town all day "without ever receiving a nod or a smile from anybody, or any recognition of his existence other than a scornful glance from a shop girl."[21]

EARLE DRAPER: "CITY PLANNER IN THE NEW SOUTH"

When Earle Draper first arrived in the South, he immediately entered the world of the mill owner. In 1915, John Nolen had dispatched the young landscape architect to supervise his operations in the South. Draper established his headquarters in Myers Park, the new residential suburb designed by Nolen's firm. The southern equivalent of planned subdivisions such as Baltimore's Roland Park, Myers Park, with curving tree-lined streets and large lots, had already become Charlotte's most desirable suburb. Draper built his own large house there and, through his professional work and his enthusiasm for golf, established close social and professional ties with the textile families settling there. Charlotte's central location made it the hub of the textile industry, and mill owners and their heirs commissioned expensive houses in Myers Park.[22] Draper spent one week a month in Kingsport, where he was equally successful in cultivating the town's sponsors. J. Fred Johnson enjoyed working with Draper, writing Nolen that he "had made a very favorable impression" and continued to hire him for projects at Kingsport throughout the 1920s.[23]

Draper quickly saw the professional opportunities the growing economy of the New South offered planners. After failing to convince Nolen to expand his office, Draper decided to strike out on his own. A graduate of the Landscape Architecture program at Massachusetts College (later, the University of Massachusetts), Draper, like Nolen, had immediately gravitated to the infant profession of city planning. After graduation, he had applied for a position in Nolen's firm, and, competing with sixty-five other applicants, was finally hired.[24] In Nolen's office, Draper received a broad training in the principles of city planning, including a grounding in economic and social issues. Draper, unlike Nolen, was also very interested in design. Since Nolen did not impose a particular design orientation on his staff, this left Draper free to develop his own distinctive planning style. Although he later described himself as "of the old school, the Olmsted school," oriented to the natural landscape, Draper was equally influenced by newer garden city techniques.[25]

Draper's new firm produced plans for parks, cemeteries, and private estates, and began to specialize in subdivisions like Myers Park. Mill owners were among Draper's first clients. When they turned to him for professional advice, Draper, whose own family was connected with the New England textile industry – his grandfather had owned cotton mills near Stoughton, Massachusetts – was sympathetic to their concerns. Financed by growing profits generated by the industry's expansion, the mill owners' demands were primarily technical: they needed to upgrade the physical environment and amenities of the mill village in order to improve their public image and attract and retain steady workers. Better living standards for employees, they hoped, would finally "secure an attachment for the village to decrease the migratory tendency." A mill president suggested that new mill villages would make "more loyal, better workers, better contented with their lot . . . those mills will have the best class of labor and more of it in times of stress."[26]

FROM PATERNALISM TO PROGRESSIVISM

The employment of a professional city planner was only one aspect of the continuing modernization of the textile industry. Alert to innovations in technology, southern mills also began to introduce new management practices already well known in the North. Their concern with the mill village's physical appearance indicates their increasing discomfort with their public image, in spite of the continuing success of the industry. Once electric power freed expanding mills from remote riverside sites, they began to locate near towns, although staying outside corporate limits to avoid taxes and maintain control. Their presence there began to attract the attention of the urban middle classes. Shocked by the enormous gulf between mill village and their own communities, local Progressives attacked the "mill problem." Child labor, limited education, and poor living conditions threatened the emerging "modern" and well-regulated society of the New South. Labelling the mill worker as a "social type," they called for child labor laws and compulsory education. As in other parts of the country, reforms that began as charity and "uplift work" soon became professionalized.[27]

To silence critics and keep reformers at bay, mill owners began to replace paternalism with "welfare work." They were attracted by welfare's widely advertised claims as a method of "attracting and retaining a loyal work force." After 1905, increasing labor shortages produced by the industry's rapid expansion prompted southern mills to enthusiastically adopt welfare programs designed to encourage "permanency of residence and regularity of work." In paternalistic southern industries, welfare programs expanded and institutionalized existing traditions. Focused on improving living conditions and the outward appearance of the mill village, welfare programs did not fundamentally threaten their control, unlike the workplace legislation they continued to resist. Although welfare programs were expensive, between 1905 and 1915, eight Piedmont mills ranked among the nation's leading practitioners of company-sponsored welfare work.[28]

The welfare workers hired by the mills regarded the mill families, in spite of their Anglo-Saxon ethnicity, as ignorant and backward people who needed training to prepare them for modern life, like the families of unskilled immigrants in the North. Although some programs, such as medical clinics, group insurance, and parks and playgrounds, genuinely improved the workers' lives, others were designed to integrate them into the firm. Like the Norton Company, many mills used sports as a "steadying" influence. Welfare workers reorganized informal baseball games, a favorite pastime, into mill teams and factory leagues. This structured leisure time served as a lesson in discipline and obedience to rules and, the owners hoped, transferred the workers' loyalty from the team to the mill. Programs aimed at women, such as childcare classes, mothers' clubs, and domestic science courses, taught middle-class values, habits, and aspirations. Home economists showed young women how to sew fashionable clothes and cook fancy meals, and encouraged them to treat company houses as homes. Trying to narrow the cultural gap between mill and town, these efforts ignored the economic fact that, even if they wanted them, most mill families could not afford such improvements.[29]

Inside the mill, professional expertise also replaced personal authority. The systematic and impersonal methods of the modern corporation gradually eliminated the old-fashioned management styles employed in family-owned mills. The growing number of local enterprises and the increase in northern mills relocating to the Piedmont imposed new standards of efficiency and profitability. Other northern imports, such as scientific management, focused on increased productivity using techniques that substituted objectively determined rules and standards for informal agreements negotiated by foremen and workers. As the pace of production was rationalized, workers were continually assigned larger production quotas – a process called the "stretch-out." Once a new generation of college-educated mill men trained in northern business schools or in local textile colleges took over, experience no longer guaranteed advancement. Supervisors did not come up through the ranks, but were hired straight from school, eliminating the possibility of upward mobility within the mill.[30]

After 1915, the mills' newly rationalized order faced additional challenges. As in the North, the war boom generated an enormous demand for textiles which exceeded local labor markets. Military contracts promised unprecedented profits impossible to realize without additional labor. Without access to immigrant labor, already employing women, and unable to hire blacks, manufacturers raised wages and introduced bonuses to entice reluctant workers to work longer hours. The workers' newfound power revived union organization, dormant since the 1901 American Federation of Labor defeat in Danville,

Cover of the 1923 "Health and Happiness" issue of *Southern Textile Bulletin.* Widely distributed to schools, public libraries, and Chambers of Commerce, these special issues were an important publicity vehicle for the textile industry. Showcasing welfare work, they featured a full range of "improvement" initiatives, from upgraded housing, community buildings, and medical centers to baseball teams, mothers' clubs, and baby contests.

Virginia. The Union of Textile Workers began to organize and, between 1918 and 1920, a series of strikes erupted in mill towns across the Piedmont.[31] Welfare activities, advertised as a panacea for industrial relations problems, also peaked during these years. The *Southern Textile Bulletin*'s "Health and Happiness" issues, published in 1917, 1919, and 1923, extolled the virtues of mill life, demonstrated by smiling children in well-kept villages.[32] Huge profits from the war-time boom funded ever more elaborate programs designed to attract and stabilize employment and promote industrial harmony.

A NEW PROFESSIONAL ROLE

Professional planning, based on the same values of efficiency, order, and rationality, offered yet another solution. Like Atterbury and Nolen, Draper attempted to balance the reformers' concern with improvement, the mill owners' economic priorities, and his own professional self-interest. In spite of his close social and professional ties with mill owners, Draper did not fully identify himself with their interests. Without questioning their sincerity in requesting improvements, he nonetheless considered the mill village to be the equivalent of an industrial plantation. He shared many of the reformers' concerns about the implications of this system. Like many southern observers, he believed that mill families constituted a uniquely southern "social type," an already backward population whose social development had been stunted by the inadequate and restrictive conditions of the mill village. He anticipated that planned mill villages with better housing and living conditions and expanded educational, social, and recreational opportunities would gradually "uplift" mill families to middle-class standards.[33] Eventually, the workers would "carry on themselves, take over the government of the village and gradually develop into proprietors themselves." Draper hoped that company ownership would evolve into co-partnership without going through the "era of real-estate speculation."[34]

In the meantime, improving conditions depended on the mill owner's goodwill. Draper defended proprietary ownership as in the workers' best interest, since he did not yet consider the mill workers able to manage their own lives. He judged the few existing "worker-managed" villages as "less than ideal."[35] Draper, like Atterbury, Goodhue, and many earlier Progressive reformers in the North, was suspicious of labor unions and did not consider them to be appropriate vehicles for social change. Beginning his career during the "red scare," he regarded the northern organizers coming into the Piedmont as dangerously radical. Therefore, Draper addressed his arguments for planning directly to the mill owners. Writing regularly in trade journals such as *Southern Textile Bulletin* and *Textile World*, he exhorted mill owners to upgrade their villages. Showing examples of his own work, he argued that planning was producing higher standards in mill villages each year.[36] Like other company town designers, Draper regarded the mill village as a significant professional opportunity. Highlighting his professional abilities, Draper's articles, supplemented by advertisements listing his professional services, were an excellent source of both publicity and new clients.

At the same time, unlike Atterbury, Goodhue, or Nolen, Draper drew his professional authority from his familiarity with the textile industry and the Piedmont region. Grounded in the economic realities of the textile production, Draper produced financial calculations to convince mill owners that improved villages represented a valuable investment. Providing a complex cost–benefit analysis, he demonstrated the long-term investment value of a single village lot – to be multiplied by the number of lots the mill required. Draper's Myers Park neighbors gave him connections with textile magnates all over the South. His increasing success in solving practical problems bolstered his professional standing and he quickly established himself as the only local "expert" on mill village planning. As the southern industry grew, so he prospered. By 1920, he employed more than a dozen professionals and operated a field office in Atlanta, a planning practice comparable to the largest offices in the country. His professional stationery listed community and mill village developments at the top of the firm's list of services, and, from 1917 to 1925, mill villages provided the bulk of Draper's commissions.

Beginning with the Spencer Mills in Spindale, North Carolina, his office planned more than one hundred villages, developing, extending, or improving mill villages in every southern textile state.[37] These jobs varied considerably. Preparing plans for completely new villages, Draper preferred to begin even before the site had been selected, in order to locate the most advantageous setting for the village and control its relationship to the mill. Not everyone was able to start from scratch, so Draper also provided numerous extension plans for rapidly expanding mills, usually adding amenities such as paved streets, parks, and better housing in the new areas of the village. Other villages, such as Rock Hill and Pacolet Mills, South Carolina, needed overall improvement. In some cases this only involved landscaping and other amenities; in others it included extensive improvements, including streets, sidewalks, sewer and water systems, new houses, and community buildings.[38] Unlike Nolen, who dealt in generalities, no detail was too small for Draper to consider. He arrived at an optimum lot size – 75 × 150 feet – balancing financial data – the price of land and the cost of insurance premiums based on density – with psychological – rural families' need for space – and social considerations – garden plots could supplement their poor diets.[39]

Unlike Nolen's firm which usually only supplied plans, Draper's office provided comprehensive design and development services, taking complete control of a project from conception to completion. The firm took responsibility for the town's layout, grading, and landscaping of the site, engineering of roads, drainage, and utilities, and locating and platting building sites. Working relationships with two important textile engineering firms, J.E. Sirrine of Greenville, South Carolina, and L.W. Roberts of Atlanta, gave Draper the dominant role in structuring and organizing the town, collaborating in designing and constructing mills and housing on sites selected by Draper. Sirrine also shared many of his commissions with Draper, calling him in to plan villages for factories designed by the engineering firm.[40] Draper's control over his projects allowed him to set and enforce his own priorities in the mill villages he built. By insisting on his own standards, which were considerably higher than the norm, he was able significantly to improve physical conditions in the mill towns he designed. Since he had more work than he could handle, he often refused commissions, turning away mill owners who proposed towns with less than what he considered to be minimum standards of light, water, electricity, sanitation, housing, and roads.[41] As a result, Draper, unlike most company town designers, saw many of his projects completed as designed. Subsidized by profits from the war-time boom, Draper's attractive villages served as visible proof of the benefits of professional town planning.

While practical solutions and improved living standards satisfied the limited objectives of mill owners and reformers, Draper went beyond the purely functional to create a rural planning aesthetic reflecting the unique conditions of the Piedmont mill village. The empirical lessons of his mill village experience connect Draper to an important local predecessor, Daniel Tompkins. Tompkins, a native of South Carolina who had studied and worked in the North before settling in Charlotte, was the first theorist of the cotton textile industry. In 1899, Tompkins, an engineer who had designed and constructed more than a hundred mills, published *Cotton Mill – Commercial Features*, a compendium of the accumulated wisdom of Piedmont mill building and operation. Although mills could locate anywhere, Tompkins emphasized the continuing benefits of rural settings for both workers and owners. He pointed out, "the whole matter of providing attractive and comfortable habitations for cotton operatives . . . [is] summarized in the statement that they are essentially a rural people. They have been accustomed to farm life . . . while their condition is decidedly bettered by going to the factory, the old instincts cling to them."[42] He suggested half-acre lots for each mill house, since gardening was "conducive to general contentment among the operatives."[43]

Tompkins's treatise codified vernacular practices while Draper superimposed a highly conceptual order on top of the industrial landscape described by Tompkins. Drawing on the Olmsted tradition and the English garden city for landscaping and site planning techniques, Draper adapted them to the specific conditions of the Piedmont landscape. Draper admired the naturalistic and rural qualities of Olmsted's landscapes. However, instead of recreating apparently "natural" landscapes with great effort as Olmsted had, Draper used the existing natural setting as his starting point. Organizing his plan around the topography and native vegetation, he subordinated roads, planting, and buildings to the natural terrain. Many of Parker and Unwin's concepts also lent themselves to this approach. Draper adopted the gently curving roads, low-density housing, protective greenbelt, and pedestrian circulation systems used at New Earswick and Letchworth.[44] However, once introduced into the very different social and physical setting of the textile village, these techniques acquired very different meanings. Unlike Olmsted's rural parks and suburbs and Parker and Unwin's nostalgic villages, Draper was not interested in posing alternatives to the evils of the industrial city. Instead, his rural mill villages reconnected workers to the familiar natural setting of the Piedmont. Rather than urbanizing workers or homogenizing their environment, as reformers urged, Draper, following Daniel Tompkins's counsel, validated their rural and mountain origins.

Although his exclusively southern practice kept Draper isolated from the mainstream of the landscape architecture and city planning, he continued to relate his activities to professional developments. Summarizing his mill village experiences in a 1927 article in *Landscape Architecture*, Draper argued that the landscape profession should aspire to address important social problems like the mill village. Emphasizing the regional specificity of the textile industry, he stressed the importance of a "thorough practical knowledge" of the social conditions and daily lives of the mill workers as a fundamental condition for community planning.[45] In a later article in *American City*, Draper discussed the replanning of the nine-plant Calloway Mills complex in LaGrange, Georgia as a demonstration of long-term urban planning. In spite of the fact that private clients sponsored most of his work, Draper, like Nolen, considered his activities to be public planning. He maintained his interest in large-scale urban projects by using private commissions as opportunities to create city plans. In LaGrange, he proposed a twenty-year improvement plan for the mill, which owned the entire southwest section of the city, requiring changes in street patterns, a new park system, and a program for commercial development, to be coordinated with the rest of the city and its projected growth. Describing the LaGrange project, Draper anticipated that such "enlightened" private undertakings would eventually convince southern cities and towns to introduce urban legislation and planning.[46]

THE VERNACULAR STANDARD: THE MILL HILL

Draper always measured his mill villages against the prevailing standards. Illustrating his articles with "before and after" photographs, he juxtaposed his redesigned villages with earlier villages to dramatize the improvements planning would bring. By 1920, he claimed that planning "has brought the South from a position from near the bottom to a position at the top, in the conditions of the textile villages and the welfare of the operatives."[47] The villages in the "before" photographs represented a typology that had developed by trial and error within narrow economic and environmental constraints. Rather than following existing examples, such as the New England textile town or conforming to plans or designs, southern villages had developed in response to considerations of function and economy, and relied on local building traditions and materials.

Early mill villages, located in isolated riverside sites for waterpower, were essentially rural places. Except for the substantial brick mills, three and four stories tall and lined up along the river, the villages were informally laid out. Surveyors and carpenters hired by mill owners plotted roads and lots and built according to local customs. To save money, identical houses all built at the same time were laid out in rows along roads leading from the mill up the "mill hill," a cleared site sloping up from the river. Standard mill houses duplicated the most common and inexpensive types of rural dwellings: single-story frame houses raised on brick piers with three or four rooms, a front porch, and a kitchen extension in the rear. Mill managers or the town minister occupied larger, better-built houses, strategically located to keep track of comings and goings in the village. The mills housed black employees in a group of smaller houses on the outskirts of the village. The rest of the village did not form any particular pattern. The store, churches, schoolhouse, and lodge hall clustered near the

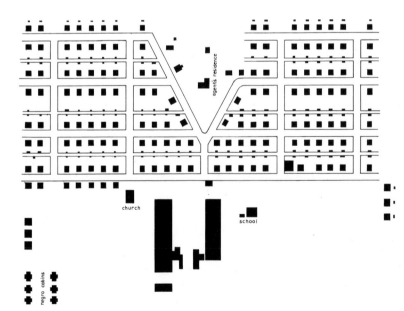

The standard layout of the vernacular textile mill village, drawn for the Bureau of Labor Statistics' survey of company housing. All the characteristic features are present: the mill at the center of the town, the strategically placed agent's house, identical rows of houses with privies lined up along an alley for company collection, and a small group of houses set aside for black workers. The church, school, and company store surround the mill.

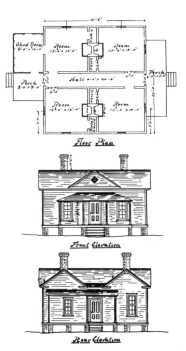

Plan and elevation of a four-room mill house featured in Daniel Tompkins's 1899 textbook on cotton mill development. Although the distinctive gables were often eliminated, the clapboard surface, brick piers, and generic rooms became standard features of subsequent mill housing.

mill or were interspersed with the houses without establishing a formal relationship to either. Compactness was the only planning requirement; since inhabitants rarely owned automobiles, the village had to be a completely pedestrian environment.[48]

As mills grew and relocated near urban areas, the villages retained rural standards of life. Infrastructure and services were extremely limited. Even after 1900, few villages had paved or graded roads; several families shared wells and pumps, brick fireplaces provided heat, and kerosene lamps, light. Indoor plumbing was unknown, and rows of privies lined the back of lots. Outdoor space was plentiful: large lots encouraged gardening and left room for pig sties, chicken coops, and cow pastures. Still, the "one worker per room" rule guaranteed overcrowded living conditions indoors; in small houses where most rooms were used for sleeping, this left the front porch as the family living room. In comparison, the average New England textile family occupied a six-room house.[49] By 1915, such conditions were standardized. Manufacturers sharing information and trade publications diffused a basic typology of village and housing across the textile belt.

Variations reflected the personal inclinations of the village owners, although differences were primarily in upkeep rather than form. Even the best villages received mixed reviews from visitors. Journalist Leonora Ellis found "cottage homes that are patterns of comfort, neatness and sanitation in Newry, South Carolina." In his 1905 survey of factory conditions, English reformer Budgett Meakin quickly passed over Pelzer, finding it well below the standards of industrial towns in other areas of the country. More typical mill villages appalled northern reformers and southern observers alike. Journalist Clare de Graffenried described one mill village as "horrible, built on malarial soil." In another, H. F. Garrett of Atlanta saw "houses in bad condition . . . with big cracks in them," unfit for family living. Another visitor concluded that the "villages are dirty, the streets unkept and the very sight of the village is a horror."[50]

REDESIGNING THE MILL VILLAGE

By the early 1920s Draper's work had completely transformed the standards of textile villages. If mill villages like those Graffenried and Garrett described still existed, they were clearly substandard when compared to Draper's improved villages. In 1925 Draper began designing Chicopee, Georgia, a mill village for the Johnson and Johnson Company. The firm's large budget and cooperative management gave Draper, who by now had designed nearly a hundred mill projects, the opportunity to develop his rural planning style fully. Transferring gauze production from the grimy textile town of Chicopee, Massachusetts to northeastern Georgia, Johnson and Johnson, a major producer of medical supplies, was typical of northern firms that, troubled by labor problems and legally mandated wages and hours, were increasingly relocating to the South. Since 1906, the firm had been a pioneer in welfare work, offering medical, legal, and social services as well as low-cost housing to employees. Johnson and Johnson intended to continue this tradition by building a model textile village in the South.[51]

Draper's first step in designing Chicopee was to eliminate the mill as the focal point of the village. Although ten years earlier, "new" company towns such as Goodyear Heights and Indian Hill had been completely separate from the plant, Chicopee was the first textile town to reverse the physical conventions of the old-style mill village, traditionally organized around the mill. Draper located the Chicopee mill, the earliest single-story plant built in the South, across the main highway from the village. A barrier of parkland and woods made it barely visible from the village. Draper's loosely curving street patterns underlined the distinction between mill and town: instead of leading directly to the mill, the dominant circulation routes led from the houses to the village center. Like Indian Hill and Tyrone, Draper's plan for Chicopee created a physically independent living sphere. The mill, shunted off to one side, was no longer a necessary condition for the village's existence, encouraging a community identity separate from the workplace.

A street in Pelzer, South Carolina, an "improved" mill village. Neat, white-washed frame cottages were provided rent-free to workers, reflecting Capt. Ellison A. Smyth's desire to make Pelzer a model textile town.

In Chicopee, Draper recreated a microcosm of the Piedmont landscape. This began with a search for the correct site. Avoiding the flat, red fields preferred by plant engineers and surveyors, Draper selected a sloping and irregular site, readily available in a region of hilly uplands. He preferred wooded sites and retained stands of second-growth timber wherever possible, based on his conviction that "a certain percentage of wooded area is always important in the South."[52] Maintaining the natural topography of Chicopee's hilly site, he made extensive use of terracing, retaining walls, and steps, constructing them from stones found on the site. This not only respected the natural contours of the site, but varied the shape of the lots so that houses could be placed at irregular intervals and elevations. This eliminated a fundamental problem of the mill village: uniformity. The village center is the only formal gesture in this landscape, focusing the town's radial streets around an axial arrangement of buildings housing services – shops, churches, clinics, and community buildings. Although in plan the combination of a formal center with informal housing areas resembles Indian Hill and Tyrone, Chicopee's center lacks the sense of enclosure that Atterbury and Goodhue, drawing on Sitte, used to convey urbanity. Instead, Draper emphasized the openness of the site, setting the village in the center of a large area of open parkland.

Chicopee's site contained a large proportion of land too steep or wooded to build on, so Draper linked these areas into a continuous system of green spaces and parkland. Salvaged woodlands, creek beds, and bottom lands were then used as buffers to isolate different parts of the village and to maintain natural vistas. Lots large enough for garden plots reduced housing densities. Although many mills discouraged workers from owning livestock, Draper encouraged the rural habit of keeping cows and pigs, proposing community stalls and pens for livestock. Draper adapted the garden city greenbelt to protect Chicopee's rural qualities. To discourage adjacent development, he persuaded Johnson and Johnson to purchase a large tract of land in order to encircle the town with a wide greenbelt.[53] Extensive woodlands, winding roads, and low-density housing, all adjusted to the existing terrain, belie their careful planning and convey the impression of a natural landscape.

Draper also encouraged the residents' engagement with the landscape, using site planning to shape experience. To accommodate the mill town's daily pedestrian traffic of workers to the mill, children to school, and housewives to the store, Draper, following Olmsted's example, created separate pedestrian paths, with dense rows of trees separating the wide sidewalks from the winding streets. The trees lining the street offered shade and a micro-climate – important amenities in the southern heat. By 1925, the reduction of the work week to fifty hours gave workers more leisure time. Recognizing this, Draper included recreational areas as part of Chicopee's park system, designing facilities for organized sports such as baseball diamonds and football fields, as well as informal parks, playgrounds, and picnic areas, all set unobtrusively into the landscape.

Plan of Chicopee, Georgia, 1927. The curving streets, large areas devoted to parks, lavish landscaping, and, most importantly, the relocation of the mill to the quadrant, show Draper's reconfiguration of the basic typological elements of the mill village.

The entrance to Chicopee. A broad green common lined with shady trees separated the mill village from the plant, serving as a buffer between community and industry.

Chicopee, Georgia

Summing Up

Starting with a perfectly clean slate in mill, in village and in every home, the Chicopee Manufacturing Corporation of Georgia has taken every possible precaution to assure the COMFORT, SAFETY, HEALTH, HAPPINESS and WELFARE of its workers. In return for these provisions, we ask every employee and every member of his family to:

KEEP CLEAN
KEEP WELL
KEEP THE PEACE
KEEP STRICT OBSERVANCE OF THE FOLLOWING HOUSEHOLD, VILLAGE AND MILL REGULATIONS—

Household Regulations

1. Keep wash basins, bath tubs and water closet clean. (Special brushes are provided for this purpose.)
2. Keep your cook stoves and ice boxes *clean*.
3. Keep walls and ceilings *clean* in every room.
4. Keep porches *clean*.
5. Keep screens in windows through the summer.
6. Report at once any trouble with the lights or plumbing.
7. Keep grass on lawns cut, and grounds around house clean and free from rubbish.
8. Do not allow garbage or ashes to collect upon the premises. Put them in the cans provided for this purpose. These cans will be collected and their contents disposed of daily without charge.
9. Do not waste water and electric current. Turn off all electric lights, water faucets and electric stoves or heaters as soon as you are through with them.
10. Follow all directions of the visiting nurse when she makes her regular inspection of the premises.

Village Regulations

1. Keep sidewalks swept.
2. Help to keep all streets, parks and playgrounds clean. Do not scatter papers or other rubbish on any part of the property.
3. Never park an automobile in front of a fire hydrant.
4. Do not tamper with fire hydrants or the village telephones.
5. Do not damage trees, shrubs, roadways or any other public property.
6. Cows, mules, horses and goats must not be kept upon the property and household pets must not include a vicious dog or any other animal which can menace or annoy your neighbors.
7. Know where your children are and what they are doing when not in school or in charge of a director at the playgrounds.
8. Use village telephones to instantly report an outbreak of fire.
9. Report immediately to the trained nurse in every case of sickness.
10. Report all public nuisances, disturbances and violations of the law to the Department of Public Safety.
11. Use village telephones to report accidents.

List of household and village regulations distributed to Chicopee's residents. Note the emphasis on cleanliness and the implied role of the company nurse as enforcer of these regulations.

Draper sought a careful balance between modern improvements and traditional images. His attempts "to blend modern forms with the long-existing living habits and social customs of the locality"[54] became more acute as new technologies such as automobiles appeared in the mill village. By 1920, many mill workers could afford to purchase an automobile, even if it was "a limping old jalopy." At Chicopee, Draper built group garages hidden at the end of blocks. Even the modern functional improvements that Draper insisted on, such as drainage, modern utilities, and paved roads, were never allowed to undermine the rural character of the villages. To overcome the problems of the notorious red clay soil of the area, which regularly alternated between mud and dust, Draper provided Chicopee with an elaborate drainage system, with street gutters and storm drains faced with local stone. He limited automobile roads to a minimum width. The roads followed the natural contours of the land in gentle curves and inclines which also provided additional drainage. In order not to disturb the natural landscape, Draper placed power lines and utilities underground.

Chicopee's housing balanced modern improvements with traditional habits. Although Draper did not design housing, he exercised considerable control over the choice of housing type; he favored the ground-hugging bungalow as an improvement over the frame mill house on piers. The bungalow style, which lent itself easily to innumerable variations in detail and finish – in Chicopee, thirty-one different types were built – overcame the uniformity of company housing.[55] Improved housing began to erase the social boundaries between living conditions in mill villages and those of urban areas and gradually included mill workers as part of the Piedmont culture. The popularity of the ubiquitous bungalow in the South also removed much of the stigma attached to easily identifiable mill houses, suggesting equality between mill workers and their urban neighbors.

Chicopee's brick houses, featuring indoor plumbing, electricity, and hot water, established a standard of accommodation much higher than most of the housing in nearby Gainesville. If large front and rear porches remained standard features, they no longer had to be used as primary family living spaces, since the plans for four- and five-room houses now differentiated space into private and public zones, just as middle-class dwellings had done a quarter of a century earlier.[56]

Like Goodhue and Nolen, Draper encountered fundamental problems that design could not address. The company assigned blacks to smaller and cruder dwellings than the rest of the workers, leaving them segregated on the outskirts of the village. Improved living conditions were accompanied by increased surveillance, impersonally administered from within a corporate structure. The company kept order on its property with a private police force known locally for its willingness to use force. The mill kept close watch over the village's inhabitants. According to one mill worker, boys who had been disciplined in the village school would not be hired when they applied for work in the mill.[57] Johnson and Johnson, producing surgical gauze for medical use, imposed cleanliness and health as the guiding principles of the town. Resident nurses employed by the mill conducted regular inspections to enforce the village's extensive list of regulations, governing everything from cleaning toilets to supervising children.[58] Instead of allowing workers to keep their own cows as Draper suggested, the mill opened a model dairy farm to supply free milk to each house. Despite the excellence of his designs, Draper's imagery and amenities could not efface the reality of the mill village system.

POSTSCRIPT: THE MILL VILLAGE IN THE NEW DEAL

In 1920, Draper claimed that his villages had helped create social peace:

> While it is too early to definitely state that village improvement has had a strong effect in combating bolshevism and minimizing the serious labor difficulties which have attended industrial development in other sections of the country, it is only fair to state that in the opinion of some of the best informed mill men in the South the general improvement work has been a not inconsiderable factor in reducing the labor unrest to the minimum.[59]

Soon, however, events proved his optimistic assessment wrong. After 1925, the textile industry went into deep depression, abruptly curtailing Draper's mill village practice. The 1929
depression exacerbated the situation of the already overextended industry. To survive in a
contracting market, mills continued to rationalize production and extended the stretch-out
even further. But even such extreme measures had little effect, and, in 1932, the Roosevelt
administration's new program for economic revitalization, the NIRA (National Industrial
Recovery Act), first directed its attention to the cotton textile industry. The Cotton Textile
Code, designed to stimulate production, clearly represented the mill owners' interests,
but, after much debate, also included labor provisions imposed by pro-labor New Dealers.
Clauses that required minimum wages and hours and gave workers the right to collective
bargaining clearly threatened the owners' control of the mill villages. The Code also struck
at the heart of regional wage differences and the "mill problem" by suggesting that southern mills dispose of their villages.[60]

   To textile workers, the benefits promised by the NIRA proved to be illusory. The stretch-
out worsened, mills rarely paid even minimum wages, and the mill owners negated the legal
right to organize in practice, firing any worker who joined a union. In spite of this, membership in the Union of Textile Workers (UTW) grew from 40,000 in September 1933 to
270,000 in August 1934, and workers grew restive. On 12 February 1934, workers at
Spindale, North Carolina, residents of one of Earle Draper's earliest villages, were the first

The 1934 general
strike led by the
United Textile
Workers. During the
height of the
Depression, more
than 400,000 textile
workers walked out
of the mills, the
largest single strike
in American history.
Although the strike
ended in defeat for
the workers, it
marked the
beginning of the end
for the mill village.

to walk out. Although the outraged mill owner, K.S. Tanner, fought back by firing union members, Spindale union leaders warned that a general strike was inevitable. By Labor Day, the UTW had led more than 400,000 mill workers off the job, the largest single labor conflict in American history. UTW "flying squadron" automobile convoys sped from mill to mill organizing walk-outs, and radio talks by union leaders spread strike news across the Piedmont.[61]

Chicopee workers did not participate in the General Strike, which was barely felt in Gainesville, but violence broke out the next year when the mill introduced the Bedaux system, a time and motion study system similar to Taylorism. After a series of beatings and a spontaneous strike prompted by the new work rules, Chicopee management shut down the plant "indefinitely." Two months later, after the company fired the strikers and evicted them from their company houses, most of the workers left the village for work elsewhere. The plant resumed production. Newly hired workers had to sign pledges accepting the "time study system."[62] Thus in spite of a dramatic outburst from previously silent workers, the protests ended in defeat without leading to subsequent unionization.

All over the South, workers returned to their jobs. However, the mill village system gradually dissolved as its social and economic rationale disappeared. The NIRA was declared unconstitutional, but other New Deal legislation, such as the Wagner Act, maintained labor's right to organize. Owners turned to different methods to fend off the threat of unionization. With the spread of automobile ownership, workers began to commute to work, so reducing the need to provide housing to attract labor. In the wake of the general strike, mills began to dismantle their villages and sell off their housing; ten years later, Harriet Herring was able to catalogue the "passing of the mill village."[63] During the 1950s, Johnson and Johnson sold the Chicopee houses to the workers.[64]

EARLE DRAPER AND THE NEW DEAL

The New Deal represented a unique opportunity for planners. Once in office, Franklin Roosevelt, a strong advocate of urban planning since the 1909 Chicago plan, immediately instituted state planning on a scale few had ever imagined possible. After decades of privately sponsored planning efforts, the massive shift to public sector planning was a dramatic change. During Roosevelt's first one hundred days in office, among other far-reaching programs, he established the Tennessee Valley Authority, the most ambitious claim of public control over private territory in the nation's history. The bill authorizing the new program, passed in 1932, directed the agency to promote "the economic and social well-being of the people in [the] river basin" of the Tennessee River, an area covering 42,000 square miles and running through seven southern states. Its work would include encouraging industry and agriculture, producing hydroelectric power, improving navigation, flood control, reforestation, and, not incidentally, building towns and highways.[65]

Roosevelt appointed Arthur Morgan, an engineer and president of Antioch College, as the TVA's chairman. Looking for a planner to direct the agency's regional planning and housing activities, Morgan passed over such nationally known figures as John Nolen to select Earle Draper for the coveted post – a position many planners considered to be the most desirable job in the New Deal. Although little known outside the South, Draper's familiarity with southern conditions and his extensive mill village experience made him an ideal choice. Draper began working with Morgan immediately, without pay or formal authorization.[66] At its first meeting, Draper convinced the new TVA to build a permanent settlement instead of a temporary construction camp at Norris, their first dam site, named after Tennessee Senator George Norris. After housing workers on the dam, the settlement would become a self-sufficient community with Morgan's ideal combination of small-scale industry and subsistence farming as its economic base.[67]

Draper began assembling a large staff; he hired – in addition to nearly twenty landscape architects – engineers, social scientists, planners, geographers, and architects. As head architect, he selected Roland Wank, a Hungarian immigrant known for monumental art deco buildings, whom he considered "an architectural genius." Morgan advised Draper not to take on "people who might embarrass us by being tied to the New York group" – a clear reference to Lewis Mumford's Regional Planning Association of America, the group including Clarence Stein, Henry Wright, Frederick Ackerman, and Charles Whitaker, who considered themselves to be the only true authorities on regional planning. However, the planner ignored his advice and hired RPAA members Tracy Auger, a fellow Nolen alumnus, who became his assistant at Norris, and Benton MacKay, hired in 1934 to study Tennessee folk culture.[68]

Before beginning work, Draper and Auger briefly considered Kingsport and the RPAA-sponsored new town of Radburn, New Jersey, designed by Wright and Stein, as possible models for Norris. They rejected both as inappropriate for the rough terrain of the area. Instead, Draper expanded on his earlier work in textile villages, and Norris became the ultimate expression of his rural planning style. Just across the Great Smoky Mountains from the Piedmont cotton belt, Norris, situated in a rural upland settled by a homogeneous Appalachian population, addressed a set of regional conditions similar to those of the Piedmont.[69] Given a free hand by the TVA and without the social and industrial constraints of textile production, Draper created a town plan that pushed the techniques he had developed in mill villages toward an even greater regional specificity.

Norris's plan synthesized the Olmsted tradition of naturalistic planning with English

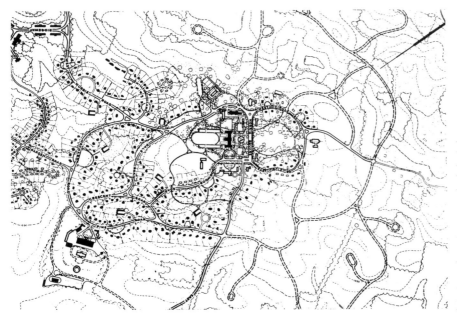

Draper's plan for the Tennessee Valley Authority town of Norris, Tennessee pushes the rural style and regional specificity of his planning beyond his textile villages. The roads snake across the top of ridges and houses are clustered according to topography.

garden city techniques and Draper's own rural preferences. Using much more open space than building, Draper designed the town around the natural landscape, with architecture playing a secondary role. Although Chicopee and other Draper textile towns were "walking villages," the entire village of Norris, like Central Park, was linked by a pedestrian circulation system. Completely separated from automobile traffic, pedestrian paths went under the main road and snaked in and out of the woods. In Norris, Draper expanded the greenbelt, already a trademark of his mill town planning, to 2,000 acres of parkland which circled the town, acting as a woodland barrier against development. Large and irregular lots with space for gardens emphasized the town's rural character and generous areas of green space reduced the density of the housing even further than the twelve houses per acre recommended by Raymond Unwin, the garden city designer. An additional protective buffer, a limited-access parkway, connected Norris to Knoxville. The first freeway built in the United States, the Norris parkway, allowing quick access from the rural village to the city, eliminated the isolation that had been characteristic of many textile towns.

Abandoning even the vestige of formal planning that had remained in Chicopee's town center, Draper pushed naturalistic planning techniques even further. The contours of the land determined the plan. Adjusted to the uneven topography of the heavily wooded site, a loose network of roads ran along the top of ridges and into valleys. A series of looping circles and cul-de-sacs provided road frontage without imposing an urban block pattern. Draper and Auger also selected the house sites according to topography rather than street lines. Instead of drawing lots on a plan, they laid out the lot lines by walking the site and staking them out. This produced irregular setbacks – some houses were angled to the sun while others clustered together. In spite of the cost savings, Draper vetoed group houses as unsuitable for a rural setting and unacceptable to local people. As at Chicopee, he directed Wank and his staff to produce a large variety of single family house types. The architects designed thirty different plans. Styles based on indigenous types replaced generic bungalows, a reference to the earlier vernacular dwellings of the area, which had been submerged under Norris Lake, an artificial lake created by a TVA dam. Dog-trot plans (for houses which featured a central open porch through which dogs could trot) and traditional materials such as hickory shakes split by hand echoed the log cabin tradition and, although criticized by modernists, offered residents familiar images of shelter, now supplemented with fully electric kitchens.[70]

At the center of the plan, a 14-acre green common circled Norris's only monumental building, the consolidated school, which replaced the mill as the symbolic heart of the town. This significant change signaled Norris's new set of social intentions. Other community buildings formed an informal civic cluster scattered around the central common. Built in less than a year, Norris was complete by late 1933. The town became a showplace

House in Norris. At the same time that European modernism was beginning to influence US government housing, Roland Wank's designs for Norris moved in the opposite direction, recalling the vernacular dwellings of the area. Model D-2 – the "Dog-Trot" – had walls clad with hand-split shakes.

of New Deal regionalism and community planning. Eleanor Roosevelt officiated at its inauguration. The following year, Sir Raymond Unwin visited the town and announced that it was "America's best example of the English garden city ideas."[71] Unwin's praise recognized not only Draper's mastery of planning technique but acknowledged that Norris, like Letchworth, was a prototype community with a new social and economic basis. Even more than the gradual disappearance of the mill village, the planning of Norris signifies the true ending of the textile mill village. The TVA's project of state-sponsored rural electrification and recreational development proposed a new social and economic paradigm as an alternative to the exploitation and cultural disruption of Piedmont industrialization, and opened up a new era of development that would once again transform the economic landscape of the South.[72]

Earle Draper, now a Norris resident, remained at the TVA for eight years. Coordinating with other TVA departments and the state planning boards in seven states, he established the broad regional powers of the agency. Buying huge tracts of land around the new lakes created by TVA dams, he was instrumental in establishing recreation as one of TVA's priorities. Draper's study, *The Scenic Resources of the Tennessee Valley*, proposed a strategy for developing tourism in a region that was, for the first time, accessible not only to outsiders but to its own residents. With planning now established as a permanent function of the national government, Draper moved to Washington DC to become Assistant Administrator of the Federal Housing Authority. Like John Nolen, committed to the expansion of the planning function in government, Draper applauded the profession's move from the private to public sector. Instead of depending on the goodwill of individual employers, housing for low-income families became a responsibility guaranteed by Federal and city governments.[73] As Draper administered Federal housing policies, absorbed in national debates about housing issues, his earlier concerns for a regional planning style disappeared. By the 1950s, rural planning was no longer a viable alternative in a professional discourse now preoccupied with urban problems and suburban developments.

CONCLUSION:
THE END OF THE
COMPANY TOWN

The year 1929 marked the end of the "new" company town. Over the preceding twenty years, designers had produced more than forty new industrial towns.[1] These towns, significantly different from earlier company towns, constitute a distinct chapter in the history of the American company town. Although many were never finished as planned, virtually all had been designed as complete communities, including housing, shops and services, public spaces, and recreational facilities. In addition, nearly all were physically and conceptually separate from their industrial purpose – the factory or mine. Almost obsessively avoiding the monotonous gridirons and repetitive rows of identical houses typical of earlier company towns, architects designed numerous varieties of inexpensive, single family houses while planners and landscape architects perfected site plans complete with parks and extensive landscaping. Architects, planners, and landscape architects collaborated to produce comprehensively designed company towns whose appearance denied their industrial origins, resembling exclusive suburbs more than earlier industrial towns such as Lowell or Pullman.

FROM WELFARE CAPITALISM TO FORDISM

In spite of their increasing sophistication, by the mid-1920s such towns had become less necessary to their sponsors. During the 1920s, William Wood, chairman of the American Woolen Company, began construction of Shawsheen Village in Andover, Mass., an ambitious project that housed both unskilled workers and executives. Other firms, such as the Endicott Johnson Company of Binghamton, New York, expanded their housing and welfare programs, known as the "Square Deal." However, these projects were exceptions to a general decline in company housing, the result of charismatic management styles rather than a trend. Many other firms began to eliminate or reduce programs providing housing, medical care, and recreation. A National Industrial Conference Board study showed that few companies added new welfare programs between 1925 and 1930 and many companies dropped their existing programs. Employers replaced housing and welfare activities with other company ventures that produced more directly practical results: pension plans, personnel departments, or, more importantly, employee representation schemes or company unions. Unlike the delayed effects and variable results of welfare work, these methods were inexpensive and confronted the threat of unions head on. During the war, many companies had introduced employee representation programs to comply with government regulations, and, finding them a useful means of improving labor relations and an effective safety-valve for grievances, continued them voluntarily. At a moment when the spread of "Bolshevism" was alarming capitalists, they adopted company unions as a safe way to introduce at least nominally democratic principles into the workplace.[2]

During the prosperous 1920s, the implicit assumption behind many welfare programs – that employees could not afford these services for themselves – was also eroding. In spite of great income inequality and a relatively low standard of living, overall, most workers' material well-being improved. National distribution of increasing numbers of consumer goods gradually incorporated workers into the market. Installment buying allowed even cash-poor workers to acquire products such as automobiles, radios, vacuum cleaners, and electric ice boxes as well as improved medical care and life insurance. As they became part of a national culture linked by the popular media of radio, magazines, and advertising, workers began to find welfare capitalism's offerings demeaning rather than welcome. Employees increasingly demanded a larger paycheck in lieu of company expenditures on welfare programs.[3]

The availability of inexpensive automobiles greatly reduced the workers' dependence on their employer. Used cars or Model T and A Fords bought on credit freed workers from the need to shop at the company store, worship at the company church, and, finally, to live in company houses. Visitors to company towns during the 1920s reported finding numerous houses left vacant by employees who had moved away and now commuted to work. The automobile affected company towns in a number of ways. Increasingly mobile workers gained access to a broader range of job opportunities. Automobiles lessened both the physical and social distances between residents of company towns and their neighbors. By connecting residents with the world outside, the automobile mitigated the repressive aspects of the company town. This new mobility encouraged individual mores instead of the community ethos that formed the social basis of the company town. As a consumer durable and a form of transportation, the automobile tended to blur class consciousness, an apparent equality of consumption and mobility masking continuing economic inequalities.[4]

Company-sponsored services became less important than they had been earlier. As automobiles reduced their isolation, company town residents gained access to greatly improved social services that state and municipal governments were beginning to provide: public schools, libraries, parks, playgrounds, and recreation programs.[5]

Welfare capitalism, always responsive to changes in labor conditions and business cycles, contracted during the 1920s as the rate of labor turnover significantly slowed and the incidence of strikes became much lower. As the strike wave of the early 1920s ebbed, employers increasingly dispensed with welfare expenditures. After 1929, the dramatic economic downturn and the deterioration of business conditions affected welfare capitalism more profoundly. Welfare expenditures were usually the first item to be eliminated as companies reduced spending and contracted production simply in order to survive. Business conditions did not begin to improve until more than a decade later, but few firms reinstated their welfare programs.[6]

If company towns and welfare capitalism declined during the 1920s, the New Deal dealt them a more serious blow. Early in the "hundred days," the new Roosevelt administration began a vigorous attack on company-sponsored housing and welfare programs. The Cotton Textile Code stated bluntly:

> There is something feudal and repugnant to American principles in the practice of employer ownership of employee homes . . . . It is hoped that, with the creation of real industrial self-government and improvement in the minimum wage, an impetus will be given by employers to independent home ownership and the conversion of the differential into a wage equivalent.

The Code required textile companies to "consider the question of plans for eventual employee ownership of homes in mill villages." The Bituminous Coal Industry Code also sought to end company requirements that miners live in company houses and shop at company stores. Legislation culminating in the Buffey–Vinson Bituminous Coal Act 1937 protected the coal miners' right to peaceful assembly and to their choice of housing. It also permitted independent stores to locate in mining towns.[7]

Even more significantly, repeated government attempts to guarantee the workers' right to collective bargaining attacked the anti-union premises of many company towns. Although Section 7a of the National Industrial Recovery Act declared "that employees shall have the right to organize and bargain collectively through representatives of their own choosing," a loophole allowed company-sponsored employee representation plans to satisfy the requirement. The Supreme Court declared the NIRA unconstitutional in May 1935, but two months later the far stronger Wagner Act reasserted the workers' right to collective bargaining and reclassified company-run employee representation as an unfair labor practice. The new National Labor Relations Board began to issue cease and desist orders which eliminated company social and recreational clubs, stating: "Good business, fair play and good sportsmanship demand that the employer divorce from his recreation programs any attempt to interfere with the serious business of self-organization and collective bargaining."[8] These policies cleared the way for unions to expand their membership dramatically. From 1935 to 1943, union membership tripled. Having lost the battle against unions, companies discontinued welfare programs and gradually began to sell off their houses.[9]

Less directly, New Deal mortgage insurance programs also affected company housing by transforming housing finance. The National Housing Act of 1934 established the Federal Housing Administration to stimulate the moderate-cost private housing market by insuring low-interest long-term mortgages. FHA-insured loans covered up to 80 percent of a house's value and were repayable over twenty years with low monthly payments of 5–6 percent interest. These programs replaced bank loans that had covered less than 50 percent of a house's value and were repayable in only three to five years at much higher interest rates. Although the growth of the program was interrupted by the Second World War, the FHA eventually extended the possibility of home ownership to a large segment of the working class, thus eliminating the need for industry-subsidized home ownership programs. Postwar Veterans Administration mortgage guarantee programs, which eliminated even the need for a down-payment, expanded home ownership even further.

The New Deal also dramatically expanded the roles professionals could play in providing low-income housing and town planning. Beginning with the TVA, new government programs such as the Division of Subsistence Homesteads, the Federal Emergency Relief Administration, the Housing Division of the Public Works Administrations, and the Resettlement Administration began to construct housing and entire communities. The government initially focused on housing three separate groups: distressed rural families, the unemployed in large cities, and "stranded populations," those who had lost their jobs in single-industry communities.[10] These programs acknowledged, for the first time, the government's responsibility to provide shelter for low-wage workers and the unemployed. New Deal community development programs built on the experiences of the designers who had created the "new" company towns. John Nolen served as an adviser to the Subsistence Homesteads program and designed several of its settlements. Earle Draper, Tracy Augur, Russell Van Ness Black, and Clarence Stein served as advisers to the best-known New Deal program, the Greenbelt communities sponsored by the Suburban Resettlement Division under Rexford Tugwell.[11] The towns of Greenbelt, Maryland, Greenhills, Ohio, and Greendale, Wisconsin – the latter designed by Elbert Peets, planner of the company town of Kohler, Wisconsin – incorporated many of the planning concepts developed in "new" company towns twenty years earlier. Increasing levels of Federal support reflected Interior

Secretary Harold Ickes's conviction that "it is not possible without a subsidy to produce housing for the lower income groups."[12] Subsidies previously supplied by employers now became the responsibility of federal and state governments.

As World War I housing programs had done, the New Deal agencies brought architects, planners, and landscape architects together in collaborative projects. Government work not only enhanced the status of the design professions but expanded their professional domain. This produced different results in each profession. Although increased government involvement in housing and community planning provided architects with a new group of clients, state support did not alter the structure of the profession. For landscape architects and city planners, however, the New Deal transformed their professional possibilities. Programs such as the Public Works Administration, the Civilian Conservation Corps, and the Federal Emergency Relief Administration supplied both funds and workers to national and state park systems, providing new jobs in park planning for landscape architects. By 1940 the National Park Service became the largest employer of landscape architects in the history of the profession. Working with large-scale land development also expanded the scope of the landscape profession, adding regional and environmental planning to designers' skills. For city planners, the benefits of the New Deal were even more pronounced. Public patronage almost completely replaced private clients. In spite of its *ex officio* status, the National Resource Planning Board, active from 1933 to 1942, represented the first permanent Federal commitment to publicly supported planning at all levels of government. This legitimized planning activities that had previously existed only at the sufferance of municipal governments. Planning acquired a widely recognized value as, all over the country, government agencies began to produce all types of plan. Encouraged by the New Deal's broad definition of planning, these were no longer limited to coordinating physical growth but now dealt with social and economic policies.[13]

EVALUATING THE "NEW" COMPANY TOWN

The New Deal also sponsored the first serious evaluation of the "new" company town. The Urbanism Committee, set up by the National Resource Planning Board, conducted an exhaustive survey of 144 planned towns, garden suburbs, and residential areas under the direction of landscape architect Arthur Comey – planner of Billerica Garden Suburb – and researcher Max S. Wehrly.[14] The largest percentage (53.3 percent) of the towns the committee examined were industrial company towns. They selected Fairfield, Torrance, Goodyear Heights, Indian Hill, Kingsport, and Chicopee for detailed case-studies. Based on questionnaires, interviews, and site visits, the committee analyzed the physical, social, and economic development of the towns as well as conducting post-occupancy evaluations. The report reflected the biases of New Deal planners, who supported community planning but were critical of paternalism and company ownership. Nevertheless, the authors concluded that the planned company towns they had studied, in spite of the social and economic restrictions imposed by their industrial sponsors, were successful communities. The main beneficiaries of the expense and expertise that had gone into the construction of these towns were their residents: "free from overcrowding . . . their inhabitants enjoy greater efficiency, greater safety, and a more healthful and in *very great measure*, a more attractive environment."[15]

It is difficult to disagree with this assessment. From 1910 to 1925, the "new" company town significantly raised the standard of living in company towns. Industrial houses were larger, better built, and provided with more services than ever before. Architectural attention to planning and comfort gradually reduced the previously wide gap between company housing and middle-class dwellings. Since the housing in the earliest "new" company towns was designed to be sold to workers, designers had to treat skilled workers as clients and consumers. With the workers' rather than the capitalists' tastes and preferences establishing the criteria for housing design, single family houses, "artistic" styles, and large lots became standard features in company towns. First introduced into higher priced workers' housing, these design standards trickled down into rental housing built for unskilled laborers. For both groups, the economic advantages of company housing were clear. Since affordability had been a fundamental consideration in their design, these improvements in quality did not raise the cost of housing. The percentage of workers' salaries necessary to cover housing costs remained stable, or, in many instances, was actually lowered.

Comprehensive planning offered other advantages. Designed to be a unified and coherent community, the "new" company town had a distinctive identity separate from the factory or mine. Like the garden city, these towns balanced a naturalistic setting with contour planning, curving streets, and extensive landscaping with communal spaces such as parks, recreation areas, shops, and services. In terms of design and environmental quality the closest equivalents were expensive middle-class suburbs. At the same time, of course, these communities were fundamentally coercive, their unified design expressing the employers' desire for control. How well these controls operated is not clear, however. The Urbanism Committee's report suggests that, by the mid-1930s, employers no longer operated many of the "new" company towns. Owner-occupied housing, political incorporation, and labor struggles had reduced the employers' degree of control and, as a result, their interest in maintaining their towns.

Thus, for employers, the benefits of the "new" company town were ambiguous. Historians disagree about the effectiveness of industrial welfare. Some scholars, such as Stewart

Brandes and Irving Bernstein, conclude that welfare capitalism was not successful in capturing workers' loyalty. Emphasizing that employers were increasingly confronted with evidence that employees instinctively rejected welfare work, they see welfare capitalism as an unstable and temporary system that could not stave off the inevitability of unionization. Others, such as Daniel Nelson and David Brody, argue that welfare capitalism succeeded in increasing management's control over workers and in generating worker loyalty. Asserting that millions of workers gladly accepted paternalism, Brody claimed that, if the Depression had not shattered the prevailing assumptions of corporate paternalism, welfare capitalism rather than unionization might have become the dominant feature of American industrialism. A recent study by Gerald Zahavi takes a third position. After intensive study of a major welfare employer, the Endicott Johnson Corporation, Zahavi claims that welfare created mutual loyalty between labor and management. In exchange for their loyalty, workers were able to extract the maximum advantages from their employer.[16]

This study does not support such clear alternatives, but suggests that other issues need to be considered to evaluate the company town's effectiveness from the employer's point of view. Searching for general conclusions, all these arguments ignore the economic, social, and geographic diversity of American industry during the early decades of the twentieth century. Like most managerial and reform ideologies of the Progressive era, the "new" company town proposed generalized and standardized solutions for situations that were local and specific. This research suggests that the success or failure of company towns usually depended on the industrial context in which they were introduced. Rather than occupying an abstract setting, every firm is located in a unique industrial context composed of a number of elements. Production processes, the size and organization of the firm, as well as such considerations as local labor markets, the local economy, and the socio-cultural environment, all shape the nature of an industrial enterprise. Designed by outsiders unfamiliar with industrial processes, unacquainted with local conditions and already committed to standard solutions, "new" company towns rarely addressed these issues. Thus, as Zahavi's study of a single firm suggests, in some industrial settings, workers can acquire the power to negotiate over a firm's welfare responsibilities. In other situations, however, different relationships between employers and workers can result in different policies and responses.

The "new" company town followed a similar pattern. Some northern manufacturing towns, such as Indian Hill and Kistler, and many southern textile villages attracted stable populations of long-term residents who resisted the unions. Other companies, building company towns in the hope of maintaining a stable group of workers and avoiding unions, were largely disappointed. In some industries improved living conditions and attractive settings in company towns had little effect on labor relations: Vandergrift, Fairfield, and Morgan Park joined other steel towns in the massive 1919 steel strike. In other places, company towns exacerbated labor disputes and intensified conflict. During the 1930s, for example, after an intense struggle, Kingsport's plants became unionized and Kohler's workers began a long and bitter strike.[17]

From the designers' point of view, the "new" company town produced equally inconclusive results. As a single commission, company towns proved disappointing. Although they appeared to offer designers the freedom to design complete communities without the restrictions of the marketplace, in practice this did not usually occur. Cost-conscious clients rarely followed plans completely. Short-term changes in labor relations and profitability affected the implementation of long-term plans. As a result, towns like Torrance, Indian Hill, Tyrone, and Kistler were never more than partial – and therefore frustrating – realizations of their designers' intentions. As a demonstration of professional achievement, the "new" company town was more successful. Designing entire communities, even in collaboration with other professions, gave credence to professional assertions of social commitment and technical expertise. Focused on the problem of the industrial community and the workers' house, designers had produced an impressive body of systematized and standardized information. Textbooks, plans, housing designs, and, most importantly, actual towns bolstered the newly expanded professional claims of architects, landscape architects, and city planners.

The "new" company town was most successful in expanding the formal and technical scope of the design professions. Placed in the larger historical context of housing design and town planning, these towns represented a significant advancement. In a period when architecture and planning operated exclusively in the marketplace, these towns provided important opportunities to plan and build comprehensively designed communities. Unlike the other main venue for community planning – the upper-middle-class suburb – industrial sponsorship at least partially removed the necessity to realize profits. As a result, company towns were testing grounds for the design of small, low-cost houses. This kept interest in low-income housing alive in the absence of state subsidies and moved architects away from the narrow concerns of tenement reform to address the entire living environment. Although the social and economic premises under which these towns were built were highly restrictive, nonetheless company town commissions encouraged designers to consider social and economic factors as fundamental elements of physical design. The boom in company town construction focused an enormous amount of professional interest and expertise on important issues of low-cost housing and community development. The need to work within exacting cost margins made these tasks even more challenging. The "new" company town greatly expanded the designers' arena and directly informed subsequent housing and community design.

Critical and historical discussions of American architecture and planning have tended to ignore the "new" company town, instead identifying the Regional Planning Association of America as the real pioneers of community planning in the United States. In 1923 Alexander Bing, Henry Wright, and Clarence Stein, who would later become members of the RPAA, praised the "new" company town in an unpublished proposal for Sunnyside, specifically singling out Neponset Garden Village, Indian Hill, Tyrone, and Kistler for their high quality design.[18] However, in general, the RPAA's insistence on a narrow definition of "community" and Lewis Mumford's dislike of industrialism limited their appreciation of the important role company town design had played in creating new housing and planning solutions.[19] Supported by limited profit financing, RPAA designers like Wright and Stein, had little reason to respond to the preferences of working-class occupants, and insisted on building group housing and communal open spaces. The RPAA's interest in regionalism did not extend to housing typologies or architectural styles. Instead, they increasingly looked to Dutch and German examples of large-scale, state-supported housing projects for inspiration.[20]

The appearance of European modernism further obscured the role of the "new" company town in the history of American planning. By the end of the 1930s, the new abstract style and powerful ideology of modernism, which equated standardization and repetition with an egalitarian social order, overshadowed earlier attempts to incorporate historical and regional influences and provide individualized dwellings for industrial workers. In the 1970s, the advent of post-modernism reversed this critical tide, fostering a renewed interest in regional imagery and housing typologies, Beaux Arts urban design, and picturesque urban planning.[21] The plans of "new" company towns were rediscovered and republished, along with the work of Parker and Unwin and Camillo Sitte. Robert A.M. Stern's *The Anglo-American Suburb*, published in 1981, and Hegemann and Peet's *American Vitruvius*, reissued in 1989, served as inspiration for a new generation of neo-traditional town planners attempting to give American cities and suburbs a new coherence and unity.

Thus, in hindsight, the "new" company town can be recognized as an episode in the continuing tradition of picturesque design. Rather than constituting a specific style, the picturesque is a method of using and combining different styles chosen for their associative meanings. As an artificially created "instant" place simulating an older form of community, the "new" company town is a direct descendant of picturesque planned villages such as Blaise Hamlet. Designed by John Nash in 1810, Blaise was an apparently casual assemblage of carefully designed, "quaint" rural cottages. Built to house the banker John Harford's retired employees, the absence of schools, church, inn, and shop underlined the village's unreal quality. According to architectural historian David Watkin, this quality of deception is one of the dominant themes of the picturesque.[22] In picturesque villages, the element of make-believe usually took the form of a preoccupation with the past and with the creation of a *genius loci*. Expressed through architectural form and landscape design, cliché, nostalgia, and escapism served as defenses against the dramatic social and environmental changes brought by industrialization. The picturesque village conveyed a reassuring social meaning by projecting a heightened image of a carefully structured society, held together by traditional values. Throughout the nineteenth century picturesque images were repeatedly invoked at moments of acute social and economic upheaval to defuse class conflict, successively producing Central Park, Riverside, and the "new" company town. Today, this tradition of fictional landscape continues in "themed" environments, such as Disneyland, Las Vegas, and shopping malls, as well as in neo-traditional towns like Seaside, Florida.

REMAINS AND SURVIVALS

The company town slowly disappeared from the American landscape. Employees who purchased company houses altered them to fit their needs, so undermining the unique physical coherence characteristic of company towns. The remains of company towns can be found all over the United States. Even as fragments, they are still recognizable from their homogeneous quality, rare in the American landscape. Their ruins are often long-lived. As the New England textile industry slowly died, its substantial mills and housing, built to last, endured long after the machinery had been shipped to the South or the Third World, mute testimony to a now anachronistic productive system. As firms went into liquidation, they often put entire towns under the auctioneer's hammer. Abandoned factories littered the region, but some textile production remained, although with far smaller workforces than in the industry's prime. Some enterprising towns succeeded in attracting new high-technology industries to occupy vacant mills. Nashua, New Hampshire, and North Andover and Lawrence, Massachusetts, became regional centers for electronics and plastics firms. In prosperous areas, mills were adapted and reused as residential, office, or commercial space. In other towns, however, textile mills have been converted into shoe and garment factories with sweatshop conditions and low wages. Other mills have simply been left to decay, corpses of industrial progress.[23]

In other parts of the country, companies continued to rent houses to their workers. A survey of Georgia mills in 1952 showed that many still retained and rented housing, although only 40 percent of their workers lived in them. A surprising number of companies continued to operate old-style company towns. In 1968, the US Civil Rights Commission discovered Bellamy, Georgia, completely owned by the American Can Company, who operated a high-priced company store and company school, and rented company houses to workers who, after deductions for rent and food, received minimal paychecks.[24] From 1887 until 1982, when it finally sold its 1,785 clapboard mill houses, the Cannon family, owners of Cannon Textile Mills, completely controlled Kannopolis, North Carolina. In the west, mining and lumber companies operated numerous resource-extraction towns until the 1980s. The mining industry, restructuring after a dramatic downtown in the early 1980s, eliminated more than 50 percent of their workers, shut down plants, and left rows of company houses to decay.[25] Since the late 1960s, the number of lumber towns in the northwest has declined along with the wood products industry.[26] In 1991, the Bechtel Corporation purchased Gilchrist, Oregon's last remaining company town, saving it from destruction. Scotia, the last company town in California, was recently acquired by the Maxxam Group, narrowly escaping a similar fate.[27] Tourism is bringing new life to western company towns in scenic areas. Scotia's neat white houses have begun to attract travelers on Interstate highway 101 in northern California. Southwestern mining towns are being resettled by artists and other self-employed residents. After the Phelps-Dodge mine closed, Ajo, Arizona became a popular destination for "snowbirds," retirees seeking inexpensive winter lodging.

Beginning in the 1960s, trends in historical scholarship have also renewed interest in company towns. Focusing on groups and issues previously neglected by mainstream American history, scholars began to examine the history of ordinary people. New approaches in urban, social and labor history focused attention on the history of "the masses, not the classes." Faced with new subjects of history, scholars posed new questions, discovered new sources, and created new methodologies such as oral history. These approaches encouraged detailed studies of working-class communities including company towns, and provided a deeper knowledge of working-class life, in particular revealing the enormous diversity of ethnic subcultures and the range of their responses to industrial life. Gradually, this historical orientation expanded to include the built environment. Using measured drawings and artifacts as the basis for interpretation, scholars of vernacular architecture and material culture studies discovered social and cultural meaning in the everyday environment. Architectural history, a discipline traditionally devoted to the study of monuments, gradually widened its scope to include industrial structures and company towns.

Influenced by this scholarship, in the 1960s the historic preservation movement looked beyond landmarks and notable houses to consider as historically significant the architectural fabric of entire neighborhoods and districts. Industrial sites and company towns were part of this newly discovered heritage. In 1976, the National Trust for Historic Preservation asserted that "workers' housing in the shadow of a factory is as much a part of America's architectural heritage as more readily acknowledged landmarks."[28] By the end of the decade, the National Park Service, the Federal agency responsible for historic landmarks, designated many of the towns discussed in the early chapters of this book as historical monuments, historic districts, or heritage areas. This included the Slater Mill and other early mills along the Blackstone River Valley in Rhode Island, Lowell, Massachusetts, Homestead, Pennsylvania, the Calumet Industrial District in Michigan, and Pullman. Other National Park Service programs such as the Historic American Building Survey and the Historic American Engineering Record are in the process of documenting industrial projects and company towns by means of photographs, drawings, and written histories. America's Industrial Heritage Project, a detailed survey of industrial sites in southwestern Pennsylvania, has produced publications on the steel mill city of Johnstown, and Iron, Coal, and Refactory company towns. Local groups like the Illinois Labor History Society produced a series of interpretive guides to Chicago labor history sites, written from the workers' point of view. In Connecticut, the Brass Workers History Project have also produced several books and a documentary film based on oral histories with workers in the Naugatuck Valley.[29] This has helped generate a growing public interest in the industrial past and working-class life, leading to the creation and expansion of local and regional museums. In New England the Merrimack Valley Textile Museum and Old Sturbridge Village attract both scholars and tourists. A recent Federal initiative designated several industrial regions as historic sites to encourage local and regional economic development. If this strategy is effective, company towns may acquire a new economic role as anchors for tourism, recreation, and commercial revitalization.[30]

THE REBIRTH OF THE COMPANY TOWN?

The impulses that generated company towns during the early decades of the twentieth century have not completely vanished. In 1980 Charles Crowder, a Texas real-estate developer, began planning an ambitious new industrial town, Santa Teresa, to be built on the border near El Paso, half in Mexico, half in the United States. Santa Teresa's industrial base was to be based on *maquiladoras*, American and Japanese-owned assembly plants that locate just across the Mexican border to take advantage of low-wage Mexican workers. Crowder's plan for the town included an industrial district on the Mexican side of the border, a border crossing, and a complete living environment for the entire workforce. Santa Teresa resembles earlier company towns in many respects. Like those towns it attempts to improve efficiency and reduce labor turnover among low-wage, unskilled workers. In Ciudad Juarez, where most *maquiladora* workers live, water is in short supply and cholera is a constant threat. The annual turnover rate at *maquiladoras* is over 100 percent. Crowder's rhetoric is reminiscent of earlier employers: "How can you be efficient if you wake up with no plumbing, walk through a slum to work, and worry about your grandmother's safety?"[31] Santa Teresa, providing good housing at low rents near workplaces and ample supplies of water, would significantly improve living and working conditions for Mexican *maquiladora* workers.[32]

Santa Teresa's planning also recalls western mining towns such as Tyrone and Ajo in its explicit provision of dual housing and services for Mexican and American workers. Management, mostly American, will live north of the border, provided with suburban houses and golf courses. On the other side, Mexican workers will be housed in dense urban dwellings, organized around a central plaza. Significantly, like earlier capitalists, Crowder called on professionals to design the town. In 1992, teams of students and professors from Harvard University's Graduate School of Design and the University of New Mexico's School of Architecture and Urban Planning visited the site and prepared proposals for town plans, housing and neighborhood development. Beaux Arts town centers, central plazas surrounded by arcades, parks, landscaping, and recreational areas figured prominently in all of the schemes.[33] In 1992, however, Sunwest Bank foreclosed on Charles Crowder's multi-million-dollar loans, making it unlikely that Santa Teresa will become the first of a new generation of company towns.[34] The enthusiastic participation of designers, unconcerned about the social and economic issues the town's premises raise, suggests that, seventy-five years after the "new" company town, the lack of awareness among a new generation of architects and planners of their own professional circumstances could allow history to repeat itself.

NOTES

INTRODUCTION

1. Horace P. Davis, "Company Towns," in the *Encyclopedia of the Social Sciences*, vol. 4, New York: The Macmillan Co. 1930, p. 119.

2. Carnegie Steel intentionally located its Homestead plant outside town limits and only later, after the 1909 steel strike, began building housing. By this time, the town was almost completely developed. Eric Monkonnen, *America Becomes Urban*, Berkeley: University of California Press 1988, p. 224; Margaret Byington, *Homestead: the Households of a Mill Town*, New York: Russell Sage Foundation 1910.

3. Leifur Magnussen,"Company Housing," in the *Encyclopedia of the Social Sciences*, vol. 4, pp. 117–19.

4. This definition of the "model town" comes from Arthur C. Comey and Max Wehrly, *Planned Communities*, Part 1, vol. II of the *Supplementary Report of the Urbanism Committee*, Washington DC: Government Printing Office 1938: "a concrete demonstration of a definite preconceived theory of physical or social planning" (p. 70). A less specific, but common use of the term "model" is John S. Garner's explanation: "some of these towns were superior to others and therefore termed 'models' ". *The Model Company Town*, Amherst: The University of Massachusetts Press 1984, p. xii. This usage is exemplified in numerous articles and books dealing with company towns and industrial welfare published during the late nineteenth century.

5. Accounts of industrial betterment include Stuart Brandes, *American Welfare Capitalism*, Chicago: University of Chicago Press 1976; Daniel Nelson, *Managers and Workers*, Madison: University of Wisconsin Press 1975; Gerald Zahavi, *Workers, Managers and Welfare Capitalism: The Shoeworkers and Tanners of Endicott-Johnson*, Urbana: University of Illinois Press 1988.

6. See Tamara K. Haraven and Randolph Langenbach, *Amoskeag: Life and Work in an American Factory City*, New York: Pantheon Books 1978; John Borden Armstrong, *Factory under the Elms: A History of Harrisville, New Hampshire*, Cambridge, Mass.: Harvard University Press 1976; Gary Kulik, Roger Parks, and Theodore Penn, eds, *The New England Mill Village, 1790–1860*, Cambridge, Mass.: Harvard University Press 1982; John Coolidge, *Mill and Mansion: A Study of Architecture and Society in Lowell, 1820–1865*, New York: Columbia University Press 1942; Donald B. Cole, *Immigrant City, Lawrence, Mass. 1845–1921*, Chapel Hill: University of North Carolina Press 1963; Katherine A. Harvey, *The Best Dressed Miners*, Ithaca, NY: Cornell University Press 1968; Anthony F.C. Wallace, *Rockdale*, New York: Columbia University Press 1978; Joseph Walker, *Hopewell Village, A Social and Economic History of an Ironmaking Community*, Philadephia: University of Pennsylvania Press 1966; David Carlton, *Mill and Town in South Carolina*, Baton Rouge: Southern Louisiana University Press 1982; and Stanley Buder,

Pullman: An Experiment in Industrial Order and Community Planning, New York: Oxford University Press 1967.

7. Architectural works include Leland Roth, "Three Industrial Towns by McKim, Mead and White," *Journal of the Society of Architectural Historians* 38 (December 1979), pp. 317–47; John S. Garner, *The Model Company Town*, Amherst: University of Massachusetts Press 1984; John S. Garner, ed., *The Company Town: Architecture and Society in the Early Industrial Age*, New York: Oxford University Press 1992; John Reps, "The Towns the Companies Built," in *The Making of Urban America*, Princeton, NJ: Princeton University Press 1965; William Pierson, "The New Industrial Order: The Factory and the Factory Town," in *American Buildings and their Architects: Technology and the Picturesque: The Corporate and Early Gothic Style*, Garden City, NY: Anchor Books 1978, pp. 60–90; Robert A.M. Stern, "Industrial Villages," in *The Anglo-American Suburb*, London: Architectural Design 1980.

8. Reps, "The Towns the Companies Built"; Stern, "Industrial Villages."

9. Norman Newton, "Town Planning in the U.S. 1915–1929," in *Design on the Land*, Cambridge, Mass: Harvard University Press 1971; Mel Scott, *American City Planning since 1890*, Berkeley: University of California Press 1969; John Hancock, "Planners in the Changing American City: 1900–1940," *American Insitute of Planners Journal* 33 (September 1967); and "John Nolen: The Background of a Pioneer Planner," *American Institute of Planners Journal* 26 (November 1960).

10. Examples of the first include Francesco Dal Co, "From the Park to the Region," in Giorgio Ciucci, Francesco Dal Co, Mario Manieri-Elia, and Manfredo Tafuri, eds, *The American City*, Cambridge, Mass.: MIT Press 1978; and Marino Folin, "La citta di fondazione industriale: le ragione del fallimento di una forma urbanistica del capital-ismo," in *L'urbanistica del reformismo U.S.A. 1890–1940*, Milano: Mazzotta 1975; and of the lat-ter: David Handlin, "The House Beautiful," in *The American Home: Architecture and Society, 1845–1915*, Boston, Mass.: Little, Brown and Company 1979;

and Gwendolyn Wright, "Welfare Capitalism and the Company Town," in *Building the Dream*, New York: Pantheon 1981.

11. Scholars of the New England textile industry emphasize the effects of change, but attribute it to technological development. See John Coolidge, *Mill and Mansion: A Study of Architecture and Society in Lowell: 1820–1865*, New York: Columbia University Press 1942; Steve Dunwell, *The Run of the Mill*, Boston, Mass.: David R. Godine 1978; Richard M. Candee, "New Towns of the Early New England Textile Industry," in Camille Wells, ed., *Perspectives in Vernacular Architecture*, Annapolis, Md: Vernacular Architecture Forum 1982, pp. 31–50.

12. Marco Cenzatti, *Motorcycles of Postmodernity; The Restructuring of Industry and Theory*, PhD Dissertation, UCLA 1993.

13. Michel Aglietta, *A Theory of Capitalist Regulation: The U.S. Experience*, London: New Left Books 1979.

14. David Harvey, *The Limits to Capital*, Chicago: University of Chicago Press 1982, pp. 415, 431–8.

15. Michael Storper and Richard Walker, *The Capitalist Imperative*, New York: Basil Blackwell 1989, p. 6.

16. Craig Littler, *The Development of the Labour Process in Capitalist Societies*, London: Heinemann Educational Books 1982, pp. 30–31.

17. Herbert Gutman, *Work, Culture and Society in Industrializing America*, New York: Vintage Books 1977; Philip S. Foner, *The AFL in the Progressive Era: 1910–1915, The History of the Labor Movement in the United States*, vol. 5, New York: International Publishers 1980; Philip S. Foner, *On the Eve of America's Entrance into World War I, The History of the Labor Movement in the United States*, vol. 6, New York: International Publishers 1982; Philip S. Foner, *Labor and World War I, The History of the Labor Movement in the United States*, vol. 7, New York: International Publishers 1987; Philip S. Foner, *Postwar Struggles, The History of the Labor Movement in the United States*, vol. 8, New York: International Publishers 1988.

18. Samuel Haber, *Efficiency and Uplift*, Chicago: University of Chicago Press 1964.

19. David Noble, *America by Design: Science, Technology and the Rise of Corporate Capitalism*, New York: Oxford University Press 1977; James Weinstein, *The Corporate Ideal in the Liberal State*, Boston, Mass.: Beacon Press 1968; Robert Weibe, *The Search for Order, 1877–1920*, New York: Hill and Wang 1967; Magali Sarfatti Larson, *The Rise of Professionalism*, Berkeley: University of California Press 1983.

20. Monkonnen, *America Becomes Urban*, p. 14.

21. *United States Strike Commission Report on the Chicago Strike of June–July, 1894*, Senate Executive Document no. 7, 53rd Congress, 3rd Session, Washington DC: Government Printing Office, 1895, p. xxxv.

1 TEXTILE LANDSCAPES: 1790–1850

1. An enormous literature deals with the social problems that accompanied English industrialization; notable examples include Thomas Carlyle, *Chartism* (1839) and *Past and Present* (1843). Friedrich Engels's *The Condition of the Working Class in England*, first published in 1845, draws on many earlier sources (London: Penguin Books, 1987).

2. Zachariah Allen, "The Practical Tourist" (1832), reprinted in Michael Folsom and Steven D. Lubar, eds, *The Philosophy of Manufactures: Early Debates over Industrialization in the United States*, Cambridge, Mass.: MIT Press 1982, p. 342.

3. For a full account of these debates, see Folson and Lubar, eds, *The Philosophy of Manufactures*.

4. Societies for the "encouragement of domestic industry" began to form as early as 1790. Groups existed in Philadelphia, New York City, Baltimore, Wilmington, Boston and Morristown, Newark and Burlington, New Jersey. The journal, *The American Museum*, promoted the "manufactory" point of view. Caroline Ware, *The Early New England Cotton Manufacture*, Boston: Houghton Mifflin 1931, p. 9.

5. John Kleinig, *Paternalism*, Totowa, New Jersey: Rowman & Allanheld 1984, pp. 6–13; for important discussions of the nature of paternalism see: Patrick Joyce, *Work, Society and Politics*, Hemel Hempstead: Harvester Wheatsheaf 1980, pp. 134–57; Eugene D. Genovese, *Roll, Jordan, Roll: The World the Slaves Made*, New York: Vintage 1976, pp. 3–7; 661–6; Richard Sennett, *Authority*, New York: Alfred A. Knopf 1980, pp. 50–83.

6. See Introduction, note 4, p. 213 this volume.

7. US Treasury Department, ed. Jacob E. Cooke, *The Reports of Alexander Hamilton*, New York: Harper & Row 1953. L'Enfant was hired as superintendent for the project for one year at a salary of 1,500 dollars. He was to lay out the waterworks and town and oversee the building program. Broadus Mitchell, *Alexander Hamilton: The National Adventure, 1788–1804*, New York: Macmillan 1962, p. 186.

8. Hamilton's was not the only plan for a manufactory. His associate Tench Coxe proposed a series of similarly ambitious schemes. In 1791, Coxe published a description of a manufactory in the *American Museum*, suggesting a textile manufacturing town laid out in the center of 500 or 1,000 acres. In a letter to Jefferson, Coxe outlined a similar town to be located somewhere in the new District of Columbia. In 1793 he elaborated these plans in his essay "Some Ideas Concerning the Creation of Manufacturing Towns in the United States, Applied, by Way of Example, to a Position on the River Susquehannah." This described an ideal town, very similar to Paterson, in great detail; it would have a comprehensive industrial base with examples of nearly fifty types of manufacturing. Set on an imaginary 2,000 acre site above Philadelphia, the town was to be laid out in a rectangular grid of spacious streets defining oblong blocks. Coxe's ideals undoubtedly influenced Hamilton's concept for Paterson. See Tenche Coxe, *A View of the United States of America*, New York: Augustus M. Kelley 1965, pp. 380–404.

9. My description of Paterson relies primarily on William Nelson and C.A. Shriner, *History of Paterson and Its Environs*, vol. I, New York: Lewis Historical Publishing Company 1920. Hamilton's prospectus for Paterson is reprinted in Folson and Lubar, eds, *The Philosophy of Manufactures*.

10. John Reps, *The Making of Urban America*, Princeton, NJ: Princeton University Press 1965,

p. 263; H. Paul Caemmer, *The Life of Pierre L'Enfant*, Washington DC: National Republic Publishing Company 1950, pp. 50–52.

11. Nelson and Shriner, *History of Paterson*, pp. 48–60.

12. Ibid., p. 49.

13. Ibid., p. 65. Paterson later developed into a major industrial city, the center of silk production in the United States. The city achieved industrial fame a second time in 1913, when the Industrial Workers of the World tried to organize immigrant silk workers.

14. Logan's and Coxe's exchange can be found in Folson and Lubar, eds, *The Philosophy of Manufactures*, pp. 103–21.

15. Frank Landon Humphreys, *Life and Times of David Humphreys*, vol. 2, New York: G.P. Putnam's Sons 1917, pp. 365–6.

16. Timothy Dwight, *Travels in New England and New York*, vol. 3, New Haven, Conn.: n.p. 1822, p. 275.

17. Folson and Lubar, eds, *The Philosophy of Manfactures*, pp. 131–41.

18. Humphreys, *Life and Times*, p. 387.

19. William R. Bagnall, *The Textile Industries of the United States including Sketches of Cotton, Woolen, Silk and Linen Manufacters in the Colonial Period*, vol. I, Cambridge, Mass.: Riverside Press 1893, p. 355.

20. Ibid., p. 358.

21. Richard Sennett, *Authority*, New York: Alfred A. Knopf 1980, pp. 57–9.

22. Dwight, *Travels*, p. 277.

23. Humphreys, *Life and Times*, p. 372.

24. This concluded a long struggle to obtain the Arkwright process. Tench Coxe had unsuccessfully attempted to smuggle models of Arkwright's machinery from England to France and continually advertised in English newspapers for technicians with "special knowledge of textile manufacturing," offering bonuses for their immigration. Ironically, Samuel Slater's arrival in American was prompted by one of Coxe's advertisements. Bagnall, *Textile Industries*, pp. 75–6.

25. Caroline Ware, *The Early New England Cotton Manufacture*, Boston and New York: Houghton Mifflin 1931, is an excellent account of the development of the early textile industry. See also Gary Kulik, Roger Parks, and Theodore Z. Penn, eds, *The New England Mill Village 1790–1860*, Cambridge, Mass.: MIT Press 1982; and Barbara M. Tucker, *Samuel Slater and the Origins of the American Textile Industry*, Ithaca, NY: Cornell University Press 1984.

26. Ware, *Early New England Cotton Manufacture*, p. 14.

27. Kulik et al., *New England Mill Village*, p. 40.

28. The most complete description of a mid-Atlantic textile town can be found in Anthony F.C. Wallace, *Rockdale*, New York: Alfred A. Knopf 1972.

29. Steve Dunwell, *Run of the Mill*, Boston: David R. Godine 1982, pp. 33–9.

30. For descriptions of Rhode Island villages, see John Coolidge,"Low Cost Housing: The New England Tradition," *New England Quarterly* 5 (March 1941), pp. 6–24; Henry Russell Hitchcock, *Rhode Island Architecture*, New York: Da Capo 1968; Richard M. Candee, "The Early New England Textile Village in Art," *Antiques* 98 (December 1970), pp. 910–15; "New Towns of the Early New England Textile Industry," in Camille Wells, ed., *Perspectives in Vernacular Architecture*, Annapolis, Md.: The Vernacular Architecture Forum 1982; "The New Industrial Order: The Factory and the Factory Town," in William Pierson, *American Buildings and Their Architects: Technology and the Picturesque, The Corporate and Early Gothic Styles*, Garden City, New York: Anchor Books 1980.

31. Kulik et al., *New England Mill Village*, p. 14

32. George S. White, *The Memoirs of Samuel Slater*, Philadelphia 1836, p. 120.

33. Ibid.

34. George S. White, "The Moral Influence of Manufacturing Establishments," reprinted in Kulik et al., *New England Mill Village*, pp. 345–70.

35. Tucker, *Samuel Slater*, pp. 164–9. Mill owners very early recognized the benefits that evangelical religions provided in support of industrial discipline and consistently encouraged the construction of churches and church-going in mill villages.

36. Kulik et al., *New England Mill Village*, p. 24.

37. Gary Kulik, "Pawtucket Village and the Strike of 1824: The Origins of Class Conflict in Rhode

Island," *Radical History Review* 17 (Spring 1978), pp. 5–37. For an opposing view, see Tucker, *Samuel Slater*, pp. 214–60.

38. Ware, *Early New England Textile Industry*, p. 63.

39. Dunwell, *Run of the Mill*, p. 48.

40. John Coolidge, *Mill and Mansion: A Study of Architecture and Society in Lowell, Massachusetts*, New York: Columbia University Press 1942, p. 25.

41. See Thomas Bender's discussion of Lowell in *Towards an Urban Vision*, Louisville: University of Kentucky Press 1975, pp. 71–128.

42. Although John Coolidge notes the mill yard's similarity to the quadrangles of Harvard University, this spacious order did not last long. By 1830, both mill yards and streets were increasingly filled in with densely packed brick structures. Coolidge, *Mill and Mansion*, p. 49.

43. Thomas Dublin, *Women at Work: The Transformation of Work and Community in Lowell, Massachusetts, 1826–1860*, New York: Columbia University Press 1979, pp. 78–9.

44. Henry Miles, a Unitarian minister in Lowell and an apologist for the mills. Quoted in Dublin, *Women at Work*, pp. 77–8.

45. Bender, *Urban Vision*, p. 110.

46. Hannah Josephson, *The Golden Threads*, New York: Russell and Russell 1949, p. 73. Josephson, Dublin, *Women at Work*, and Coolidge, *Mill and Mansion* all contain good descriptions of Lowell's physical organization and daily life, although Richard Candee, "Early New England Mill Towns of the Piscataqua River Valley," in John Garner, ed., *The Company Town: Architecture and Society in the Early Industrial Age*, New York: Oxford University Press 1992, corrects several of Coolidge's assumptions.

47. Josephson, *Golden Threads*, pp. 81, 92–3.

48. Dublin, *Women at Work*, pp. 108–12.

49. Josephson, *Golden Threads*, p. 183.

50. Ibid., p. 184.

51. Dublin, *Women at Work*, pp. 123–30; Josephson, *Golden Threads*, pp. 185–203.

52. "Speed-up" refers to methods of increasing the workload of each worker by increasing the pace of work and assigning extra duties.

53. Dublin, *Women at Work*, pp. 108–31.

54. Coolidge, *Mill and Mansion*, p. 48.

55. Bender, *Urban Vision*, p. 108.

56. Folson and Lubar, eds, *The Philosophy of Manufactures*, p. xxxii.

57. Wallace, *Rockdale*, pp. 396–7. Some of the most interesting critiques of industrialization were made by followers of Fourier and Owen, associationists, "freethinkers," and other Enlightenment "radicals." Rather than simply rejecting industrialization, they opposed the domination of its technology by the capitalist class. Both Wallace, *Rockdale*, pp. 243–94, and Norman Ware, *The Industrial Worker*, Boston: Houghton Mifflin 1924, pp. 163–97, outline these objections to industrial capitalism. Although fascinating, such alternatives remained marginal.

58. This formulation was credited to Amos Blanchard, a resident of Lowell, quoted in Bender, *Urban Vision*, p. 111. See Stephan Thernstrom, in *Poverty and Progress*, Cambridge, Mass.: Harvard University Press 1964; and Herbert Gutman, "The Reality of the Rags-to-Riches 'Myth'," in *Work, Culture and Society in Industrializing America*, New York: Vintage Books 1966, pp. 211–33 for studies of actual social mobility during this period.

59. Reinhard Bendix, *Work and Authority in Industry*, Berkeley: University of California Press 1974, pp. 255–7. See also Richard Hofstadter, *Social Darwinism in American Thought*, Philadelphia: University of Pennsylvania Press 1945.

2 THE COMPANY TOWN IN AN ERA OF INDUSTRIAL EXPANSION

1. Victor Clark, *History of Manufactures in the United States*, vol. 3, Washington DC: Carnegie Institution 1929, pp. 154–91.

2. Ibid., p. 182.

3. James McFarlane, *The Coal Regions of America*, New York: D. Appleton 1873, pp. 176–8.

4. Clark, *History of Manufactures*, pp. 21–219; William B. Gates, *Michigan Copper and Boston Dollars*, New York: Russell and Russell 1951, pp. 102–5.

5. Herbert Gutman, "Two Lockouts in

Pennsylvania, 1873–1874," in *Work Culture and Society in Industrializing America*, New York: Vintage Books 1977, pp. 321–42.

6. Ibid., p. 328.

7. Stuart Brandes, *American Welfare Capitalism*, Chicago: University of Chicago Press 1976, p. 45.

8. Katharine A. Harvey, *The Best Dressed Miners*, Ithaca, NY: Cornell University Press 1989, pp. 104–5.

9. Brandes, *Welfare Capitalism*, p. 45.

10. Angus Murdoch, *Boom Copper*, New York: Macmillan 1943, p. 159.

11. Kim E. Wallace, ed., *The Character of a Steel Mill City*, Washington DC: Historic American Buildings Survey 1989, pp. 39–100.

12. Murdoch, *Boom Copper*, pp. 156–7.

13. Gates, *Michigan Copper*, p. 113.

14. Gutman, "Two Lockouts," pp. 334–5.

15. Murdoch, *Boom Copper*, p. 153.

16. Gates, *Michigan Copper*, p. 112.

17. Daniel Nelson, *Managers and Workers*, Madison: University of Wisconsin Press 1975, p. 92.

18. Wallace, ed., *Steel Mill Town*, p. 21.

19. Murdoch, *Boom Copper*, pp. 145–6.

20. Nelson, *Managers and Workers*, p. 103.

21. Richard Sennett, *Authority*, New York: Alfred A. Knopf 1980, p. 77.

22. Brandes, *Welfare Capitalism*, pp. 83–91; Nelson, *Managers and Workers*, pp. 105–6. Profit-sharing, imported from Europe, was one of the earliest welfare programs. Proctor & Gamble, the Peacedale Maufacturing Company, and the N.O. Nelson Company were pioneers in the 1880s. Later, Nicholas P. Gilman's books, *Industrial Partnership of Profit Sharing: A Word to the Employer*, Boston: Press of George H. Ellis 1890, and *A Dividend to Labor: A Study of Employer's Welfare Institutions*, Boston: Houghton Mifflin 1899 popularized the movement.

23. Nelson, *Managers and Workers*, p. 95.

24. Descriptions of these towns have been taken from Budgett Meakin, *Model Factories and Villages*, London: T. Fisher Unwin 1905, pp. 383–416; E.R.L. Gould, "The Housing of the Working People," in *Eighth Special Report of the Commissioner of Labor*, US Bureau of Labor, Washington DC: Government Printing Office 1895; Thomas R. Navin, *The Whitin Machine Works Since 1831*, Cambridge, Mass.: Harvard University Press 1950. Secondary sources include Nelson, *Managers and Workers*, pp. 90–95; and Garner, *The Model Company Town*.

25. Gates, *Michigan Copper*, p. 110.

26. H.L. Nelson, "The Cheney Village at South Manchester, Connecticut," *Harpers Weekly* 34 (1 February 1890) pp. 87–8; Meakin, *Model Factories*, pp. 397–8.

27. Nelson, *Managers and Workers*, p. 104.

28. G.W.W. Hangar, "Housing of the Working People by Employers," *Bulletin of the Bureau of Labor* 21, Washington DC: Government Printing Office 1904, p. 1209.

29. Gould, "Housing" pp. 327–8.

30. Ibid., p. 328.

31. Meakin, *Model Factories*, p. 387.

32. Hangar, "Housing by Employers," pp. 1222–3; Gilman, *Dividend*, pp. 334–5; Nelson, *Managers and Workers*, pp. 102–3; Henry Roland, "Six Examples of Successful Shop Management," *Engineering Magazine* 12 (October 1896) p. 81.

33. Garner, *Model Company Town*, pp. 77–82.

34. These civic ensembles were less well known than those in North Easton, Massachusetts, and Naugatuck, Connecticut, designed by H.H. Richardson and McKim, Mead and White. Although not located in company towns, these philanthropic endeavors were sponsored by major employers in each town, the Ames family of the Ames Tool and Shovel Company, and John Howard Whittemore of Tuttle and Whittemore, also producers of iron implements. Interestingly, McKim, Mead and White also designed houses in South Manchester for members of the Cheney family. Leland Roth suggests that Whittmore may have been influenced by the nearby examples of Willimatic, South Manchester and Peace Dale. See Leland Roth, "Three Company Towns by McKim, Mead and White," *Journal of the Society of Architectural Historians* 38 (December 1979), pp. 317–46; and Robert F. Brown, *The Architecture of Henry Hobson Richardson in North Easton, Massachusetts*, North Easton, Mass.: The Oakes Ames Memorial Hall

Association and the Easton Historical Society 1969.

35. Meakin, *Model Factories*, p. 397.

36. Nelson, *Managers and Workers*, p. 103.

37. Hangar, *Housing by Employers*, p. 1209.

38. Stanley Buder, *Pullman: An Experiment in Industrial Order and Community Planning*, New York: Oxford University Press 1967, p. 61.

39. Ibid., p. 43. Advocates of philanthropic housing claimed that "model" housing projects offering a clean and healthy environment could provide high-quality housing for workers and still produce a reasonable rate of return. See Roy Lubove, *The Progressives and the Slums: Tenement House Reform in New York City, 1890–1917*, Pittsburgh: University of Pittsburgh Press 1963, pp. 10–26.

40. Thomas J. Schlereth, "Solon Spencer Beman, Pullman, and the European Influence on and Interest in his Chicago Architecture," in *Chicago Architecture 1872–1922*, ed. John Zukowsky, Munich: Prestel Verlag 1987, pp.175–7.

41. Buder, *Pullman*, p. 43.

42. Henry Adams, *The Education of Henry Adams* [1907], Boston: Houghton Mifflin 1973.

43. Buder, *Pullman*, pp. 42–3.

44. Descriptions of Pullman's architecture can be found in Schlereth, "Beman, Pullman," and Robert M. Lillibridge, "Pullman: Town Development in an Age of Eclecticism," *Journal of the Society of Architectural Historians* 12 (September 1954), pp. 17–22.

45. Buder, *Pullman*, p. 96.

46. *Report of Commissioners of the State Bureaus of Labor Statistics of the Industrial, Social and Economic Conditions of Pullman, Illinois* (1884), p. 22.

47. Richard T. Ely, "Pullman: A Social Study," *Harper's Monthly* 70 (1885), pp. 452–66.

48. *United States Strike Commission's Report on the Chicago Strike of June–July, 1894*, Senate Executive Document no. 7, 53rd Congress, 3rd Session, Washington DC: Government Printing Office 1895, p. xvii. (Subsequently cited as *Strike Report*.)

49. Buder, *Pullman*, pp. 118–23.

50. Thomas R. Brooks, *Toil and Trouble*, New York: Delacorte Press 1964, p. 97.

51. James Leiby, *Carroll Wright and Labor Reform*, Cambridge, Mass.: Harvard University Press 1960, p. 160.

52. *Strike Report*, p. xviii.

53. Ibid., pp. xlvii–iii; New York *Sun*, 9 December 1883, quoted in Buder, *Pullman*, p. 42.

54. *Strike Report*, p. xxxv.

55. Jane Addams, "A Modern Lear," in Graham Taylor, ed., *Satellite Cities*, New York: D. Appleton 1915, pp. 68–90.

56. Almont Lindsey, *The Pullman Strike*, Chicago: University of Chicago Press 1942, pp. 342–3.

57. Buder, *Pullman*, pp. 131–2.

58. Addams, "Modern Lear," p. 73.

59. This was in 1883. Later, Procter & Gamble became an important proponent of "industrial betterment" programs. In this instance, Procter hired S.S. Beman to design a model factory with extensively landscaped grounds as part of their factory district, "Ivorydale." Procter & Gamble initiated a wide range of betterment activities, but never built houses. Buder, *Pullman*, pp. 132–3.

60. An interesting exception was Leclaire, Illinois, founded in 1890. Like Pullman, which partly inspired it, Leclaire was built in response to labor unrest. In 1886, N.O. Nelson introduced profit-sharing after heavy losses from railroad strikes. In 1890, he built a new plant and company town, Leclaire, near Edwardsville, Illinois. Leclaire was supplied with all the usual features: schools, clubs, recreation, a library, and a relief fund. Significantly, however, Nelson encouraged private home ownership. Far more sensitive than Pullman to his much smaller workforce, Nelson avoided coercion and operated his town successfully until 1934. Leclaire's picturesque planning and varied architecture were also notable for the period. See John S. Garner, "Leclaire, Illinois: A Model Company Town," *Journal of the Society of Architectural Historians* 30 (October 1971), pp. 219–27.

61. Eugene Buffington, "Making Cities for Workmen," *Harper's Weekly* 53 (8 May 1909), pp. 15–17. This article also describes Vandergrift and Ambridge after their acquisition by US Steel.

62. Taylor, *Satellite Cities*, pp. 63–80, provides a detailed critique of Gary.

63. Raymond A. Mohl and Neil Betten, "The Failure of Industrial City Planning: Gary Indiana, 1906–10," *American Institute of Planners Journal* (July 1972), pp. 206–15.

64. See Taylor, *Satellite Cities*, pp. 29–67; Charles H. Eaton, "Pullman and Paternalism," *American Journal of Politics* 5 (August 1894), p.575; Thomas B. Grant, "Pullman and its Lessons," *American Journal of Politics* 5 (August 1894), pp. 190–204; Meakin, *Model Factories*, pp. 385–89.

65. *Strike Report*, pp. 87–91.

66. Both Buder's otherwise well-documented study of Pullman and Richard Fogelsong's Marxist interpretation of American city planning suggest that this was the case. Richard Fogelsong, *Planning the Capitalist City*, Princeton, NJ: Princeton University Press 1986.

67. Meakin, *Model Factories*, pp. 382–414.

68. *Supplementary Report of the Urbanism Committee to the National Resources Commitee. Vol. II: Urban Planning and Land Policies*, Washington DC: Government Printing Office 1939, pp. 2–4.

3 WELFARE CAPITALISM, HOUSING REFORM, AND THE COMPANY TOWN

1. As the "new" urban middle class – clerical workers, salespeople, government employees, technicians, and professionals – replaced the "old" middle class – primarily independent businessmen – it grew far more rapidly than the population as a whole, from 756,000 in 1870 to 5,609,000 in 1910. Samuel Hays, *The Response to Industrialism*, Chicago: University of Chicago Press 1972, p. 73.

2. Ibid., p. 86.

3. Ibid.

4. Samuel Haber, *Efficiency and Uplift*, Chicago: University of Chicago Press 1964, outlines the broad intellectual and institutional connections between Taylorism and the Progressive Movement.

5. Accounts of the industrial betterment movement include: Stuart Brandes, *American Welfare Capitalism*, Chicago: University of Chicago Press 1976; Daniel Nelson, *Managers and Workers*, Madison: University of Wisconsin Press 1975; Gerald Zahavi, *Workers, Managers and Welfare Capitalism: The Shoeworkers and Tanners of Endicott Johnson*, Chicago: University of Illinois Press 1988. Sources on housing reform include James Ford, *Slums and Housing*, vols I and II, Cambridge, Mass.: Harvard University Press 1936; Roy Lubove, *The Progressives and the Slums*, Pittsburgh: University of Pittsburgh Press 1962; and Anthony Jackson, *A Place Called Home: A History of Low Cost Housing in Manhattan*, Cambridge, Mass.: MIT Press 1976.

6. Lubove, *The Progressives*, p. 247.

7. "Welfare Work for Employees in Industrial Establishments in the United States," US Bureau of Labor Statistics *Bulletin* 250 (1919), p. 8.

8. The Young Men's Christian Association (YMCA) was another important precursor of welfare work. Beginning with organizing religious programs for railroad workers in the 1870s, the YMCA introduced services such as infirmaries, lunch rooms, and recreational programs. They later branched out into other industries, in 1902, establishing an Industrial Department which provided welfare activities in cities, lumber camps, and mining and mill towns. Although the YMCA often considered itself more independent than company welfare programs, it was still tightly tied to its corporate sponsors. Sanford Jacoby, *Employing Bureaucracy*, New York: Columbia University Press 1988, pp. 57–9.

9. Marguerite Green, *The National Civic Federation and the American Labor Movement 1900–1925*, Washington DC: The Catholic University of America Press 1956. For a more detailed discussion of the meaning of the NCF in the Progressive era, see James Weinstein, *The Corporate Ideal in the Liberal State*, Boston: Beacon Press 1968.

10. Brandes, *Welfare Capitalism*, pp. 21–3.

11. Nelson, *Managers and Workers*, p. 111.

12. Ibid., p. 112.

13. Brandes, *Welfare Capitalism*, p. 23.

14. Ibid., pp. 111–17.

15. William Tolman, *Social Engineering*, New York: Macmillan 1909; Gertrude Beeks, *National Civic Federation Conference on Welfare Work*, New York:

National Civic Federation 1904; Nicholas Gilman, *A Dividend to Labor*, Boston: Houghton Mifflin 1899; Edwin Shuey, *Factory People and their Employers*, New York: Lentilon 1900; Budgett Meakin, *Model Factories and Villages*, London: T. Fisher Unwin, 1905.

16. Elizabeth L. Otey, "Employers' Welfare Work," Bureau of Labor Statistics, Bulletin 123 (1913); "Welfare Work for Employees in Industrial Establishments in the United States," Bulletin 250 (1919).

17. Nelson, *Managers and Workers*, pp. 117–18. N.O. Nelson's profit-sharing plan is an interesting example of the selective use of welfare policies. Widely considered to be a liberal and humane employer, Nelson altered the rules of his profit-sharing plan so that dividends were given only to employees who saved 10 percent of their wages and invested this in the company's stock. Nelson stated that his purpose for doing this was "to offer a substantial inducement for men . . . to save something for the future and also to make the sharing in the business profits dependent on each one doing something toward it in a direct and personal way." G.W. Hangar, "Housing of the Working People by Employers," Bureau of Labor Special Report, p. 1217.

18. Brandes, *Welfare Capitalism*, p. 140; Nelson, *Managers and Workers*, p. 118.

19. Jacoby, *Employing Bureaucracy*, p. 50; Nelson, *Managers and Workers*, pp. 117–19; Zahavi, *Workers, Managers*, pp. 50–51; Samuel Crowther, *John H. Patterson, Pioneer in Industrial Welfare*, Garden City, NY: Doubleday Page 1934, p. 48.

20. Meakin, *Model Factories*, pp. 400–407.

21. Ibid., pp. 389–96; Ida M. Tarbell, *New Ideals in Business*, New York: Macmillan 1916, p. 154.

22. Not all of these were strictly steel towns. Granite City, for example, was a mixed-industry town. The town was initially developed by the Niedringhaus Brothers, manufacturers of enameled kitchenware. After the Pullman strike, the Niedringhauses sold property to their workers and encouraged other companies to locate in Granite City. Granite City Steel became a major employer.

Graham Taylor, *Satellite Cities*, New York: Appleton–Century–Crofts, 1915, p. 140. Most companies were not concerned with profits. At Aliquippa, Jones and Laughlin, for example, limited their return to 5 percent. David Brody, *Steel Workers in America: The Non-Union Years*, Cambridge, Mass.: Harvard University Press 1960, p. 88.

23. Jacoby, *Bureaucracy*, p. 53.

24. Taylor, *Satellite Cities*, p. 266; Brody, *Steelworkers*, p. 102.

25. Meakin, *Model Factories*, p. 394.

26. Nelson, *Managers and Workers*, pp. 48–54.

27. Haber, *Efficiency and Uplift*, p. 24; For a more sustained argument about the deskilling effects of Taylorism, see Harry Braverman, *Labor and Monopoly Capital*, New York: Monthly Review Press 1974.

28. Haber, *Efficiency and Uplift*, p. 64.

29. Daniel Nelson and Stuart Campbell, "Welfare work vs. Taylorism in American Industry: H.L. Gantt and the Bancrofts," *Business History Review* 46 (Spring 1972). Companies that combined welfare work with Taylorism include Amoskeag Mills, Cheney Brothers Silk, Joseph and Feiss, and the Bancroft Company. This list was compiled from Daniel Nelson's lists of major welfare and scientific management firms, *Managers and Workers*, pp. 7, 116.

30. Brandes, *Welfare Capitalism*, p. 30.

31. National Industrial Conference Board, *Industrial Relations*, New York 1931, p. 104.

32. Leifur Magnussen, *Housing by Employers in the United States*, Bulletin of the US Bureau of Labor Statistics, Washington DC: Government Printing Office, October 1920, p. 20.

33. David Brody, "The Rise and Decline of Welfare Capitalism," in John Braeman, Robert Bremner, and David Brody, eds, *Change and Continuity in Twentieth Century America: The 1920s*, Columbus: Ohio State University Press 1968, p. 153.

34. Ibid., p.154.

35. Brandes, *Welfare Capitalism*, p. 31.

36. Brody, "Rise and Decline," pp. 157–8.

37. Brandes, *Welfare Capitalism*, p. 32. Later, the AFL consistently attacked welfare capitalism in the

pages of its magazine, *American Federationist*. See *American Federationist* 30 (September 1923), pp. 760–61.

38. Brody, *Steelworkers*, p. 88.

39. Nelson, *Managers and Workers*, p.120; Brandes, *Welfare Capitalism*, pp.138–9.

40. Zahavi, *Workers, Managers*, pp. 102–5; Zahavi summarizes the debates about the success or failures of welfare capitalism, pp.102–21. See also Jeremy Brecher et al., "Uncovering the Hidden History of the American Workplace," *Review of Radical Political Economics* 10 (Winter 1978) p. 3; Irving Bernstein, *The Lean Years: A History of the American Worker, 1920–1933*, Boston: Houghton Mifflin 1960, pp. 157–89.

41. Brandes, *Welfare Capitalism*, p. 139.

42. Zahavi, *Workers, Managers*, pp. 100–101. The original version, including the first two verses, was printed in the *Masses*, then reprinted in labor magazines throughout the 1920s:

Sing a song of "Welfare,"
A pocket full of tricks
To sooth the weary worker
When he groans and kicks.
If he asks for shorter hours
Or for better pay,
Little stunts of welfare
Turn his thoughts away

Sing a song of "Welfare,"
Sound the horn and drum
Anything to keep the mind
Fixed on Kingdom Come.
"Welfare" loots your pocket
While you dream and sing;
"Welfare" to your pay check
Doesn't do a thing.

43. Tarbell, *New Ideals*, pp. 3–5; Lincoln Steffens, *The Autobiography of Lincoln Steffens*, New York: Harcourt, Brace 1931, pp. 489–94.

44. Haber, *Efficiency and Uplift*, p. 2.

45. Beeks, *NCF Welfare Conference*, pp. vi–vii.

46. Richard Ely, "Industrial Betterment," *Harper's Monthly* 105 (September 1902), pp. 548–53.

47. Jackson, *Place Called Home*, p. 3.

48. Gould, *Housing*, p. 18.

49. Lubove, *Progressives*, pp. 104–10.

50. Jackson, *Place Called Home*, pp. 116–18.

51. Lubove, *Progressives*, p. 228.

4 DESIGNERS AND THE "NEW" COMPANY TOWN

1. See Roy Lubove, "I.N. Phelps-Stokes: Tenement Architect, Economist, Planner," *Journal of the Society of Architectural Historians* 23 (May 1964), pp. 75–87; Marges Bacon, *Ernest Flagg*, Cambridge, Mass.: MIT Press 1986, pp. 234–66. Designing low-income urban housing was a particularly interesting architectural problem during the period 1890–1910: William Mead of McKim, Mead, and White entered tenement design contests (Anthony Jackson, *A Place Called Home*, Cambridge, Mass.: MIT Press 1976, p. 117); in 1895, Frank Lloyd Wright designed Francisco Terrace, a philanthropic project of low-cost units (Grant Manson, *Frank Lloyd Wright to 1910*, New York: Van Nostrand Reinhold 1958, pp. 81–3); Phelps-Stokes, Flagg, and Atterbury, all wealthy and well-connected, were more consistently active. All three served on New York Tenement House Commissions. Flagg designed the Alfred Corning Clark Buildings (1896) for City and Suburban Homes, several Fireproof Tenement Association Model Tenements (1899, 1909, 1911), and Mills Houses No. 1 and 2, hotels for workers (both 1896). Atterbury designed the Phipps Houses (1906) and the Rogers Model Dwellings (1913). See Grosvenor Atterbury, "The Phipps Model Tenement Houses," *Charities* 17 (October 1906), pp. 62–5.

2. Mel Scott, *American City Planning since 1890*, Berkeley: University of California Press 1969, pp. 95–6; Gwendolyn Wright, *Moralism and the Model House*, Chicago: University of Chicago Press 1980, p. 226.

3. For general discussions of American professionalism, see Magali Sarfatti Larson, *The Rise of Professionalism*, Berkeley, University of California

Press 1977; and Burton Bledstein, *The Culture of Professionalism*, New York: Norton 1976.

4. More specific accounts of architectural professionalization include: Magali Sarfatti Larson, "Emblem and Exception: the Historical Definition of the Architect's Professional Role," in Judith Blau, Mark LaGory, and John Pipkin, eds, *Professionals and Urban Form*, Albany: State University of New York Press 1983; Bernard Boyle, "Architectural Practice in America: 1865–1965: Ideal and Reality," in Spiro Kostof, ed., *The Architect*, New York: Oxford University Press 1977.

5. Sibel Bozdogan, "The Rise of the Architectural Profession in Chicago 1871–1909," Paper delivered at the Society of Architectural Historians' Annual Meeting, Chicago, April 1989, p. 4.

6. Herbert Croly, "American Artists and their Public," *Architectural Record* 10 (January 1901), p. 257; "Rich Men and their Houses," *Architectural Record* 11 (May 1902), pp. 27–32.

7. Herbert Croly, *The Promise of American Life*, New York: Macmillan 1909. Croly expanded on his study of the architect, stating: "the case of the statesman, the man of letters, the philanthropist, or the reformer does not differ essentially from that of the architect" (p. 446).

8. Norman T. Newton, *Design on the Land: The Development of Landscape Architecture*, Cambridge, Mass.: Harvard University Press 1971, pp. 385–90; Roy Lubove, "Social History and the History of Landscape Architecture," *Journal of Social History* 23 (Fall 1983), p. 273; Geoffrey Blodgett, "Landscape Design as Conservative Reform," in Bruce Kelly, Gail Travis Guillet, and Mary Ellen Hern, eds, *Art of the Olmsted Landscape*, New York: New York City Landmarks Preservation Commission 1981, pp. 111–21; J.B. Jackson, "The American Public Space," *The Public Interest* (Winter 1984), pp. 52–65.

9. Thomas Bender, *Towards an Urban Vision*, Louisville: University of Kentucky Press 1975, p. 180.

10. Blodgett, "Landscape Design," p. 114.

11. Olmsted, Vaux, and Co.,"Preliminary Report upon the Proposed Suburban Village of Riverside, near Chicago" (New York 1868), reprinted in S.B. Sutton, ed., *Civilizing American Cities: A Selection of Frederick Law Olmsted's Writings on City Landscapes*, Cambridge, Mass.: MIT Press 1971, p. 295. See David Schuyler, *The New Urban Landscape*, Baltimore: The Johns Hopkins University Press 1986, pp. 162–6 for a detailed discussion of Riverside.

12. Olmsted explicitly rejected the model offered by both the English picturesque suburb and the earlier American suburb of Llewlyn Park. Olmsted objected to the English custom of walled villas, and prescribed that each house at Riverside should be set back at least thirty feet from the road and that each owner should maintain one or two living trees between their house and the road. He objected equally to the Llewlyn Park model of setting houses in an open park without fences. At Riverside, he felt that fences were necessary to establish the domestic containment necessary for the privacy of a family home. Olmsted, Vaux and Co., "Preliminary Report," pp. 288–90; Bender, *Urban Vision*, p. 162; Lubove, "Social History," p. 273; Walter Creese, *The Crowning of the American Landscape*, Princeton, NJ: Princeton University Press 1985, pp. 81–9.

13. Scott, *American City Planning*, p. 118.

14. Ibid., pp. 122–3; "Efficiency in City Planning," *American City* 7 (February 1913), p. 139.

15. Bender, *Urban Vision*, p. 179; Blodgett, "Landscape Design," p. 109.

16. Ibid., p. 124.

17. Scott, *City Planning*, p. 84.

18. The Russell Sage Foundation was established by Mrs Russell Sage in 1907 with the aim of "improving social and living conditions in the United States." John M. Glenn, *Russell Sage Foundation, 1907–1946*, New York: Russell Sage Foundation 1947, p. 11.

19. Paul U. Kellog, ed., *Pittsburgh Survey*, 6 vols, New York: Russell Sage Foundation 1909–14. The Survey's staff came from settlement houses, charity societies, and universities. The Survey was first published in three special monthly issues of *Charities and the Commons*, beginning 2 January 1909 and, in the next year, as six separate volumes.

20. Philip S. Foner, *On the Eve of America's Entrance*

into World War 1, The History of the Labor Movement in the United States, vol. 6, New York: International Publishers 1982, p. 28.

21. Margaret Byington, *Homestead: The Households of a Mill Town*, New York: Russell Sage Foundation 1910, p. 48.

22. "The Pittsburgh Survey," *Survey* 19 (7 March 1908), p. 1666.

23. See Raymond Williams, *The Country and the City*, London: Paladin 1973, for a thorough discussion of this duality.

24. See Gillian Darley, *Villages of Vision*, London: Granada Publishing 1978, pp. 137–47; Walter Creese, *The Search for Environment*, New Haven, Conn.: Yale University Press 1966, pp. 108–43; Peter Batchelor, "The Origins of the Garden City Concept of Urban Form," *Journal of the Society of Architectural Historians* 18 (Fall 1969), pp. 184–200.

25. Darley, *Villages of Vision*, p. 139; Alexander Harvey, *Model Village: Bournville*, London: Batsford 1906.

26. Polly Toynbee, *A Working Life*, London: Macmillan 1971; see also W.L. George, *Labour and Housing at Port Sunlight*, London: Alston Rivers 1909.

27. Creese, *Search for Environment*, p. 130.

28. See Barry Parker, "Site Planning at New Earswick," *Town Planning Review* (February 1937), pp. 2–9.

29. Robert Fishman, *Urban Utopias in the Twentieth Century*, Cambridge, Mass.: MIT Press 1982, p. 69.

30. Ibid., p. 68.

31. Creese, *Search for Environment*, pp. 207–18.

32. Barry Parker and Raymond Unwin, *The Art of Building a Home*, London: Longmans, Green and Co. 1901; C.B. Purdom, *The Garden City: A Study in the Development of a Modern Town*, London: Dent 1913, pp. 52–98.

33. For a discussion of the cooperative quadrangle, see Dolores Hayden, *The Grand Domestic Revolution*, Cambridge, Mass.: MIT Press 1981, pp. 230–37.

34. Roy Lubove, *The Progressives and the Slums*, Pittsburgh: University of Pittsburgh Press 1962, p. 224.

35. Glenn, *The Russell Sage Foundation*, p. 4.

36. Ibid., p. 8.

37. Richard Plunz, *A History of Housing in New York City*, New York; Columbia University Press 1990, pp. 117–18.

38. Arthur Comey, "Billerica Garden Suburb," *Landscape Architecture* 4 (July 1915), pp. 145–9; Massachusetts Homestead Commission, *Fourth Annual Report*, Boston: Wright and Potter 1917, pp. 56–61.

39. Scott, *City Planning*, p. 310.

5 THE SEARCH FOR A STYLE

1. See Leland Roth, "Three Company Towns by McKim, Mead and White," *Journal of the Society of Architectural Historians* 38 (December 1979), pp. 317–47. Also G.W.W. Hangar, "Housing of the Working People by Employers," *Bulletin of the Bureau of Labor* 54, Washington DC: Government Printing Office 1904, pp. 1218–20; William A. Tolman, "Workmen's Cities in the United States," *Bericht, 9th International Housing Congress*, Vienna: 1910, pp. 1084–5; Budgett Meakin, *Model Factories and Villages*, London: T. Fisher Unwin 1905, p. 411.

2. John S. Garner, *The Model Company Town*, Amherst: University of Massachusetts Press 1984, pp. 158–61.

3. Letter from Apollo Steel to Frederick Law Olmsted, Jr, File 204. Olmsted Collection, Library of Congress, Washington DC. See also Arthur C. Comey and Max Wehrly, *Planned Communities, Supplementary Report of the Urbanism Committee*, Part I, vol. II, Washington DC: Government Printing Office 1938, pp. 47–50. John Reps considers Vandergrift to be one of the few poorly designed projects to come out of the Olmsted office, *The Making of Urban America: A History of City Planning in America*, Princeton, NJ: Princeton University Press 1965, p. 242.

4. William B. Gates, *Michigan Copper and Boston Dollars*, New York: Russell and Russell 1951, pp.128–34; Philip S. Foner, *The AFL in the Progressive Era: 1910–1915, The History of the Labor Movement in the United States*, vol. 5, New York: International Publishers 1980, pp. 197, 215.

5. Foner, *The AFL in the Progressive Era*, pp. 196–213.

6. *The Survey* (30 December 1911), pp. 1430–31.

7. Burton Bledstein, *The Culture of Professionalism*, New York: Norton 1976, p. 100.

8. Philip S. Foner, *On the Eve of America's Entrance into World War I, The History of the Labor Movement in the United States*, vol. 6, New York: International Publishers 1982, p. 28; Philip S. Foner, *The Industrial Workers of the World, History of the Labor Movement in the United States*, vol. 4, New York: International Publishers 1965, pp. 282–95; John A. Garraty, "The US Steel Corporation versus Labor: The Early Years," *Labor History* 1 (Winter 1960), pp. 3–38. Like most employers with extensive welfare programs, under Gary, US Steel was strongly opposed to unions. The corporation was successful in avoiding unionization until the great steel strike of 1919, in which the AFL effectively organized workers, leading them on a strike in which more than 365,000 steel workers participated.

9. Graham Taylor, *Satellite Cities*, New York: Appleton–Century–Croft 1915, p. 237.

10. George H. Miller, "Fairfield: A Town with a Purpose," *American City* 9 (September 1913), pp. 213–19; Comey and Wehrly, *Planned Communities*, pp. 27–9.

11. "Fairfield, Alabama," *Homes for Workmen*, New Orleans: The Southern Pine Association 1919, pp. 103–10; Taylor, *Satellite Cities*, pp. 243–4.

12. Eileen Boris, *Art and Labor: Ruskin, Morris and the Craftsman Ideal in America*, Philadelphia: Temple University Press 1986, pp. 78–9.

13. *Housing Labor*, Davenport, Iowa: Gordon-Van Tine Company 1918; *The Aladdin Plan of Industrial Housing*, Bay City, Michigan: The Aladdin Company 1917; Katherine Cole Stevenson and H. Ward Jandl, *Houses by Mail*, Washington DC: Preservation Press 1986, p. 196.

14. Miller, "Fairfield," p. 28.

15. Geoffrey Cowan, *The People vs. Clarence Darrow*, Los Angeles: Times Books 1993, p. 48.

16. For discussions of the strike and the McNamara trial, see Foner, *The AFL in the Progressive Era*, pp. 7–31; Graham Adams Jr, *Age of Industrial Violence*, New York: Columbia University Press 1956, pp. 1–24; Louis Adamic, *Dynamite: The Story of Class Violence in America*, New York: Viking 1931, pp. 187–243. Llewellyn Steel owned 15 percent of the Dominguez Land Company.

17. "Dictation of J.S. Torrance," August 1916, on file at the Torrance Public Library. Union Tool estimated that relocating to Torrance would reduce the cost of production by 18 percent and increase output by 20 percent without hiring a single new employee.

18. Walter Willard, "Moving the Factory Back to the Land," *Sunset* 30 (March 1913), p. 301; Dana Bartlett, "An Industrial Garden City: Torrance," *American City* 10 (October 1913), p. 314.

19. Bartlett, "An Industrial Garden City," p. 313.

20. Los Angeles *Examiner* (5 October 1911), p. 1. The actual fee was 5,000 dollars a year plus expenses. File 5354.1, Olmsted Collection, Manuscript Division, Library of Congress.

21. File 5354, Olmsted Collection.

22. Ibid.

23. Ibid.

24. Ibid.

25. Based on a limited competition with four Los Angeles architects, R.D. Farquhar, Elmer Grey, Sumner Hunt, and Parker Wright. Richard Oliver, *Bertram Grosvenor Goodhue*, Cambridge, Mass.: MIT Press 1983, pp. 109–19. Also see Kevin Starr, *Americans and the California Dream: 1850–1915*, New York: Oxford University Press 1973, pp. 403–7.

26. Bartlett, "An Industrial Garden City," p. 311.

27. Irving Gill, "The Home of the Future: The New Architecture of the West: Small Homes for a Great Country," *The Craftsman* (May 1916), pp. 310–12.

28. Willard, "Moving the Factory," pp. 303–4. Esther McCoy also reports that the construction workers for the houses objected to Gill's plans because of their extreme simplicity. A public meeting was held in which the architect faced a hostile audience criticizing the design of the dwellings. *Five California Architects*, New York: Reinhold Press 1960, p. 87.

29. Rudolph Schindler and Frank Lloyd Wright

also explored the possibilities of concrete architecture in 1919 in a set of fascinating designs for experimental workers' houses. Schindler, in charge of Wright's Chicago office while Wright was away in Japan and California, was primarily responsible for the design of simple cubic houses for what was labeled a "Workingmen's Colony of Concrete Monolith Houses," designed for a former Prairie House client, Thomas P. Hardy, to be built in Racine, Wisconsin. Cast concrete was used throughout on the exterior and interior for floors, walls, and roof. Unlike both Gill's and Morrill's cubic designs, Schindler juxtaposed vertical and horizontal concrete planes leaving openings for two floor-to-ceiling corner windows. See Kathryn Smith, "Chicago–Los Angeles: The Concrete Connection," in *Concrete California*, Los Angeles: Carpenters/Contractors Cooperation Committee of Southern California 1990, pp. 6–7, 10.

30. Milton Dana Morrill, "Inexpensive Homes of Reinforced Concrete," *Western Architect* 16 (1910), pp. 103–6.

31. Winthrop Hamlin, *Low Cost Cottage Construction In America*, Cambridge, Mass.: Harvard Social Museum 1917, pp. 16–23.

32. "An Improvement in Poured Concrete Houses for Workingmen," *Square Deal* 13 (September 1913), p. 108.

33. "Concrete for Industrial Housing – A Review," *Concrete* 12 (January 1918), pp. 30–31.

34. "Industrial Housing for Employees," *Engineering and Cement World* 12 (15 February 1918), pp. 32–3; *Industrial Houses of Concrete and Stucco*, New York and Chicago: Atlas Portland Cement Company 1918.

35. Foner, *The Industrial Workers of the World*, p. 373.

36. Ibid., p. 374.

37. In 1917 Firestone also built a settlement, Firestone Park, designed by landscape architect Alling DeForest. Although its plan is more coherent than that of Goodyear Heights, Firestone Park followed the earlier example closely. As at Goodyear Heights, houses were sold to skilled employees. Harvey S. Firestone, "Firestone Park, Akron, Ohio,"

in *Homes for Workmen*, pp. 199–202.

38. Warren H. Manning, "A Step Towards Solving the Industrial Housing Problem," *American City* 12 (April 1915), pp. 321–5; "Goodyear Heights," in Comey and Wehrly, *Planned Communities*, pp. 51–3.

39. Manning, "Industrial Housing," pp. 322–3.

40. Ibid., p. 324.

41. Ibid., p. 325.

42. Taylor, *Satellite Cities*, pp. 289–300.

43. Ibid. pp. 303–24.

44. Stuart Brandes, *American Welfare Capitalism*, Chicago: University of Chicago Press 1976, p. 142.

6 AMERICANIZING THE GARDEN CITY: GROSVENOR ATTERBURY AND INDIAN HILL

1. *Worcester Sunday Telegram* (10 October 1915), p. 2.

2. William Zeuch, "An Investigation of the Metal Trades Strike of Worcester, 1915," MA thesis, Clark University, 1916, p. 13.

3. Charles W. Cheape, *Family Firm to Multinational: Norton Company, a New England Enterprise*, Cambridge, Mass.: Harvard University Press 1985, pp. 128–9.

4. Ibid., p. 2.

5. Clifford Anderson, *Indian Hill: An Industrial Village*, Worcester, Mass.: The Norton Company n.d., p. 2.

6. Mildred McClary Tymeson, *The Norton Story*, Worcester, Mass.: The Norton Company 1953, pp. 66–7.

7. Ibid., p. 124.

8. Ibid., p. 106.

9. Cheape, *Family Firm*, pp. 141–9.

10. David Noble, *America by Design: Science, Technology and the Rise of Corporate Capitalism*, New York: Oxford University Press 1977, p. 307.

11. Cheape, *Family Firm*, p. 43.

12. Ibid., pp. 126–8.

13. Ibid., p. 131.

14. Ibid.

15. Ibid., p. 135; *Norton Spirit* (May 1915), p. 2.

16. Cheape, *Family Firm*, p. 135.

17. Ibid., p. 4.

18. Examples of the first category include the New York town houses of John Williams Robbins and John S. Fitch, the Yale Medical Library and University Hall, Johns Hopkins University. Atterbury's houses include a series of shingle houses on Long Island: the Rice house in Easthampton, the Claflin house in Southampton, and the Swayne, Soley, and Atterbury houses in Shinnecock Hills. For descriptions of Atterbury's work, see: "Examples of the Work of Grosvenor Atterbury," *American Architect and Building News* 94 (30 May 1908), pp. 1104–7; C. Matlack Price, "The Development of a National Architecture: The Work of Grosvenor Atterbury," *Arts and Decorations* 2 (October 1912), pp. 176–9; "Portrait of Grosvenor Atterbury," *Country Life in America* 47 (June 1912), p. 78.

19. "The Residence of Aldus C. Higgins," *Country Life in America* (March 1926), pp. 47–9.

20. "Rogers Model Dwellings," *American Architect* 104 (29 October 1913), p. 198; Grosvenor Atterbury, "The Phipps Model Tenement Houses," *Charities* 17 (October 1906), pp. 62–5.

21. For contemporary discussions of Forest Hills Gardens, see: Edward Hale Brush, "A Garden City for the Man of Moderate Means," *The Craftsman* (January 1911), pp. 445–51; Grosvenor Atterbury, "Forest Hills Gardens, Long Island," *Brickbuilder* 21 (December 1911), pp. 13–20; Charles C. May, "Forest Hills Gardens from the Town Planning Viewpoint," *Architecture* (August 1916), pp. 161–82; Samuel Howe, "Forest Hills Gardens," *Architectural Record* 67 (January 1930), pp. 13–20.

22. Grosvenor Atterbury, "Model Towns in America," *Scribner's* 7 (March 1912), pp. 20–35.

23. Atterbury's skillful handling of contained urban spaces suggest that he was familiar with the urban design principles of Camillo Sitte, who emphasized the perceptual experience of defined and bounded space. Atterbury probably first encountered Sitte in Raymond Unwin's *Town Planning in Practice*, London: Unwin 1909, the first comprehensive treatment of Sitte's work in English.

24. See Gerd Korman, *Industrialization, Immigrants and Americanizers*, Madison: The State Historical Society of Wisconsin 1967; John Higham, *Strangers in the Land: Patterns of American Nativism: 1860–1925*, New York: Atheneum 1963.

25. Atterbury, "Model Towns," p. 23.

26. Charles C. May, "Indian Hill, an Industrial Village at Worcester, Mass.," *Architectural Record* 41 (January 1917), p. 25.

27. Ibid., p. 28.

28. Walter Creese, *The Search for Environment*, New Haven, Conn.: Yale University Press 1966, pp. 227–8.

29. May, "Indian Hill," p. 28.

30. *Norton Spirit* (May 1915), p. 3.

31. May, "Indian Hill," p. 27 ; Anderson, "Indian Hill," p. 4.

32. *Norton Spirit* (September 1915) p. 3.

33. For a discussion of the colonial revival's symbolic qualities, see Alan Gowans, *The Comfortable House: North American Suburban Architecture 1890–1930*, Cambridge, Mass.: MIT Press 1986, pp. 101–80.

34. May, "Indian Hill," p. 25.

35. *Norton Spirit* (May 1915), p. 2.

36. *Norton Spirit* (September 1916), p. 5.

37. May, "Indian Hill," p. 30.

38. Tymeson, *Norton Story*, p. 46.

39. George B. Ford, "Indian Hill: A Garden Village near Worcester, Mass.," *Journal of the American Insitutute of Architects* 5 (January 1917), p. 29.

40. *Norton Spirit* (May 1915), p. 3; (June 1915), pp. 2–3.

41. *Norton Spirit* (June 1915), p. 1.

42. Anderson, "Indian Hill," p. 9.

43. Ibid.

44. *Norton Spirit* (October 1915), p. 2.

45. Tymeson, *Norton Story*, pp. 10–11, 288.

46. Zeuch, "An Investigation," p. 18.

47. Based on an informal survey comparing the buyers with members of Norton groups listed in the *Norton Spirit*.

48. At Echota, for example, the Niagara Falls Power Company furnished one of Stanford White's cottages with basic furniture. The price of each item was clearly marked to instruct employees in

how to furnish an appropriately modest, but tasteful home inexpensively. A welfare worker lived in the houses, offering advice about all aspects of homemaking and home economics to Echota's residents. Stuart Brandes, *American Welfare Capitalism*, Chicago: University of Chicago Press 1976, p. 113. "Upgrading" working-class taste – or standardizing it to American middle-class norms – was a consistent theme in reform activities. See Anderson, "Indian Hill," p. 9.

49. W.E. Freedland, "New Housing Development at Worcester," *Iron Age* 97 (18 May 1916), p.1188; *Norton Spirit* (June 1917), p. 3.

50. *Norton Spirit* (June 1917), p. 3.

51. Tymeson, *Norton Story*, p. 35.

52. David Brody, *Steelworkers in America: The Non-union Era*, Cambridge, Mass.: Harvard University Press 1960, p. 188.

53. Cheape, *Family Firm*, p. 126.

54. Ibid., p. 129.

55. Ibid., p. 135.

56. Tymeson, *Norton Story*, p. 79.

57. "Conference with Mr. Grosvenor Atterbury: July 3, 1917," Works Managers' Papers, Norton Company Archives, Worcester Historical Museum, Worcester, Mass.

58. Ibid., p. 3.

59. Grosvenor Atterbury, *The Economic Production of Workingmen's Houses*, New York: Russell Sage Foundation 1930, p. 974.

60. Ida Tarbell, *New Ideals in Business*, New York: Macmillan 1916, pp. 160–62.

61. "Conference with Atterbury," pp. 3–4.

62. Tymeson, *Norton Story*, p. 35; *Norton Spirit* (June 1917), p. 3.

63. Cheape, *Family Firm*, p. 131.

64. Tymeson, *Norton Story*, p. 85.

65. Arthur C. Comey and Max Wehrly, *Planned Communities*, Part 1, vol. II of the *Supplementary Report of the Urbanism Committee*, Washington DC: Government Printing Office 1938, p. 55.

66. Grosvenor Atterbury, "Bricks without Brains," *Architecture* 73 (April 1936), p. 195.

67. Grosvenor Atterbury, "Garden Cities," in *Housing Problems in America: Proceedings of the Second National Conference on Housing*, Philadelphia: National Housing Association 1912, pp. 106–13.

68. Grosvenor Atterbury, "How To Get Low Cost Houses," in *Housing Problems in America: Proceedings of the Fifth National Conference on Housing*, Providence, RI: National Housing Association 1916, pp. 91–101.

69. Lawrence Veiller, "A Research Institute for Economic Housing," *Housing* (December 1926), p. 369.

70. Adele Atterbury, telephone interview with author, 6 January 1984.

71. "The Industry Capitalism Forgot," *Fortune* 36 (August 1947), p. 19.

72. John Burchard and Albert Bush-Brown, *The Architecture of America*, Boston: Little, Brown 1966, p. 328.

73. Lewis Mumford, "Mass Production and Housing," in *City Development*, New York: Vintage Books 1971, p. 128.

74. Burchard and Bush-Brown, *The Architecture of America*, p. 330; "The Industry Capitalism Forgot," pp. 61–7.

75. Freeland, "New Housing Development," p. 1190; May, "Indian Hill"; George B. Ford, "Indian Hill: A Garden Village near Worcester, Mass.," *Journal of the American Institute of Architects* 5 (January 1917) p. 29; Tarbell, *New Ideals*, p. 156; Comey and Wehrly, *Planned Communities*, p. 55.

76. For a more complete description of Kohler, see L.L. Smith, "The Industrial Garden City of Kohler, Wisconsin," *American Landscape Architect* 3 (September 1930), pp. 11–19; Arnold R. Alanen and Thomas J. Peltin, "Kohler, Wisconsin: Planning and Paternalism in a Model Industrial Village," *American Institute of Planning Journal* (April 1978), pp. 145–59. Walter Kohler, the town's sponsor, toured European garden cities with his architect, Richard Phillips, before beginning to plan the town. The Kohler Company pursued welfare and housing programs very similar to those of the Norton Company. Kohler, later Governor of Wisconsin, however, far exceeded Norton's Americanization efforts. He built a large "hotel," housing more than three hundred, mostly single,

foreign-born workers, who were bombarded with patriotic exhortation. They ate in a large dining hall decorated with American flags, while a victrola played patriotic marches.

77. For a description of Midland, see "Midland, Pennsylvania," *Architectural Review* 4 (February 1916), pp. 33–9.

78. "The Immigrant Housing Competition," *Architectural Review* (January 1917), pp. 4–24.

79. In spite of his preoccupation with prefabrication, Atterbury developed the Indian Hill housing type in two different directions. In 1917, he designed a group of inexpensive miners' houses for the West End Coal Company of Westmoreland, Pennsylvania. These were compactly planned minimal dwellings, with four rooms, a kitchen and bath, as well as a shower for the returning miner. Although the houses were limited in size and price, Atterbury managed to imbue them with Indian Hill's cozy domesticity, using textured shingle walls and roofs and adding ivy-covered trellised gates. The same year, he elaborated on the Indian Hill type in a small development at Erwin, Tennessee. Although the town planned for the area was never built, he envisioned larger houses that were more picturesque than those at Indian Hill. A southern interpretation of the colonial revival, the houses exhibited an even greater variety of materials, colors, and detailing than those at Indian Hill. At Kingsport, Tennessee, Atterbury designed larger variants of this southern colonial house for White City, one of the industrial town's elite neighborhoods. File no. 3762, Nolen Papers, Regional Planning Archives, Olin Library, Cornell University, Ithaca, New York.

80. For a discussion of Kistler, see Chapter 6; descriptions of the other projects can be found in *Homes for Workmen*, New Orleans: The Southern Pine Association 1919; Winthrop Hamlin, *Low Cost Cottage Construction in America*, Cambridge, Mass.: Harvard Social Museum 1917; "The Workingman and His House," *Architectural Record* (January 1917), pp. 302–25; Marcia Mead, "The Architecture of the Small House," *Architecture* 37 (June 1918), pp. 145–53.

7 REDESIGNING THE MINING TOWN: BERTRAM GOODHUE AND TYRONE, NEW MEXICO

1. Karl B. Lohman, "New Era for Mining Towns," *Coal Age* (13 November 1915), p. 799. Lohman was a landscape architect.

2. Vernon Jensen, *Heritage of Conflict: Labor Relations in the Nonferrous Metals Industry Up to 1930*, Ithaca, NY: Cornell University Press 1950, p. 357.

3. Robert Cleland, *A History of Phelps-Dodge*, New York: Alfred A. Knopf 1952, pp. 355–9.

4. Excellent descriptions of Bisbee and Warren can be found in John Pastier, "The Mining Towns," *Architecture* (March 1984) pp. 106–12 and *Art and Architecture*, "Urban Guidemap No. 3: Bisbee, Arizona."

5. James W. Byrkit, *Forging the Copper Collar*, Tucson: University of Arizona Press 1982, pp. 64–6.

6. Ibid., pp. 71–3.

7. Philip Foner, *On the Eve of America's Entry into World War I, The History of the Labor Movement in the United States*, vol. 6 New York: International Publishers 1982, pp. 13–24; Walter Douglas, "The Arizona Strike," *New Republic* 6 (18 March 1916) pp. 185–6; George Hunt, "The Arizona Strike," *New Republic* 6 (14 April 1916), p. 293.

8. Jensen, *Conflict*, pp. 355–6; Y.S. Leong, "Technology, Employment and Output in Copper Mining," WPA National Research Project, Department of Statistics, Bureau of Mines, Philadelphia: Bureau of Mines 1940.

9. Foner, *On the Eve*, p. 269.

10. Bertram Goodhue (henceforth BGG), letter to Cecil C. Brewer, 18 August 1915; letter to Walter Douglas, 12 August 1915: Goodhue Papers, Avery Library, Columbia University, New York. All citations from letters, unless otherwise noted, are from the Goodhue Papers.

11. Richard Oliver, *Bertram Goodhue*, Cambridge, Mass.: MIT Press 1985, pp. 25–31. Ralph Adams Cram, *My Life in Architecture*, Boston: Little, Brown 1936, pp. 78–9.

12. Cram, *My Life*, p. 78; Sylvester Baxter, *Spanish Colonial Architecture in Mexico*, Boston: J.B. Millet

1901; Oliver, *Goodhue*, pp. 31–42; *A Book of Architectural and Decorative Drawings by Bertram Grosvenor Goodhue*, New York: The Architectural Book Publishing Company 1914.

13. These include West Point, the Taft School, Rice Institute, and the Virginia Military Institute.

14. Cram, *My Life*, p. 79.

15. Kevin Starr, *Americans and the California Dream: 1850–1915*, New York: Oxford University Press 1973, pp. 403–5.

16. Ibid., p. 404.

17. Oliver, *Goodhue*, p. 113.

18. Starr, *California Dream*, p. 404.

19. In 1911, Goodhue, after completing designs for a hotel at Colon, Panama, had sailed back to New Orleans with his friend, Frederick Law Olmsted, Jr and his wife, then on their honeymoon. The Olmsted brothers were strong supporters of Goodhue's efforts to be appointed designer of the Panama–California Exhibition. Oliver, *Goodhue*, pp. 108–9. BGG, letter to Frederick Law Olmsted, Jr, 7 January 1911; BGG, letter to Herbert Croly, 4 April 1916.

20. By 1916, copper producers had made 400 percent greater profits than two years before. "Copper," *Review of Reviews* 54 (October 1916), pp. 429–32.

21. In 1915, in Arizona mines, Americans worked for a minimum of $3.50 a day while Mexicans earned only $1.62. Foner, *On the Eve*, p. 15.

22. Byrkit, *Copper Collar*, p. 21.

23. Foner, *On the Eve*, pp. 13–24.

24. Charles Willis, "The Life of a Mining Community," *Engineering and Mining Journal* 151 (28 October 1918), p. 733.

25. Phelps-Dodge Company Annual Reports, 1915, 1916, 1917.

26. "Tyrone, the Booming Mining Center of the Burro Mountain District, Grant County, N.M.," *El Paso Morning Times* (13 September 1917).

27. Like Atterbury, Goodhue probably was influenced by his direct contact with the work of the Olmsted brothers.

28. Bertram G. Goodhue, *The Architecture and the Gardens of the San Diego Exposition*, San Francisco: Paul Elder 1916, p. 80.

29. BGG, letter to George W. Horsefield, 6 February 1919.

30. Bertram Goodhue, "The Home of the Future: A Study of America in Relation to the Architect," *The Craftsman* 29 (February 1916), p. 543.

31. BGG, letter to Christian Brinton, 17 August 1915.

32. Oliver, *Goodhue*, p. 154.

33. Marcia Mead, "The Architecture of the Small House," *Architecture* 37 (June 1918), p. 145.

34. Leifur Magnussen, "A Modern Copper Mining Town," *Monthly Labor Review* 7 (September 1918), p. 280.

35. Mead, "Small House," pp. 145–8.

36. Magnussen, "Copper Mining Town," pp. 279–80.

37. Charles F. Willis, "Housing at Tyrone, New Mexico," *Chemical and Metallurgical Engineering* 19 (15 October 1918), pp. 629–30.

38. Ibid., p. 629.

39. Clarence Stein later became a notable community planner. See *Towards New Towns in America*, Cambridge, Mass.: MIT Press 1957, and discussion in conclusion.

40. "Tyrone," *El Paso Morning Times*.

41. BGG, letter to John D. Moore, 9 August 1915.

42. "The LeBrun Travelling Scholarship," *Architecture* 34 (December 1916), pp. 256–61. In fact, the winner, Austin Whittlesey, was working in Goodhue's office and Goodhue's influence is clearly visible in his entry. Oliver, *Goodhue*, p. 270.

43. Magnussen, "Copper Mining Town," p. 283. Goodhue did not design the hospital, a mission-style structure which *Architectural Review* described as "clearly of engineering origin." "New Mining Community of Tyrone, New Mexico," *Architectural Review* 6 (March 1918), p. 60.

44. Willis, "Housing at Tyrone," p. 627.

45. Magnussen, "Copper Mining Town," p. 283; Robert Riley, "Gone Forever: Goodhue's Beaux Arts Ghost Town," *A.I.A. Journal* 50 (August 1968), pp. 67–70.

46. Willis, "Housing at Tyrone," p. 629.

47. "Tyrone N.M., the Development of Phelps-Dodge Corporation," *Architectural Forum* 28 (April

1918), pp. 131–40; "New Mining Community," pp. 59–62; Marcia Mead, "Small House"; "The Workingman's House," pp. 311, 314–17; Werner Hegemann and Elbert Peets, *The American Vitruvius*, New York: The Architectural Book Publishing Company 1922, pp. 108–9.

48. Magnussen, "Copper Mining Town," p. 283.

49. Charles Willis, "The Life of a Mining Community," *Engineering and Mining Journal* 106 (26 October 1918), pp. 731–3; Willis, "Housing at Tyrone," p. 629.

50. Byrkit, *Copper Collar*, p. 99.

51. Philip S. Foner, *Labor and World War I, The History of the Labor Movement in the United States*, vol. 7, New York: International Publishers 1987, pp. 265–6.

52. L.W. Casaday, "The Economics of a One-Industry Town," *Arizona Business and Economic Review* 3 (December 1954), pp. 1–5.

53. Janet Ball, "Company Built Copper Communities in the American Southwest, 1910–1920," MA thesis, University of Utah, 1989, p. 46.

54. William Kenyon, "Ajo, Arizona," *Architecture* 39 (January 1919), p. 10.

55. Ibid.

56. Ball, "Company Built Communities," pp. 61–4.

57. Foner, *Labor and World War I*, pp. 269–70.

58. Ball, "Company Built Communities," p. 30.

59. Irving F. Morrow, "Two Town Planning Projects in Arizona: Herding and Boyd," *The Architect and Engineer* 58 (December 1920), pp. 50–52.

60. Ibid., p. 53.

61. Ibid., p. 63.

62. Ibid., p. 61.

63. For different perspectives on the Bisbee deportations, see: Jensen, *Heritage*, pp. 398–406; Foner, *Labor and World War I*, pp. 270–79; Byrkit, *Copper Collar*, pp. 280–97; and Melvyn Dubofsky, *We Shall Be All*, New York: Quadrangle Books 1969, pp. 385–9.

64. Foner, *Labor and World War I*, p. 278.

65. Ibid., p. 280.

66. Even before the United States entered the war, Goodhue's letters indicated a strong hostility to Germans.

67. Goodhue, "Home of the Future," p. 452.

68. Phelps-Dodge Company Annual Report, 1921; Ralph Looney, *Haunted Highways: The Ghost Towns of New Mexico*, Albuquerque: University of New Mexico Press 1968, p. 188.

69. "Tyrone," *Pay Dirt* (Summer 1981), p. 74.

70. Riley, "Ghost Town," p. 67.

8 PROFESSIONAL SOLUTIONS: JOHN NOLEN AND THE STANDARDIZATION OF COMPANY TOWN PLANNING

1. John L. Hancock, "John Nolen and the American City Planning Movement: A History of Culture Change and Community Response, 1900–1940" PhD dissertation, University of Pennsylvania 1964, pp. 3–15.

2. Ibid., p. 43.

3. Richard Foglesong, *Planning the Capitalist City*, Princeton, NJ: Princeton University Press 1986, pp. 202–3.

4. Hancock, "Nolen," p. 189.

5. John L. Hancock, *John Nolen: A Bibliographical Record of Achievement*, Ithaca, NY: Cornell University Program in Urban and Regional Studies 1976, p. 16.

6. Ibid., pp. 35–43.

7. Ibid.

8. Although John Hancock claims that Nolen's office *was* the largest firm in the nation, other planning firms, including that of the Olmsted brothers and Earle S. Draper, were probably equal in size. Hancock, "Nolen," p. 295.

9. Earle S. Draper, interview with author, Vero Beach, Florida, 19 March 1984.

10. Hancock, "Nolen," p. 232.

11. Ibid., p. 255.

12. George B. Ford, ed., *City Planning Progress in the United States*, Washington DC: American Institute of Architects 1917, pp. ii–iii.

13. Hancock, *Bibliographical Record*, pp. 7–12. For a discussion of the conservative NAM, see James

Weinstein, *The Corporate Ideal in the Liberal State 1900–1918*, Boston: Beacon Press 1968.

14. Hancock, "Nolen," p. 235.

15. Robert Walker, *The Planning Function in Urban Government*, Chicago: University of Chicago Press 1950, pp. 235–41.

16. Foglesong, *Capitalist City*, pp. 225–9.

17. See John Nolen, *Replanning Reading: An Industrial City of a Hundred Thousand*, Boston: George H. Ellis, 1910.

18. Mel Scott, *American City Planning Since 1890*, Berkeley: University of California Press 1969, pp. 110–16; Item no. 2903, John Nolen Papers, John M. Olin Library, Cornell University, Ithaca, New York.

19. Hancock, "Nolen," p. 260.

20. "Garden Village is Promising," *Christian Science Monitor* (13 November 1913), pp. 441–4.

21. Ibid., p. 442.

22. C.S. Bird, *Town Planning for Small Communities* New York: D. Appleton 1917, pp. 168–72.

23. Bird reprinted Mann and MacNeille's report in *Town Planning for Small Communities*, pp. 173–231.

24. Ibid., p. 200.

25. Ibid., pp. 178, 205.

26. Ibid., p. 189.

27. *Architectural Forum* 28 (April 1918), p. 1.

28. See: *Housing Problems in America: Proceedings of the Fifth National Conference on Housing*, Providence RI: National Housing Association 1916; and *Housing Problems in America: Proceedings of the Sixth National Congress on Housing*, Chicago: National Housing Association 1917.

29. *Homes for Workmen*, New Orleans: The Southern Pine Association 1919; Morris Knowles, *Industrial Housing*, New York: Knickerbocker Press 1920; R.S. Whiting, *Housing and Industry*, Chicago: Engineering Bureau, National Lumber Manufacturers Association 1918; Leslie Allen, *Industrial Housing Problems*, Boston: Aberthaw Construction Company 1917; F.T. Ley, *Home Building for Wage Earners; A Financial and Economic Problem*, New York and Boston: F.T. Ley and Company 1920.

30. Leifur Magnussen, "A Modern Copper Mining Town" and "A Model Industrial Suburb," *Monthly Review of Labor Statistics* 6 (April 1918), pp. 729–53.

31. *Architectural Review* 5 (January 1917); *Architectural Forum* 28 (April 1918).

32. John Nolen, *New Towns for Old: Achievements in Civic Improvements to Some American Small Towns and Neighborhoods*, Boston: Marshall Jones 1927, pp. 66–7; Ed Kurtz, plant manager, Mt Union Refactory, interview with author, Mt Union, Pennsylvania, 4 August 1987.

33. Kim E. Wallace, *Brickyard Towns: A History of Refractories Industry Communities in South-Central Pennsylvania*, Washington DC: Historic American Buildings Survey 1993, p. 122.

34. Frank J. Mulvihill, "Kistler Industrial Village," *Wildwood Magazine* 3 (Autumn 1916), pp. 14–15.

35. John Nolen, *The Industrial Village*, National Housing Association Publication 50, Washington DC: National Housing Association 1918, pp. 18–19.

36. Nolen, *New Towns*, pp. 69–70.

37. Ibid., pp. 67–8.

38. *A Bicentennial Keepsake*, Mt Union, Penn., Mt Union Historical Society 1976, p. 31; Wallace, *Brickyard Towns*, p. 130.

39. "Model factory town is planned in Pennsylvania," *Christian Science Monitor* (24 May 1916), p. 13.

40. Winthrop Hamlin, *Low Cost Cottage Construction in America*, Cambridge, Mass.: Harvard Social Museum 1917, pp. 8–9, 28–9.

41. Perry MacNeille, "Industrial Housing – What Types of Houses to Build," *Housing Problems in America: Proceedings of the Fifth National Congress on Housing*, Providence, RI: National Housing Association 1916, pp. 67–79.

42. Bird, *Small Communities*, p. 176.

43. MacNeille, "Types of Houses," p. 72.

44. Ibid.

45. Mrs Florence Alexander, interview with author, Kistler, Pennsylvania, 4 August 1987.

46. Kurtz interview; Alexander interview.

47. "Model factory town," *Christian Science Monitor*, p. 13.

48. MacNeille, "Types of Houses," p. 74; *Homes for Workmen*, pp. 188–96.

49. John Nolen, "Low Cost Houses for Employees," *American Industries* 17 (November 1917), pp. 13–17; "The Low-Cost Housing Problem," *American Industries* 18 (April 1917), p. 19; "The Problem of Industrial Housing," *American Industries* 19 (March 1918), p. 225; "Industrial Housing," *Housing Problems in America: Proceedings of the Fifth National Conference on Housing*, Providence, RI: National Housing Association 1916, pp. 5–24; "The Essential Principles of Industrial Village Development," *Architectural Forum* 28 (April 1918), pp. 97–102; "Industrial Village Communities in the United States," *Garden Cities and Town Planning* 11 (January 1921), pp. 6–9.

50. Clinton Mackenzie, *Industrial Housing*, New York: The Knickerbocker Press 1920, pp. 49–52.

51. File no. 2903, Nolen Papers.

52. Hancock, "Nolen," pp. 271–3; File no. 2903, Nolen Papers.

53. File no. 2903, Nolen Papers.

54. Kingsport has generated a large literature. The most reliable account of its development can be found in Margaret Ripley Wolfe, *Kingsport, Tennessee: A Planned American City*, Lexington: The University Press of Kentucky 1987. Other accounts include: Isaac Shuman, "Kingsport, an Unusual City, Built to Make Business for a Railroad," *American City* 22 (May 1920), pp. 471–3; *Kingsport: City of Industries Schools Churches and Homes*, Kingsport: Rotary Club of Kingsport 1936; Ray Holcombe, "Industrial City Building," *Southern Architect and Building News* (March 1927), pp. 53–8; Ralph Palette, "Keeping Main Street on the Map," *Nations Business* (May 1929), pp. 89–94 ; Mary Frances Hughes, "Where Planned Beauty Blossoms in an Industrial Community," *American City* (December 1930), pp. 140–41.

55. Ibid., p. 43.

56. Hancock, "Nolen," pp. 455–61.

57. Mackenzie, *Industrial Housing*, pp. 19–32.

58. Wolfe, *Kingsport*, p. 44.

59. Margaret Wolfe's discussion of Nolen's role in Kingsport's planning serves as an important corrective to John Hancock's extremely positive, if often inaccurate, reading of Nolen's career.

Hancock appears to have taken many of Nolen's over-optimistic assessments of his planning work at face value. See Wolfe, *Kingsport*, pp. 221–2.

60. John Nolen, "Kingsport, Tennessee: An Industrial City Built to Order," *Review of Reviews* 75 (March 1927) pp. 286–92;

61. Mackenzie, *Industrial Housing*, p. 4.

62. Wolfe, *Kingsport*, pp. 51–3; Hancock, "Nolen," p. 466.

63. John Nolen, "Kingsport, Tennessee: An Industrial Town," *Town Planning Review* 16 (July 1934), pp. 16–24; Charles Stevenson, "A Contrast in 'Perfect' Towns," *Nation's Business* (December 1937), pp. 18–20, 124–8. This article cited Kingsport as a triumph of business organization and labor harmony compared to the just-built TVA town of Norris, Tennessee, which it judged an expensive failure. Kingsport's success was debated during the 1920s and early 1930s. Its supporters lauded the town's welfare programs, loyal workers and economic prosperity, while critics pointed out its oligarchical control – which extended to politics, with only 1,300 registered voters in a town of 18,000 – and low wages. Arthur C. Comey and Max Wehrly, *Planned Communities*, Part 1, vol. II of the *Supplementary Report of the Urbanism Committee*, Washington DC: Government Printing Office 1938, p. 39.

64. John Nolen, "Industrial Village Communities in the United States," *Garden Cities and Town Planning* (October 1918), pp. 6–9.

65. Ibid., p. 142.

66. Ibid., p. 155.

67. Philip S. Foner, *Labor and World War I, The History of the Labor Movement in the United States*, vol. 7, New York: International Publishers 1987, pp. 174–5.

68. Samuel Haber, *Efficiency and Uplift*, p. 121; Sanford Jacoby, *Employing Bureaucracy*, New York: Columbia University Press 1988, pp. 121–30; Stuart Brandes, *American Welfare Capitalism*, Chicago: University of Chicago Press 1976, p.26.

69. Roy Lubove, "Homes and 'A Few Well Placed Fruit Trees': An Object Lesson in Federal Housing," *Social Research* 27 (Winter 1960), pp. 469–86.

70. Ibid., p. 471.

71. Charles Whitaker, *The Housing Problem in War and Peace*, Washington DC: American Institute of Architects 1918; Francesco Dal Co, "From the Park to the Region," in Giorgio Ciucci, Francesco Dal Co, Mario Manieri-Elia, and Manfredo Tafuri, eds, *The American City*, Cambridge, Mass.: MIT Press 1979, p. 223.

72. Many writers, such as Lewis Mumford and other RPAA members, ignoring the considerable amount of American activity in industrial housing and town planning that had taken place in the years since 1910, overestimated the influence of the English war towns on the American government-sponsored programs. Although their private sponsorship rendered them suspect to advocates of government support, most of the English measures, including cooperative ownership and group housing, had already been widely proposed and discussed by company town architects.

73. See Mackenzie, *Industrial Housing*, pp. 43–9.

74. Hancock, "Nolen," pp. 280–82.

75. William E. Groben, "Union Park Gardens: A Model Garden Suburb for Shipworkers of Wilmington, Del.," *Architectural Record* 45 (January 1919), p. 102; Emile G. Perrot, "Recent Government Housing Developments: Union Park Gardens," *Housing Problems in America: Proceedings of the Seventh National Conference on Housing*, Philadelphia: National Housing Association 1918, pp. 101–17.

76. William E. Groben, *Modern Industrial Housing*, Philadelphia: Ballinger and Perrot 1918; "Industrial Village at Marcus Hook, Pa.," *Brickbuilder* 25 (December 1916), pp. 329–30.

77. Nolen, *New Towns*, pp. 90–92.

78. Groben, "Union Park Gardens," pp. 46–60.

79. Ibid., p. 48.

80. Comey and Wehrly, *Planned Communities*, pp. 67–9.

81. Most observers consider Yorkship Village, designed by Electus D. Litchfield, to be the best of the EFC projects. See Robert Stern, *The Anglo-American Suburb*, London: Architectural Design 1980, p. 62; Ralph F. Warner, "Yorkship, A New War Town for the Emergency Fleet Corporation," *Architectural Review* 23 (June 1918), pp. 91–4.

82. Lubove, "Homes and a Few Fruit Trees," pp. 482–4.

83. Ibid., p. 485.

84. Hancock, "Nolen," pp. 290–91.

85. Comey and Wehrly, *Planned Communities*, p. 67.

86. Lewis Mumford, "Introduction," in Clarence Stein, *Towards New Towns for America*, Cambridge, Mass.: MIT Press 1957, pp. 11–12.

87. Stern, *The Anglo-American Suburb*, p. 81.

88. Nolen, *New Towns for Old*.

89. Hancock, "Nolen," pp. 573–9.

90. Ibid., pp. 603–7.

9 REGIONAL ALTERNATIVES: EARLE S. DRAPER AND THE SOUTHERN TEXTILE MILL VILLAGE

1. Broadus Mitchell, *The Rise of Cotton Mills in the South*, Baltimore, Md: Johns Hopkins University Press 1921, is the classic account of this process; more recent work has challenged Mitchell's assessment of the philanthropic motives of southern textile entrepreneurs: Melton A. McLaurin, *Paternalism and Protest*, Westport, Conn.: Greenwood Publishing 1971.

2. For a detailed account of this process, see Jacquelyn Dowd Hall, James Leloudis, Robert Korstad, Mary Murphy, Lu Ann Jones, and Christopher B. Daly, *Like a Family: The Making of a Southern Cotton Mill World*, Chapel Hill: University of North Carolina Press 1987, pp. 44–113.

3. The post-Civil War shortage of cash forced small farmers to turn to local merchants for cash or credit. To guarantee their investment, lenders demanded a lien on the crop. The crop-lien system, legalized in 1866, increased cotton crops while decreasing prices. Unable to repay their loans, indebted farmers lost their land and turned into tenants, cultivating shares of land that they had once owned. Mill work provided one way out of this continuing cycle. McLaurin, *Paternalism and Protest*, p. 13.

4. In 1910, southern mill workers born of foreign parents constituted 0.4 percent of the labor force, foreign born operatives, 0.3 percent. McLaurin, *Paternalism and Protest*, p. 20.

5. Herbert Lahne, *The Cotton Mill Worker*, New York: Farrar and Rinehart 1944, p. 41.

6. McLaurin, *Paternalism and Protest*, p. 22; Hall et al., *Like a Family*, p. 61.

7. McLaurin, *Paternalism and Protest*, p. 8; David Carlton, *Mill and Town in South Carolina 1880–1920*, Baton Rouge: Louisiana State University Press 1982, p. 152.

8. McLaurin, *Paternalism and Protest*, pp. 60–67.

9. Lahne, *Cotton Mill Worker*, pp. 36–9.

10. Ibid.

11. Hall et al., *Like a Family*, p. 115.

12. Lahne, *Cotton Mill Worker*, p. 61; Hall et al., *Like a Family*, pp. 127–9.

13. Harriet Herring, *Welfare Work in Mill Villages*, Chapel Hill, NC: University of North Carolina Press 1930, p. 99.

14. Hall et al., *Like a Family*, p. 126; the classic study of religion in the mill village is Liston Pope, *Millhands and Preachers*, New Haven, Conn.: Yale University Press 1941.

15. Daniel Tompkins, *Cotton Mill, Commercial Features*, Charlotte, NC: published by the author 1899, p. 35.

16. McLaurin, *Paternalism and Protest*, pp. 43–8.

17. Ibid., pp. 38, 45.

18. Richard Ely, "An American Industrial Experiment," *Harper's Magazine* 105 (1902), pp. 39–45; McLaurin, *Paternalism and Protest*, p. 48.

19. Hall et al., *Like a Family*, pp. 14, 140–45.

20. Lahne, *Cotton Mill Worker*, p. 66.

21. W.J. Cash, *The Mind of the South*, New York: Vintage 1941, p. 274.

22. Charles E. Augur, "Earle S. Draper: Unsung Hero of American Planned Community and Regional Development," paper presented at the Annual Meeting of the Society for American City and Regional Planning History, September 1987; Thomas W. Hanchett, "Earle Sumner Draper: City Planner of the New South," in Catherine W. Bishir and Lawrence S. Early, eds, *Early Twentieth-Century Suburbs in North Carolina*, Raleigh: North Carolina Department of Cultural Resources 1985; Earle S. Draper, interview with author, Vero Beach, Florida, 19 March 1984. As Augur's title suggests, Draper's work is just beginning to be studied by historians of urban planning. See also Norman T. Newton, *Design on the Land*, Cambridge, Mass.: Harvard University Press 1971, pp. 486–9.

23. Margaret Ripley Wolfe, *Kingsport, Tenessee: A Planned American City*, Lexington: The University Press of Kentucky 1987, pp. 39–45.

24. Auger, "Earle S. Draper," p. 212.

25. Ibid., p. 216; Draper interview.

26. Hall et al., *Like a Family*, p. 264.

27. Carlton, *Mill and Town*, pp. 171–200.

28. Hall et al., *Like a Family*, pp. 131–2, 107; Herring, *Welfare Work*, pp. 108–10.

29. Herring, *Welfare Work*, pp. 135–9, 206.

30. Hall et al., *Like a Family*, p. 210.

31. Ibid., p. 212.

32. Herring, *Welfare Work*, pp. 115, 123–4, 126.

33. Draper interview.

34. Earle S. Draper, "Southern Textile Mill Village Planning," *Landscape Architecture* 18 (October 1927), p. 5.

35. Earle S. Draper, "Practical Value of Mill Village Planning," *Southern Textile Bulletin* (4 January 1923), pp. 48–9.

36. Earle S. Draper, "Much Activity in Mill Village Improvement Work," *Southern Textile Bulletin,* (22 June 1919), pp. 3–4; "Southern Mill Village Development," *Textile World* (4 February 1922), p. 5; "Mill Village Developments," *Textile World* (3 February 1923), p. 2; "Mill Village Developments," *Textile World* (9 February 1924), pp. 4–5.

37. Augur, "Earle S. Draper," p. 214.

38. Earle S. Draper, "Activity in Southern Mill Development," *Textile World* (7 February 1920), pp. 2–4.

39. Draper, "Southern Mill Village Planning," p. 16.

40. Draper interview; Draper, "Southern Textile Village Planning," pp. 1–27; Earle S. Draper, "Community Work in Southern Mill Villages," *Southern Textile Bulletin* (8 May 1919), p. 31.

41. Draper interview.

42. Tompkins, *Cotton Mill*, p. 117.

43. Ibid.

44. Draper interview; Auger, "Earle S. Draper," p. 224.

45. Draper, "Textile Village Planning," p. 26.

46. Earle S. Draper, "Proposed City Planning Improvements for an Industrial Section of LaGrange, Ga." *American City* 20 (June 1930), pp. 112–16.

47. Draper, "Southern Mill Village Development," p. 5.

48. Brent Glass, "Southern Mill Hills: Design in a Public Place," in Doug Swaim, ed., *Carolina Dwelling: Towards Preservation of Place: In Celebration of the North Carolina Vernacular Landscape*, Raleigh: School of Design, North Carolina State University 1978, pp. 140–42; Jennings Rhyne, *Some Southern Cotton Mill Workers and Their Villages*, Chapel Hill: University of North Carolina Press 1930, pp. 7–19; Dale Newman, "Work and Community Life in a Southern Textile Town," *Labor History* 19 (1978), p. 212; Leifur Magnussen, "Southern Cotton Mill Villages," in *Housing by Employers in the United States*, Bulletin 263, US Department of Labor, Bureau of Labor Statistics, Washington DC: Government Printing Office 1920, pp. 139–60.

49. Hall et al., *Like a Family*, p. 127.

50. Leonora Ellis, "A Model Factory Town," *Forum* 32 (1901–1902), pp. 60–61; Ely, "An American Industrial Experiment," p. 40; Budgett Meakin, *Model Factories and Villages*, London: T. Fisher Unwin 1905, pp. 329–33; Clare de Graffenried, "The Georgia Cracker in the Cotton Mill," *Century Magazine* (February 1881), p. 483; Hall et al., *Like a Family*, p. 119.

51. Lawrence G. Foster, *A Company that Cares*, New Brunswick, NJ: Johnson and Johnson 1986, pp. 34–5.

52. Draper, "Southern Textile Village Planning," p. 20.

53. Ibid., p. 21.

54. Earle S. Draper, "Applied Home Economics in TVA Houses," *Journal of Home Economics* 27 (December 1935), p. 632.

55. "Reflections – Chicopee, Georgia," Chicopee, Ga.: Johnson and Johnson Company 1986.

56. "Reflections," p. 33; Hall et al., *Like a Family*, p. 127.

57. James Winters and Barker Jones, interview with author, Chicopee, Georgia, 15 April 1991.

58. "Reflections," pp. 42–4.

59. Draper, "Activity in Mill Villages," p. 4.

60. James A. Hodges, *New Deal Labor Policy and the Southern Cotton Textile Industry*, Knoxville: University of Tennessee Press 1986, pp. 10–11.

61. Robert Dunn and Jack Hardy, *Labor and Textiles*, New York: International Publishers 1931, pp. 212–33; Tom Tippett, *When Southern Labor Stirs*, New York: Jonathan Cape and Harrison Smith 1935, pp. 210–50.

62. Gainesville, "Reflections," p. 14; Winters and Jones interview.

63. Harriet Herring, *The Passing of the Mill Village*, Chapel Hill: University of North Carolina Press 1949, p. 9.

64. Arthur C. Comey and Max Wehrly, *Planned Communities* Part I, vol. II of the *Supplementary Report of the Urbanism Committee*, Washington DC: Government Printing Office 1938, p. 26.

65. Scott, *City Planning*, pp. 300–301; Walter Creese, *TVA's Public Planning: The Vision, The Reality*, Knoxville: University of Tennessee Press 1990, pp. 42–4.

66. Auger, "Earle Draper," pp. 220–21.

67. Morgan had written a number of books outlining the ideal community, such as *The Small Community, Foundation of a Democratic Life: What It is and How to Achieve It*, Yellow Springs, Ohio: Community Service Books 1957. Draper and Morgan were in complete agreement about the social aims of the TVA, as stated by Morgan: "The mountain regions of the South are the last great bulwarks of individuality in America. . . . The Southern Highlander is different. He likes rural life. His income has been and is very small. Agriculture alone will not support him. Today great industries are settling in his midst. Some of these factories tend to destroy his type of civilization. The Southern Highlander is often regarded merely as

cheap labor to be exploited rather than as the representative of a valuable type of culture to be encouraged and protected." Quoted in Creese, *TVA Public Planning*, pp. 251–2.

68. Auger, "Earle Draper," pp. 226–9. For an account of the RPAA, see Roy Lubove, *Community Planning in the 1920s*, Pittsburgh: University of Pittsburgh Press 1963; and Carl Sussman, *Planning the Fourth Migration*, Cambridge, Mass.: MIT Press 1976.

69. For a general discussion of TVA planning, see Phoebe Cutler, *The Landscape of the New Deal*, New Haven, Conn.: Yale University Press 1985; more specific discussions of Norris include Earle S. Draper, "The New TVA Town of Norris, Tennessee," *American City* 48 (December 1933), pp. 67–8; Tracy Auger, "The Planning of the Town of Norris," *American Architect* 128 (April 1926), pp. 19–26. The TVA, however, should not be seen as necessarily democratic or totally benign. Armed with extraordinary powers, the TVA disrupted long-settled family farms. Norris Dam and Norris Lake alone displaced more than 3,500 people. The TVA commissioned the photographer Lewis Hine to document the soon to disappear way of life in the area.

70. Draper interview, author; Earle S. Draper, Jr, "The TVA's Forgotten Town: Norris, Tennessee," *Landscape Architecture* 78 (March 1988), pp. 96–102.

71. Auger, "Earle Draper," p. 224.

72. An extensive literature critically addresses the question of whether the TVA fulfilled the hopes of its early sponsors. See Philip Selznick, *TVA and the Grass Roots*, Berkeley: University of California Press 1949; Thomas K. McGraw, *Morgan vs. Lilienthal*, Chicago: Loyola University Press 1970; Erwin Hargrove and Paul Conklin, eds, *TVA: Fifty Years of Grassroots Bureaucracy*, Urbana: University of Illinois Press 1983.

73. Mel Scott, *American City Planning Since 1890*, Berkeley: University of California Press 1969, p. 315.

CONCLUSION: THE END OF THE COMPANY TOWN

1. These include: Ajo, Arizona (copper); Alcoa, Tennessee (aluminum); Atco, Georgia (textiles); Bayview, Alabama (coal mining); Chicasaw, Alabama (shipbuilding); Chicopee, Georgia (textiles); Danielson, Connecticut (textiles); Fairfield, Alabama (steel); Eclipse Park, Beloit, Wisconsin (scales); Endee Manor, Bristol, Connecticut (textiles); Firestone Park, Ohio (tires); Goodyear Heights, Ohio (tires); Happy Valley, Tennessee (textiles); Hershey, Pennsylvania (chocolate); Indian Hill, Massachusetts (abrasives); Janesville, Wisconsin (automobiles); Jefferson Rouge, Michigan (metalworking); Kaulton, Alabama (lumber); Kincaid, Illinois (coal mining); Kingsport, Tennessee (diversified industries); Kistler, Pennsylvania (brick); Kohler, Wisconsin (plumbing fixtures); Laurens, South Carolina (textiles); Lynch, Kentucky (coal mining); Massena, New York (metalworking); Marysville, Michigan (automobiles); Marcus Hook, Pennsylvania (textiles); Mark, Indiana (steel); Midland, Pennsylvania (steel); Morgan Park, Minnesota (steel); Pacolet, South Carolina (textiles); Perryville, Maryland (gunpowder); Riverdale, Rome, New York, (brass and copper manufacturing); Shawsheen Village, Lawrence, Massachusetts (textiles); Silvertown, Georgia (textiles); Spindale, North Carolina (textiles); Torrance, California (diversified industries); Tyrone, New Mexico (copper); Westfield, Alabama (coal mining); West Point, Georgia (textiles).

2. Stuart Brandes, *American Welfare Capitalism*, Chicago: University of Chicago Press 1976, pp. 128–30, 141; Irving Bernstein, *The Lean Years*, New York: Da Capo Press, 1960, p. 60.

3. Bernstein, *Lean Years*, pp. 63–5; Jacqueline Dowd Hall et al., *Like a Family: The Making of a Southern Cotton Mill World*, Chapel Hill: University of North Carolina Press 1987, pp. 259–61; Roland Marchand, *Advertising the American Dream*, Berkeley, California: University of California Press 1985, pp. 52–82.

4. For descriptions of how the automobile changed working-class life, see Robert S. Lynd and Helen M. Lynd, *Middletown: A Study in Modern American Culture*, New York: Harcourt, Brace 1929; John B. Rae, *The Road and the Car in American Life*, Cambridge, Mass.: MIT Press 1971.

5. Bernstein, *Lean Years*, p. 65; Brandes, *Welfare Capitalism*, p. 141.

6. Ibid., p. 142.

7. Ibid., p 143; James A. Hodges, *New Deal Labor Policy and the Southern Textile Industry*, Knoxville: University of Tennessee Press 1986, pp. 23–42.

8. Brandes, *Welfare Capitalism*, p. 144.

9. Harriet Herring, *The Passing of the Mill Village*, Chapel Hill: University of North Carolina Press 1949, p. 9.

10. Diane Ghirardo, *Designing New Towns: New Deal America and Fascist Italy*, Princeton, NJ: Princeton University Press 1989, pp. 195–7; Paul Conkin, *Tomorrow a New World: The New Deal Community Program*, Ithaca, NY: Cornell University Press 1959; Mel Scott, *American City Planning Since 1890*, Berkeley: University of California Press 1969, p. 111.

11. Scott, *City Planning*, p. 318.

12. Ibid.

13. Ibid.

14. Ibid.

15. Arthur C. Comey and Max Wehrly, *Planned Communities*, Part 1, vol. II of the *Supplementary Report of the Urbanism Committee*, Washington DC: Government Printing Office 1938, p. 70.

16. See Brandes, *Welfare Capitalism*; Bernstein, *Lean Years*; Daniel Nelson, *Managers and Workers*, Madison: University of Wisconsin Press 1975; David Brody, "The Rise and Decline of Welfare Capitalism," in John Braeman, Robert Bremner, and David Brody, eds, *Change and Continuity in Twentieth Century America: The 1920s*, Columbus: Ohio State University Press 1968; and Gerald Zahavi, *Workers, Managers and Welfare Capitalism*, Urbana: University of Illinois Press 1988.

17. Brandes, *Welfare Capitalism*, p. 138; Bernstein, *Lean Years*, pp. 14–20.

18. Roy Lubove, *Community Planning in the 1920's: The Contribution of the Regional Planning Association of America*, Pittsburgh: University of Pittsburgh Press 1963, p. 55.

19. Lewis Mumford, "Introduction," in C.S. Stein, *Towards New Towns for America*, Cambridge, Mass.: MIT Press 1957, pp. 11–15.

20. See Catherine Bauer, *Modern Housing*, New York: Houghton-Mifflin 1937; and United States Housing Authority, *Public Housing Design*, Washington DC: Government Printing Office 1946.

21. Robert Stern's survey, *The Anglo-American Suburb*, London: Architectural Design 1980; and the reissue of *American Vitruvius*, New York: Princeton Architectural Press 1988, indicate this interest. See Alan Colquhoun, "Twentieth Century Concepts of Urban Space," in *Modernity and the Classical Tradition*, Cambridge, Mass.: MIT Press 1989, for a more complete discussion of the change from "modern" to "post-modern" concepts of urban space.

22. David Watkin, *The English Vision: The Picturesque in Architecture, Landsape and Garden Design*, New York: Harper & Row 1982, p. ix.

23. Steve Dunwell, *The Run of the Mill*, Boston, Mass.: David R. Godine 1978, pp. 165–7.

24. Brandes, *Welfare Capitalism*, p. 145.

25. Bill Curry, "Mining Life Played Out in the West," *Los Angeles Times* (4 May 1985), p. A–1.

26. Linda Killian, "Industry Slump Cuts Down Oregon Lumber Mill Town," *Los Angeles Times* (14 June 1984), p. D–4.

27. Marc A. Stein, "Part of Past Works Well in Scotia," *Los Angeles Times* (3 February 1986), p. 1; "Small Town is Losing its Company," *New York Times* (30 December 1986), p. 6.

28. Tony Wrenn and Elizabeth Mulloy, *America's Forgotten Architecture*, New York: Pantheon Books 1976, p. 15.

29. These publications include Jeremy Brecher, Jerry Lombardi and Jan Stackhouse, eds, *Brass Valley: The Story of Working People's Lives and Struggles in an American Industrial Region*, Philadelphia: Temple University Press 1982; William Adelman, *Touring Pullman*, Chicago: Illinois Labor History Society 1977; *Haymarket Revisited*, Chicago: Illinois Labor History Society 1976; *Pilsen and the West Side: A Tour Guide*, Chicago: Illinois Labor History Society 1979.

30. HABS/HAER Annual Report (Washington DC: National Park Service 1992), pp. 28–9. The HABS publications, such as Kim E. Wallace,

Brickyard Towns: A History of Refractories Industry Communities in South-Central Pennsylvania, Washington DC: Historic American Buildings Survey 1993, are the most thorough documentation of American company towns currently available.

31. "Charlie Crowder Sees Utopia and It's a Border Town," *Business Week* (31 July 1989), pp. 35–56.

32. Roberto Suro, "Dark Cholera Fear Hovers over El Paso," *El Paso Herald-Post* (4 April 1992), p. B–1.

33. *Studio Work 1988–89*, Cambridge, Mass.: Harvard University Graduate School of Design 1989, pp. 57–8; Charles W. Harris and Jonathan S. Lane, *The Harvard Santa Teresa Study*, Cambridge, Mass.: Harvard Graduate School of Design, Spring 1989.

34. Alfredo Corchado, "Bankruptcy may be Developer's Only Way Out," *El Paso Herald-Post* (4 April 1992), p. A–1.

INDEX

Note: **bold** figures indicate illustrations